Queens & Power

Portrait of Princess Elizabeth attributed to William Scrots.
The Royal Collection © 2008, reproduced by permission of
Her Majesty Queen Elizabeth II.

Queens & Power

in Medieval and Early Modern England

Edited by CAROLE LEVIN *and*
ROBERT BUCHOLZ

Associate Editors:
Amy Gant, Shannon Meyer,
and Lisa Schuelke

University of Nebraska Press   Lincoln & London

Publication of this volume was assisted by
a grant from the University of Nebraska.

Portions of chapter 12, "'*She is the man, and Raignes*':
Popular Representations of Henrietta Maria during
the English Civil Wars," by Michelle A. White,
originally appeared in slightly different form in
the author's *Henrietta Maria and the English Civil Wars*
(Aldershot: Ashgate Publications, 2006).

Manufactured in the
United States of America

Library of Congress Cataloging-
in-Publication Data
Queens and power in medieval and early modern England
/ edited by Carole Levin and Robert Bucholz.
        p. cm.
Includes bibliographical references and index.
ISBN 978-0-8032-2968-6 (pbk. : alk. paper)
1. Queens—Great Britain—History.
2. Power (Social sciences)—Great Britain—History.
3. Great Britain—Politics and government.
I. Levin, Carole, 1948– II. Bucholz, R. O., 1958–
DA176.Q84 2009
942.009'9—dc22
2008029626

Set in Sabon by Kimberly Essman.

To
Lynn Spangler
—CL

and
Lois Noel
—RB

Contents

Illustrations

Acknowledgments

In 2003 the Newberry Library sponsored the exhibit Elizabeth I: Ruler and Legend, which had a second life as a travelling exhibit that visited forty libraries across the United States for the next three years. Carole Levin was the Senior Historical Consultant on the exhibit and was also in residence at the Newberry Library as a National Endowment for the Humanities Fellow in 2003. There she got to know Bob Bucholz, and the two presented a "dueling queens" talk at the Newberry on the relative merits of Queen Elizabeth and Queen Anne. When Love Library at the University of Nebraska was chosen to host the exhibit in the spring of 2006, Carole decided that the University of Nebraska should host a scholarly conference on queens and power to coincide, and she asked Bob to be her conference cochair. It was out of this conference that this essay collection evolved.

We owe many debts for the success of the conference that led to this collection. Joanie Barnes and Kathy Johnson, librarians at Love Library, were truly wonderful women with whom to work. Without Kim Weide, the Events Coordinator for the University of Nebraska, we could not have hosted the conference. We are deeply grateful for the support of our many cosponsors: at the University of Nebraska, we thank the Honors Program, the Department of History, the Medieval and Renaissance Studies Program, the Women's Studies Program, the Department of English, the Department of Modern Languages and Literature, the Office of the Vice Chancellor for Research, the Office of Graduate Studies, the Office of the Dean of Undergraduate Studies, and the Office of the Director of International Affairs, as well as the local chapter of Phi Beta Kappa, the University of Nebraska Press, the University of Nebraska Bookstore, the Friends of the Libraries of the University of Nebraska–Lincoln, the College of Architecture, and the College of Business Administration. We are especially grateful as well to the Nebraska Humanities Council for their funding and to Mark and Krista and the Coffee House for providing coffee not only for the conference but also for the many planning meetings that took place there. Others who supported this conference and subsequent collection are Christine Fagan, Pamela Starr, Mark Hinchman, and Bob Haller. We are deeply grateful to all who presented and attended. Our three associate editors, Amy Gant, Shannon Meyer, and Lisa Schuelke, were critical to the success of the conference and the book, and we are delighted to have them as part of this project.

In conclusion, we wish to thank the readers of the manuscript for their helpful suggestions. We could not ask for a better editor than Ladette Randolph, Interim Director of the University of Nebraska Press, who supported this project from its inception.

Introduction

It's Good to Be Queen

ROBERT BUCHOLZ & CAROLE LEVIN

Queens are much in fashion these days, receiving scholarly attention as never before. Always popular with historical novelists, dramatists, filmmakers, and their audiences, queens regnant, consort, mother, and dowager have emerged in recent years as legitimate and frequent subjects of serious academic inquiry.[1] For scholars—and perhaps for a wider audience—queens are interesting because they are anomalous and often liminal. In most places, for most of human history, the political, social, and cultural power of rulership has been accorded to males. In early modern Europe that arrangement was buttressed by a patriarchal worldview trumpeted from thousands of pulpits, propounded in hundreds of books and proverbs, manifested in gesture and dress—indeed, in almost every aspect of life. That so few women ruled in medieval and early modern England, that those who did faced obstacles unknown to their male counterparts, and that those who ruled successfully have not always been celebrated for their achievements tells us a great deal about the early modern worldview, in particular its attitudes to order, hierarchy, rulership, property, biology, and the relations between the genders. This is because queenly reigns were—like festivals or riots, albeit of a more sustained duration—extended moments of suspension in the normal working of political, social, cultural, and gender history. According to Katherine Eggert such moments established "through counterposition the possibility of another mode of shaping the basic conditions of existence."[2] As real and powerful women ruled, depictions of queens—historical and mythical—also became more multifaceted and complex. Examining together actual early modern women of power and early modern representations of queens yields a far richer understanding of the interplay of gender and power in politics and culture. No wonder that historical queens and literary depictions of them have increasingly moved center stage in the world of early modern scholarship.

Because queens were anomalous, their regimes interrupting "normal" monarchy, previous scholars have understandably treated queenly reigns as "one-offs." One of the purposes of this collection is to demonstrate more continuity than has generally been seen across queenly reigns. The expectations of queenship articulated by Michelle A. White in her paper on Henrietta Maria apply to all the women discussed in this collection. Queens themselves "talked" to each other, either literally, in the case of the "sisterly" correspondence between Catherine de' Medici and Elizabeth I, or figuratively across time, as when Cleopatra was translated into a post-Elizabethan icon, or, a century later, when Anne consciously evoked Elizabeth's style by choosing her motto and wearing clothing patterned on hers. As both Elaine Kruse and John Watkins remind us, the third quarter of the sixteenth century, the chronological heart of this collection, saw queens reigning or ruling in England, Scotland, and France, negotiating with each other, and furthering diplomatic unions across the continent via strategic marriages. Despite the horror expressed by John Knox in his *The First Blast of the Trumpet against the Monstrous Regiment of Women* (1558), for a few decades at least, female rule became the norm.

The coincidence of so many women ruling or figuring in diplomatic marriages at this moment in history allows John Watkins to interrogate the value of using gender as an analytical tool for the new diplomatic history. He argues that the negotiations for Cateau-Cambrésis may be seen as inhabiting a transitional period in which, on the one hand, consorts and mistresses were still deployed traditionally, as marital bargaining chips, quiet intercessors, or consorts, but in which, on the other hand, sovereign women like Mary I and Elizabeth I ruled in their own right. This introduced a new and potentially disruptive element to the European dynastic system. In particular, Elizabeth's apparent refusal to play by the traditional rules—to forge alliances through marriage and childbearing—cast the whole system into doubt. After Elizabeth, starting in England, such marriages increasingly became matters of public comment and, often, opposition: John Stubbs's heirs were William Prynne and Henrietta Maria's other critics as described by Michelle White. In the later seventeenth century, his intellectual and political successors called for Catherine of Braganza's divorce during the Exclusion Crisis, demonized Mary Beatrice of Modena, or, later still, complained of the political influence of Caroline of Ansbach or Marie Antoinette. In Watkins's bold vision, the Virgin Queen thus began the long process by which the authority of personal monarchy was undermined in England and on the continent, laying the foundation for a truly constitutional monarch like Anne and for solutions even more radical elsewhere. Thus, if queens were anomalous, the period covered by this book shows them to be protean, transitional, and catalytic figures, changing the landscape of European politics forever.

Traditional versus Nontraditional Queenship

Admittedly, some queens behaved as if nothing had changed, doing little to disabuse their subjects of the idea that they were conventional women in royal dress whose purpose was to produce male heirs. Michelle White usefully delineates the characteristics of the ideal early modern queen: her reproductive duties apart, she was to be obedient, passive, submissive, chaste, pious, kind, and decorous, but to retire to the background. Elisabeth de Valois seems to have been the ideal of the type: according to Watkins, her "career manifests a distinct retreat from the public task of mediation toward the more passive responsibility of bearing offspring." He argues further that this was a necessary condition of living with Philip II: "The domestic contentment that both Philip and Elisabeth seem to have enjoyed almost certainly depended on her lack of personal political ambition." In other words, Elisabeth de Valois' role was determined, as it was for so many early modern women, by what her husband, that is, the strong male given authority over her, would tolerate.

Some historians have portrayed both Mary I and Anne as similarly passive and submissive. The essays by Sarah Duncan and Robert Bucholz, however, qualify or reject the traditional view, showing each taking male advice but ultimately setting the agenda for her reign.[3] In fact, nearly every queen portrayed in this book failed to meet the expectations laid out by White. In part, this was because each operated in a vacuum created by the lack of the sort of dominating male figure those expectations presupposed. Catherine de' Medici and Elizabeth I, widow and virgin, both ruled famously and effectively without husbands. Esther's king was weak and easily (mis)led; Cleopatra's Antony was an ineffective admiral and diplomat; Matilda's brief reign was made possible by Henry I's lack of a male heir, exacerbated by her cousin Stephen's incompetence; Charles I was largely absent from the diplomatic arena inhabited so skillfully by Henrietta Maria. In fact, there was nothing new about this. Weak kings and unstable political situations often drove royal women to abandon their traditional, supplementary roles: Isabella of France and Margaret of Anjou had done so in the fourteenth and fifteenth centuries; Charlotte of Mecklenberg-Strelitz would do so in the eighteenth and nineteenth. All were compelled to suspend their domestic activities, assert themselves at court, and insert themselves into public life. In many cases, they sustained the dynasty (at least temporarily) but paid with their reputations. Indeed, Henrietta Maria's efforts on behalf of her husband rendered even her fecundity—a traditional expectation of queenship—a bone of contention because of fears that her children would be raised Catholic.[4]

Still, in the absence of a dominating male, the unusual combination of their gender and royal authority gave these women an opportunity to redefine power and gender roles (as applied to royal women, anyway) by exploiting the ambiguity involved in the status of being a female king. It is a truism of the historiography on queenship that assertive royal women faced immense obstacles, both physical and conceptual, and that the odds were stacked against their successful reigns. But perhaps we have read this all wrong. Perhaps queenly status, the possession of the attributes of both males and females, was potentially liberating. Obviously, it was good to be queen. Queenly status allowed women to assert themselves in public roles usually closed to their gender. Charles Beem articulates how Matilda practically invented regnal queenship in England. Timothy Elston's previous work has demonstrated that Catherine of Aragon pushed the limits of consortship; in this collection, he shows her pushing those of widowhood.[5] Mary followed Matilda's lead, but as in so much else, Elizabeth was the real pivotal figure: in exploiting the possibilities of her unique status and constructing a self with the most useful attributes of both males and females (nicely epitomized in Linda Shenk's "female Solomon"), she had a long and successful reign that rendered the accession of Anne and her female successors possible, even unremarkable. Moreover, the sheer originality of Elizabeth's rejection of the dynastic principle that drove her father and nearly all early modern kings and queens gave Elizabeth and England the freedom of maneuver to survive in the shark-infested waters of western northern Europe. In Watkins's reading, it also marked a step toward the desacralization of monarchy in Europe.

Watkins is careful not to argue that Elizabeth's unorthodox path was a step in the direction of the decommodification of female royal bodies: clearly, diplomatic royal marriages continued. Nevertheless, in this collection, Marjorie Swann shows how Elizabeth's choice of virginity—if it was, indeed, a choice—disrupted the early modern gender system as well.[6] Swann admits the argument that Elizabeth's royal status rendered her unique and so not as obvious a model for most early modern women. But that did not render her any less iconic a figure—a model woman if not a model for women. Examining the posthumous printed construction of Elizabeth, she finds plenty of subversion of traditional models of sexuality. Elizabeth's legitimization of virginity was corrosive enough to a Protestant world that expected every woman to marry, but John Banks's outrageous—and popular—play *The Island Queens* was even more threatening. Repudiating the time-honored belief that Elizabeth gave up the love of men for her country, Banks's Elizabeth is perfectly willing to abandon reason of state—even the state itself—as well as taboos on incest and lesbianism to consummate her love for Mary, Queen of Scots. Rather than bear children by a male husband, this Elizabeth turns traditional expectations of queenship on their head by imagining their love as procreating not heirs but "Fresh Pleasures and rich Welcomes."

In fact, it might be argued that queenship, the status of being royal, powerful, and a woman, allowed for new channels of power, not only for women, but in general. One way in which female gender (or at least consortship) may have been an asset was in patronage, especially cultural and religious patronage. In the seventeenth century, Anne of Denmark, Henrietta Maria, and Catherine of Braganza used their households to patronize political actors and coreligionists who would have had a harder go of it in the royal court.[7] As we have seen, Elizabeth exploited her gender to render herself more powerful, more able to command loyalty, than she might have done if she were a man. One way to do this was through what might be called "the appeal to chivalry"—the culturally constructed expectation that men will defend women in danger. Elizabeth I was not the only masterful exploiter of this cultural norm: other examples include Mary I in her unjustly neglected Guildhall speech, Mary II as regent; and Anne following the declaration of war on Louis XIV. Indeed, it might be argued for the beginning of the eighteenth century that it would have been far more difficult to keep England in the War of the Spanish Succession, following a controversial revolution, in the midst of bitter party and religious strife, had the main object of personal loyalty been a man. Certainly, a minority seem to have fought with any spirit or heartfelt loyalty for William III in *his* war, while Anne seems to have inspired ardent affection in hers. Thus, the existence of regnal royal women created an anomaly that made possible different constructions of image, loyalty, and power relations than were possible with kings.

Legitimacy

Nevertheless, before queens could initiate such constructions, they faced challenges unknown to or met far more easily by male rulers. The first and most obvious such challenge was legitimacy: this collection traces a progression on this issue from the first, tentative assertions of female sovereignty in England under Matilda, through the pivotal reigns of Mary I and Elizabeth I, to the uncontroversial accession of Anne. Given contemporary, but long-standing, attitudes toward the respective roles of men and women, it was inevitable that the idea of a female monarch would seem foreign[8]: as Michele Osherow and Richardine Woodall remind us, reservations about female rule and authority went back to ancient times. In this context, Henry I's decision to name his only surviving child, Matilda, as heir was a radical embrace of the hereditary principle over the claims of gender and expediency. Admittedly, as Beem points out, this was intended as a temporary expedient, since Matilda's viability was predicated on her ability to produce a male heir: that is, she could only be seen as an attractive alternative to Stephen if she promised to be succeeded by a man.

Beem's Matilda, arguably England's first queen regnant, comes across as a more subtle and skillful politician than the termagant immortalized by medieval and Renaissance chroniclers. She shrewdly skirted the issue of female legitimacy by styling herself "Lady of the English," a title that appealed to personal feudal loyalties rather than to territorial claims. Though subsequent royal women were accused, as she was, of overweening power, they exercised that power (or were thought to do so) as consorts, not queens regnant, until the succession crisis of 1553. It might be argued that the willingness of the English Privy Council to turn to, first, Jane Grey, and then Mary Tudor shows that, in the wake of the Wars of the Roses and the elaboration and centralization of the Tudor State, the English ruling class had finally embraced Henry I's principle, choosing blood legitimacy over gender legitimacy: no man was offered as a serious alternative in 1553 or 1558 because no man could claim so close a kinship to previous kings. However, it is equally true that in 1547 no one had seriously suggested Mary over her pre-adolescent brother: clearly, if blood trumped gender in the English monarchical system, gender trumped age.

The key to all subsequent female ascendancies was Elizabeth's long and successful reign—and, perhaps, the failures of her male successors. While many in 1603 seem to have welcomed James I because of his gender, by the end of the century the Stuarts' performance, in particular their divisive religious policies, rendered another female reign more palatable. For reasons that remain largely unexplored but surely have much to do with their strong reputations as Protestants, Mary II's transitional and partial ascendancy was followed in 1702 by Queen Anne's uncontested accession to undiluted sovereignty without so much as a Knoxian murmur. This is not to say that patriarchal anxiety about female rule had been allayed, but it was now more often expressed in satirical and allegorical criticism of policy rather than in Scriptural proscription of the fundamental right of women to rule.[9] Anne's triumphant reign, in turn, paved the way for Victoria and Elizabeth II—and for those who would argue that England's most successful rulers have all been women.[10]

The Limits of Self-presentation

Given the anomalous role of queens and questions about their legitimacy, a pressing issue once they were on the throne was self-definition, self-presentation, and the fashioning of the royal image. This again reminds us that the nature of queenship was protean—perhaps more so than kingship. Faced with so little precedent, regnal queens had choices as to how to present themselves and even, perhaps, how to rule: once again, Matilda appears to have been ahead of her time. Conversely, in both Timothy Elston's and Carole Levin's essays we see queens—actually a former queen and a future queen—desperately trying to forge their images when they lack complete power to do so. Just as Matilda continued to evoke her status as empress and reject that of countess, Catherine of Aragon rejected her new status as a princess-widow, clinging to the style of queen. Her position was strengthened by the pointed fashioning of her image that had taken place over the previous quarter-century: Henry VIII found it far more difficult to unmake a queen in the eyes of his people than to make one. As Elston points out, Catherine also, whether consciously or unconsciously, played off of contemporary expectations of widows as public dispensers of charity and promoters of piety. Ultimately, like Elisabeth of Valois later, Catherine was dependent on what the strong man in her life, Henry VIII, would allow—even in her religious devotions. But equally, Elston's essay shows the limits of male monarchs' control over queenly images: the king could thwart his former queen's public activities, but he could less easily influence how people felt about her. The imaginary Catherine that he had helped construct for twenty years lived on in their hearts.

Elizabeth began to craft her image long before her accession. As Carole Levin shows, a queen *in potentium* was limited in her ability to do this: Elizabeth could commission a portrait, but she did not control dissemination of her image as she would as queen. She could dress and shape her physical presence as much as she wished, but she could only display it to the public as her brother's Council and her sister allowed. She could plant the seeds for associations that she would cultivate throughout her long reign—Protestant heroine, woman alone against a hostile world, lover of her people, saint—but those seeds would bear little fruit so long as Mary lived. Levin demonstrates that Elizabeth exploited the few possibilities open to her with such prudence and skill that she not only survived Mary's reign but continued long after her own death to evoke the associations she had nurtured.

Queens as Intercessors

Conversely, Levin's piece and Mary I's reign demonstrate that not even a queen regnant with the full authority to control her image was able to do so completely. As Andrew Barclay has written, "queenship in this period was never something created only by the queen herself."[11] Sarah Duncan uncovers a veritable war of words over Mary's attempt to fulfill the long-standing association of queens as intercessors for mercy. Nearly every queen in this book took on this role. Osherow's piece on Esther discusses how the queen saves her people from a wrathful king through her masterful (and arguably deceitful) use of gesture and language. Duncan's essay shows that Catherine of Aragon uses similar methods—"with tears in her eyes and on her bended knees"—on behalf of May Day rioters in 1517. In each case, traditional expectations of womanhood—subservience, humility, emotionalism—gave the women in question agency.[12] Put another way, sometimes patriarchy sowed the seeds of its own subversion. Though not a queen, Christine, Duchess of Lorraine, became the crucial linchpin in the Cateau-Cambrésis negotiations precisely because, as a royal woman, her role was by definition liminal and unthreatening, enabling her to move back and forth across hostile lines.

Queens regnant may have been anomalous, but they were not quite so liminal. As a result, the granting of mercy carried greater consequences than it did for the intercessor, as the decision rested ultimately with the sovereign, who would have to live with it. The difficulties are highlighted by Mary I's delays in executing Jane Grey and the Wyatt conspirators, and Elizabeth I's hesitation over the fate of Mary, Queen of Scots. In the end, it was Mary I's consort, Prince Philip, who played the part of intercessor for accused traitors, including Elizabeth, at her court. Here we see the protean nature of queenship in its ability to turn around gender roles. It is also significant that having a consort enabled Mary to grant mercy, passing off some responsibility to the mediator in a way that might not have been possible were she ruling alone. One of the impressions left by Queen Elizabeth's various utterances about Mary, Queen of Scots, is the sheer loneliness of her decision. As Duncan points out, there remains much work to be done on Elizabeth's sense of and reputation for mercy. Despite executing some 450 northern rebels, 180 Catholic priests and supporters, Mary, Queen of Scots, the Duke of Norfolk, the Earls of Northumberland and Essex, and assorted members of the gentry, Elizabeth is not often thought of as bloodthirsty, leading Sara Mendelson and Patricia Crawford to argue that "for a sixteenth century regime, her reign saw very few executions."[13] This raises the question of why Elizabeth I succeeded in portraying herself as merciful where Mary I failed. In part, it would seem to be a simple matter of which side won and thus wrote the history. But also to be considered is that Elizabeth's reign spanned nearly forty-five years, while Mary burnt over three hundred Protestants in just three years of her five-year reign. The vast majority of Mary's victims were no threat politically to the state, unlike those executed in Elizabeth's reign. Still, are Elizabeth's expressions of reluctance to be taken at face value? Was there something in the "quality" of Mary's mercy that was more "strained"?

As this suggests, and as Duncan demonstrates in the case of Prince Philip, intercession and mediation were not in themselves neutral activities: they were subject to political interpretations. Michelle White's essay on Henrietta Maria illustrates the dangers. Attacked early in her marital career for pleading with her husband on behalf of Catholics, she was excoriated during the civil wars for pleading with the crowned heads of Europe on behalf of her husband. Despite the fact that, in both cases, she was only moderately successful (after all, the men and munitions she brought in 1643 did not turn the tide), she became an icon of monstrous queenship to the puritan/parliamentarian side. White's essay shows us the process by which a queen lost control of her image in a new world of print culture, and in particular during the open window of a relatively free press, 1641–50. White illuminates precisely how news gathering and dissemination had expanded since the days when Elizabeth exercised such iron control; indeed, this essay is much enhanced by its "how-it-was-done" guide to the dissemination of news. After 1641 it was simply impossible for the Crown to control what was being said about it because the many-headed hydra of a free press produced pamphlets, newsbooks, woodcuts, ballads, poems, joke-books, rhymes, and so on targeted to nearly every possible audience in England: elite and common, urban and rural, male and female, literate and illiterate. The long-term result could only expose the magic of monarchy to what Walter Bagehot thought of as the corrosive effects of daylight.

The immediate result was a portrait of Henrietta Maria that resembled the old "she-devil" depictions of Isabella of France and Margaret of Anjou in previous centuries. Similar attacks on the influence of women at the English court would be made through the reigns of George II and beyond. Their common denominator is that they criticized the queen's mediating role when it shaded into political influence. That is, female intercession was approved of as consistent with patriarchal monarchy when it involved the solicitation of mercy for individuals or, possibly, groups. Such solicitation served the purposes of patriarchal monarchy by endowing it with flexibility and crowd-pleasing mercy. But it stepped out of bounds when it translated into influence with the ruler over policy or patronage: as White notes, Henrietta Maria was accused of both. In contrast, Osherow points out that most early modern commentators were careful to construct an Esther who was obedient and subject to the advice of men, downplaying her agency and duplicity.

To some extent, these constraints applied to male favorites as well: there seems to have been a long-standing notion that any influence exerted in the closet or bedchamber, especially by someone not of cabinet rank, was inappropriate. But seventeenth-century male courtiers like the George Villiers, Duke of Buckingham, or the circle around James, Duke of York, were permitted, indeed expected, to engage in the world of military and diplomatic action—while Henrietta Maria was criticized for it. Why? White argues that a crucial factor was Henrietta Maria's religion: the "Papist" nature of her advice aimed, in her critics' eyes, at accomplishing a Popish plot. But, as White points out, gender played a role as well: attacks on the queen's ability to bear children, on her health (associating bodily consumption and corruption with that of the state), and, more overtly, the notion that Charles I was tied by apron strings all used expectations for her gender as a measuring stick with which to beat her. Opposition figures had traditionally used the charge of inappropriate influence to avoid having to say that the king was wrong—rather, his unsuitable policies were the self-evident result of bad advice from "evil counselors." It is possibly indicative of the misanthropy that was a part of the general culture that Henrietta Maria continued to be demonized in this way even after half the country had, in effect, admitted that the king was wrong by waging war against him. Whatever Charles I's crimes, his consort had committed a more fundamental one—"she is a man, and Raignes"—thus upsetting the gender hierarchy and claiming a legitimacy to which she was not entitled.

In response, Charles argued that parliamentarian writers had violated the privacy of his marriage by exposing his letters to the queen. But when it came to the substance of those letters, he felt compelled to diminish her efforts, emphasizing that she advised only on menial appointments—thus playing into a view of queenship that has been the prevalent one, but directly at odds with that argued for in this book.[14] And yet, Charles I's suggestion that Henrietta Maria might appropriately take on even a modest role in running the state was highly controversial—and received much the same reception as the Clintons' "two for one" offer in the early 1990s: the general culture still rejects vehemently the notion that a female spouse can play an active or even advisory role to a male ruler. In each case, the female is portrayed as a "she-devil," the male as submissive, weak, and, therefore, delegitimized. If Prince Philip much preferred his queen to be quiet, so has the general public for much of even recent history.

Queen's Words, Queen's Prayers

But queens have not been quiet. They fashioned themselves through their actions, but also through their words. Queens' words are a theme in the essays by Beem, Levin, Shenk, and Kruse. Beem's Matilda is very careful about words, especially titles: styling herself *Imperiatrix* to give herself the mantle of imperium, *regis Henrici filia* to claim legitimacy, and "Lady of the English" to aggrandize loyalty but avoiding "Duchess of Normandy" and "Countess of Anjou" as beneath her. In the essays by both Levin and Kruse, Elizabeth I fashions her words carefully to draw a contrast with a current nemeses, either Mary I or Catherine de' Medici. In Kruse's piece in particular, we see the last Tudor in her own words, carefully parsing language, fashioning, during the Alençon negotiations, an eager, if not yet fully committed, future daughter-in-law to Catherine, but also a virtuous, vigilant, yet ultimately self-sacrificing mother to her people—all things to all men and women. The harsh sentence her government passed on John Stubbs in 1579 when he published

The Discoverie of a Gaping Gulf Where into England is Likely to be Swallowed by another French Marriage—he lost his right hand—was a signal that she alone could do the fashioning: her people had better be wary of attempting to construct her too much according to their liking.

Another theme to queenship and, thus, this collection, is religion. Piety was an expected attribute of queens and a necessary condition for successful queenship, but, as we have seen in the case of Henrietta Maria, it was not a sufficient one and could be dangerous. Osherow's Esther, Elston's Catherine, and Levin's Elizabeth all found their reputations for piety to be validating, legitimizing images, in part because they accorded with the religious sympathies of their respective "audiences." Indeed, in Osherow's piece, it is Esther's right religion, the congruence of her purposes with God's, that frees her to violate both the truth and gender norms. Linda Shenk's Elizabeth enhances her reputation for piety with the authorization of prayer books containing what purport to be her own devotions. It is hard not to see Elizabeth performing here—not only for her God but also for her people and, indeed, for the French, the Spanish, and anyone else who might be paying attention. This is a classic case of the "theater of monarchy": what could be more theatrical than broadcasting one's most private conversations with God? Elizabeth assumes the part of Solomon, the archetypal learned, godly ruler, susceptible to good human counsel but not subject to it. The result is an image of harmony—between herself and God, herself and her counselors, herself and her people—that belied the seeming instability of her regime. In contrast, Henrietta Maria's piety—and that of the next two Stuart consorts—was destabilizing because it was out of step with the religious predilections of their subjects. Not just any piety would do.

The protean nature of queenship could pose difficulties for subjects as well as queens. Anna Riehl notes the dangers in portraying the queen: one false move and one might end up like Stubbs. The angel motif was safe: it was deeply rooted in European culture yet impeccably English; crossing confessional boundaries, it called attention to Elizabeth's semi-divinity, her sacerdotal status, her beauty, and her wisdom. It also dovetailed nicely with the intercessory function of queens. At the same time, as we have seen, queens could not always control their image and lost control of it after their deaths: while Elizabeth would certainly have approved of the many angelic elegies on her death, the essays by Woodall, Swann, and Bucholz address posthumous representations of queens of which they would not have approved.

Biological Determinism?

It might be argued that, in the end, the queens in this collection largely failed to escape the determinism of biology. After all, their very royal status derived from being the daughter or wife of a royal male. As women no less than as queens, all were expected to marry, engage in sexual relations, and have children—in that order. In Osherow's essay, Queen Vashti is banished because of her refusal to display her body like an object while Esther is forced to submit to the bed of an uncircumcised husband. Cleopatra is discounted by the Romans because of her willingness to, in effect, do both. In each case, their bodies are all these women have been allowed to work with: both Esther and Cleopatra use them to satisfy the sexual and romantic longings of male authority figures, and both costume and deport themselves carefully and effectively to achieve political ends. In contrast, Matilda's body sometimes worked against her: her marriages brought her the added prestige of the "empress" title and Geoffrey of Anjou's army but also complications and obligations that sometimes thwarted her ambitions. For example, her pregnancy in 1135 may have prevented her swift appearance in London to claim the Crown. In John Watkins's portrayal, Elisabeth de Valois, in particular, comes across as only a body: "a vehicle of dynastic perpetuation," literally a vessel for carrying heirs whose very bodily functions were the property of the Crown and its subjects. Marriage and fertility were, in the cases of Henrietta Maria and Anne, necessary but not sufficient conditions for success: the happy marriage between Charles I and Henrietta Maria only fueled speculation about her influence, while Anne's uxoriousness seems to have cast suspicion on her governing abilities. In each case, their contrasting success at childbearing became another weapon to use against them.

Ever the exception, Elizabeth tried to get beyond all this, in part by portraying herself as something other than a flesh-and-blood woman. As many writers have pointed out, she constructed a vocabulary of rule that was largely male while her most popular mythological analogues tended to be female divinities: Diana, Belphoebe, Astrea, the Fairy Queen, the Virgin Mary, female angels. Riehl's essay, along with Bucholz's, illustrates how well contemporary commentators picked up on royal themes and associations: for Elizabeth, writers took up the angelic associations; for Anne, the maternal ones.

The fashioning—even commodification—of these women continued after their deaths. For example, if Elston is correct, the tradition that Catherine encouraged the art of lace making in Ampthill grew after her decease. Less positively, Sarah Duncan confirms that Mary I's merciless reputation was mostly forged for her posthumously. Above all, even in death, the eyes of posterity fixated on queen's bodies, their sexuality, and their relationships to men: this is true of Osherow's Esther, Woodall's Cleopatra, Elston's Catherine of Aragon, White's Henrietta Maria, Bucholz's Anne, and even the woman who did so much to deny these factors: Elizabeth I. Carole Levin, John Watkins, and, in this collection, Marjorie Swann have all demonstrated that Elizabeth's sexuality in particular continued to be a matter of speculation and exploitation even after her demise.[15] Indeed, anyone who teaches the period knows that what today's undergraduates really want to know about the Virgin Queen is "Was she really a virgin"? In the case of the last monarch depicted in this collection, Queen Anne, there was no mystery about her body: it was fertile and it was fat. Bucholz argues that neither attribute was particularly damaging to the queen during her reign but that both have been used to peg her, pejoratively, ever since.

To the extent that longstanding assessments of Anne's body still determine our view of her character, abilities, and reign, it would seem that society's attitudes toward women have changed little in the last three or four centuries. As Bucholz suggests, historians and their readers are still, too often, bound by their cultural paradigms, preventing fresh appraisal of the realities they seek to describe and understand. In the end, it may be significant that the transition to monumental royal marble that Shakespeare engineers posthumously for Cleopatra seems to foreshadow that which Shekhar Kapur and Michael Hirst foist on Elizabeth in the film of the same name: in both cases, queens are stripped of their humanity—and a certain historical verisimilitude—to satisfy the needs of the drama and its audience. In both cases queens posthumously lose control of their images, their bodies becoming iconic tablets upon which later ages can write as they will. In becoming one for the ages, each has become something other than what they were. Thus, even in death, queens continue to serve, to exercise a fascination for us, fulfilling the needs of subjects as yet unborn when they reigned.

Notes

1. The literature is too vast to list in its entirety, but see C. Levin, J. E. Carney, and D. Barrett-Graves, eds., *Elizabeth I: Always Her Own Free Woman* (Aldershot: Ashgate, 2003); C. Levin, J. E. Carney, and D. Barrett-Graves, eds., *"High and Mighty Queens"*

of Early Modern England: Realities and Representations (New York: Palgrave, 2003); C. C. Orr, ed., *Queenship in Britain, 1660–1837: Royal Patronage, Court Culture and Dynastic Politics* (Manchester: Manchester University Press, 2002); C. C. Orr, ed., *Queenship in Europe, 1660–1815: The Role of the Consort* (Cambridge: Cambridge University Press, 2004); R. Warnicke, *The Rise and Fall of Anne Boleyn* (Cambridge: Cambridge University Press, 1989); R. Warnicke, *The Marrying of Anne of Cleves* (Cambridge: Cambridge University Press, 2000); S. Doran, *Monarchy and Matrimony: The Courtships of Elizabeth I* (London: Routledge, 1996); S. Doran, *Queen Elizabeth I* (New York: New York University Press, 2003); S. Doran and T. S. Freeman, eds., *The Myth of Elizabeth* (Basingstoke: Palgrave, 2003); M. H. Cole, *The Portable Queen: Elizabeth I and the Politics of Ceremony* (Amherst: University of Massachusetts Press, 2000); R. Rex, *Elizabeth I: Fortune's Bastard* (Stroud: Tempus Publishing, 2003); C. Haigh, *Elizabeth I*, 2nd ed. (Harlow: Longman, 1998); C. Levin, *"The Heart and Stomach of a King": Elizabeth I and the Politics of Sex and Power* (Philadelphia: University of Pennsylvania Press, 1994); C. Levin, *The Reign of Elizabeth I* (New York: Palgrave, 2002); D. Starkey, *Elizabeth: The Struggle for the Throne* (New York: Harper-Collins, 2001); L. Barroll, *Anna of Denmark, Queen of England: A Cultural Biography* (Philadelphia: University of Pennsylvania Press, 2001); L. Barroll, "The Court of the First Stuart Queen," in *The Mental World of the Jacobean Court*, ed. L. L. Peck (Cambridge: Cambridge University Press, 1991); C. Hibbard, "The Role of a Queen Consort: The Household and Court of Henrietta Maria, 1625–1642," in *Princes, Patronage, and the Nobility: The Court at the Beginning of the Modern Age*, ed. R. G. Asch and A. M. Birke (London: German Historical Institute and Oxford: Oxford University Press, 1991); L. G. Schwoerer, "The Queen as Regent and Patron," in *The Age of William III and Mary II: Power, Politics and Patronage, 1688–1702*, ed. R. P. Maccubin and M. Hamilton-Philips (Williamsburg: William and Mary Press, 1989); E. Gregg, *Queen Anne*, rev. ed. (New Haven: Yale University Press, 2001); M. Kroll, *Sophia, Electress of Hanover* (London: Gollancz, 1973); S. Taylor, "Queen Caroline and the Church of England," in *Hanoverian Britain and the Empire: Essays in Memory of Philip Lawson*, ed. S. Taylor, R. Connors, and C. Jones (Woodbridge: Boydell, 1999).

2. K. Eggert, *Showing Like a Queen: Female Authority and Literary Experiment in Spenser, Shakespeare, and Milton* (Philadelphia: University of Pennsylvania Press, 2000), 14.

3. For Mary, see also J. M. Richards, "Mary Tudor: Renaissance Queen of England," in *High and Mighty Queens*, ed. Levin, Carney, and Barrett-Graves, 27–44; J. M. Richards, "Mary Tudor as 'Sole Quene'?: Gendering Tudor Monarchy," *Historical Journal* 40 (1997): 895–924; D. M. Loades, *Mary Tudor: A Life*, reprint ed. (Oxford: Blackwell, 1992); for Anne, see R. O. Bucholz, "Queen Anne: Victim of Her Virtues?" in Orr, *Queenship in Britain*, 94–129.

4. The same thing would happen to Mary Beatrice of Modena, with even more serious consequences: see A. Barclay, "Mary Beatrice of Modena: The 'Second Bless'd of Woman-kind'?" in Orr, *Queenship in Britain*, 74–94.

5. T. G. Elston, "Transformation or Continuity? Sixteenth-Century Education and the Legacy of Catherine of Aragon, Mary I and Juan Luis Vives," in *High and Mighty Queens*, 11–26.

6. For another example of how Elizabeth may have destabilized the gender system, see I. Bell, "Elizabeth and the Politics of Elizabethan Courtship," in *Elizabeth I*, ed. Levin, Carney, and Barrett-Graves, 179–91.

7. See Orr, *Queenship in Britain*, introduction and chaps. 1–2; and Barroll, *Anna of Denmark*.

8. For a good, brief discussion of contemporary attitudes toward gender roles, see S. Dunn-Hemsley, "Whore Queens: The Sexualized Female Body and the State," in *High and Mighty Queens*, 102–5.

9. See esp. T. Bowers, *The Politics of Motherhood: British Writing and Culture, 1680–1780* (Cambridge: Cambridge University Press, 1996), pt. 1; R. Weil, *Political Passions: Gender, the Family, and Political Argument in England, 1680–1714* (Manchester: Manchester University Press, 1999), chaps. 7–8; and the poems in *Poems on Affairs of State*, vol. 6, ed. F. H. Ellis (New Haven: Yale University Press, 1970), and vol. 7, ed. F. H. Ellis (New Haven: Yale University Press, 1975).

10. For more on England's ruling queens, see C. Beem, *The Lioness Roared: The Problem of Female Rule in English History* (New York: Palgrave Macmillan, 2006).

11. Barclay, "Mary Beatrice of Modena," 90.

12. Similarly, Magdalena Sanchez argues that Margaret of Austria, Margaret of the Cross, and the Empress Maria used their frequent illnesses to advantage: M. S. Sanchez, *The Empress, the Queen, and the Nun: Women and Power at the Court of Philip III of Spain* (Baltimore: Johns Hopkins University Press, 1998), 5.

13. S. Mendelson and P. Crawford, *Women in Early Modern England* (Oxford: Oxford University Press, 2003), 356.

14. As Andrew Barclay points out, "defenders" of Mary Beatrice of Modena have similarly attempted to revive her reputation by deemphasizing her power: see Barclay, "Mary Beatrice of Modena," 77–78.

15. Levin, *Heart and Stomach of a King*, 66–90; J. Watkins, *Representing Elizabeth in Stuart England: Literature, History, Sovereignty* (Cambridge: Cambridge University Press, 2002). See also M. Dobson and N. J. Watson, *England's Elizabeth: An Afterlife in Fame and Fantasy* (New York: Oxford University Press, 2002); J. M. Walker, *The Elizabeth Icon, 1603–2003* (New York: Palgrave, 2004).

I

"Greater by Marriage"

The Matrimonial Career of the Empress Matilda

CHARLES BEEM

Here lies Henry's daughter,
wife and mother,
great by birth, greater by marriage,
But greatest by motherhood.

The epitaph of the empress Matilda described the summit of earthly achievement to which a twelfth-century aristocratic woman could aspire, according to the dictates of a male-dominant feudal society. As the daughter of Henry I of England, the widow of Holy Roman Emperor Henry V, and the mother to the future Henry II of England, Matilda's relationships to her male royal kinsmen were crucial and inescapable elements of her career as a female feudal lord, when she bore the title *Domina Anglorum*, "Lady of the English," during the years 1141 to 1147.[1]

While Matilda possessed a hereditary title to the English throne, she failed to gain her inheritance following her father's death in 1135, as her cousin, Stephen of Blois, rushed into the vacuum to claim the English crown. Four years later, as her second husband, Geoffrey,

Count of Anjou, labored to subjugate the duchy of Normandy, Matilda set off on her own to begin a sustained effort to displace Stephen as king. Matilda, however, was not content to exercise power on behalf of either her second husband or eldest son, or to play the role of dynast, the usual method by which women in Anglo-Saxon and Norman England enjoyed the legitimate exercise of political power. Instead, for all intents and purposes, Matilda wanted to be a *king*, in the sense that her ultimate goal was to solely possess an estate and office that had previously been occupied only by men.

Matilda's second marriage complicated her pursuit of this goal. As she presented herself as an alternative candidate for the English throne, Matilda represented herself as a single woman, amplifying her exalted position as the daughter of a king and the widow of an emperor while downplaying her status as a married woman. During the spring and summer of 1141, the pinnacle of her career as *Domina Anglorum*, Matilda exercised an autonomous historical agency completely outside the conjugal jurisdiction of the marriage not mentioned in her epitaph.

On the twelfth-century European aristocratic marriage market, Matilda was a catch. During this time, a woman's designation as a royal heir was rare, but not unknown. Matilda's contemporaries Queens Urracca of Castilla-Leon and Melinsende of Jerusalem had been designated by their fathers as successors to continue their respective dynasties through the female line.[2] To do this, they needed to be married, so they could produce the next generation of male heirs. The big problem for both of these queens, however, was attempts by both husbands and sons to encroach on the political power that each also considered their birthright.

Matilda's designation as Henry I's heir was also based primarily on her ability to force a similar dynastic link. Henry's first consort, Edith/Matilda, was a direct descendant of the Anglo-Saxon royal house of Wessex; their dynastic union represented a highly symbolic blending of Norman and Saxon royal blood.[3] Seeking to stabilize the fluid Norman succession patterns, Henry I was adamant that his successor would be his own legitimate offspring. Before her death in 1118, Edith/Matilda bore Henry two children who lived to adulthood, a daughter, Matilda, and a son, William, the *Ætheling*. In 1114, Henry I married eleven-year-old Matilda to Holy Roman Emperor Henry V. During the course of her first marriage, Matilda gained both the experience and the status that formed the building blocks for her later career as Lady of the English.[4]

Following the tragic death of William the *Ætheling* in 1120, Henry I began to consider the possibility of designating Matilda as his heir.[5] In 1125, Henry V died, leaving Matilda a still youthful but childless dowager Holy Roman empress. At her father's bidding, Matilda returned to England, an experienced woman of the world possessed with a formidable tutelage in the wide-ranging affairs of the twelfth-century empire. At the same time, Henry I's second marriage had produced no children, leaving Matilda his remaining legitimate heir general.

Primogeniture, however, had only been an intermittent feature of late Anglo-Saxon and Norman succession patterns.[6] Henry I himself had triumphed over the claims of his elder brother Robert and his heirs as he consolidated his rule over both England and Normandy. Indeed, a primary facet of Henry's French ambitions was the acquisition of further territories at the expense of his feudal overlord and bête noir, King Louis VI of France.[7]

Henry I had little difficulty getting Matilda recognized as his heir. While continental monarchs often crowned their chosen successors during their lifetimes to further ensure their eventual succession, Henry I balked at this strategy both for his son and his daughter. Instead, Henry had compelled his tenants-in-chief to swear solemn oaths recognizing William the *Ætheling* as his successor before his death in 1120. In 1127, Henry applied the same procedure to Matilda.[8] Anglo-Norman feudal society took oath taking very seriously, or at least claimed to; this represented the most secure form of contract Henry could make with his tenants-in-chief.

Henry had no need to impress upon his barons his daughter's capabilities; they doubtless already knew. Matilda was educated, intelligent, and experienced and possessed, as one anonymous and hostile chronicler later observed, "a mind steeled and unbroken in adversity."[9] Henry was undoubtedly aware of his daughter's ability to wield a royal prerogative. Matilda's biological capabilities, however, were an equally significant factor in her designation as her father's heir. Matilda's hoped for ability to produce male heirs represented the most persuasive justification for a female heiress that Henry I could hurl at his temporal and spiritual tenants-in-chief.

Henry's dynastic and territorial policies, however, were inseparable. In 1128, one year after her designation as her father's heir, Henry I married the now twenty-five-year-old Matilda, dowager Holy Roman empress, to fourteen-year-old Geoffrey Plantagenet, who had recently succeeded his father, Fulk, as Count of Anjou. The disparity in age and status were problems; a year after the marriage was celebrated, Matilda left her husband and returned to England.[10] In 1131, an English great council reconfirmed their oaths and repatriated Matilda to her husband in Anjou. Eventually, Matilda fulfilled the dynastic quid pro quo of her designation as her father's heir; in 1133 and 1134, she gave birth to two sons who survived infancy, an impressive show of reproductive achievement that certainly reinforced her candidacy for the crown.

But what about Matilda's husband? While Henry I had not necessarily arranged the match to make his son-in-law England's next king, Henry was keen to see his eldest grandson inherit England,

Normandy, *and* Anjou. As a number of scholars have argued, Henry I probably hoped he would live long enough to transmit his kingdom and duchy to his eldest grandson, Henry.[11] Geoffrey's role in the interim was unclear, but the general pattern was that a husband usually took possession of the political prerogatives vested in a wife's feudal inheritance. However, Henry I neither offered Geoffrey of Anjou any form of political office or patronage nor ever fully relinquished Matilda's dowry to him, which included a number of castles in southwestern Normandy.

In fact, Henry's immediate heir was clearly Matilda. The oaths of 1131 were given to Matilda alone and made no mention of her second marriage. Matilda herself had already begun a spirited campaign to obscure her position as a mere provincial French countess as she emphasized her more exalted position as a dowager Holy Roman empress. During the years 1128 to 1135, Matilda rarely referred to herself as Countess of Anjou in the various surviving charters she attested or assisted in attesting. Instead, she identified herself as *Mathildis Imperatrix*, "the empress Matilda," followed by *regis Henrici filia*, "daughter of King Henry."[12] This representational strategy identified Matilda as an autonomous female lord seemingly outside the formal bonds of her coverture as Geoffrey's wife; rather, she emphasized her kinship relationships to the sources of imperial and royal power.

Even Geoffrey, on occasion, took advantage of his wife's superior status, signifying himself in one charter as "the husband of Matilda, daughter of the king of the English and former wife of Henry, Roman emperor."[13] While Geoffrey eventually matured into a capable military commander, Matilda undoubtedly never let him forget the wide gap in their social status, or, it appears, in the power relations that governed their marriage. Geoffrey never appears to have imposed his will on Matilda's course of actions over the course of their twenty-two-year marriage.

Matilda seemed well poised to successfully succeed her father: her position as Henry I's only legitimate heir, the oaths of 1127 and 1131, and the birth of her two sons. When Henry I died rather suddenly in December 1135, however, Matilda was caught off guard, while a number of circumstances came together to prevent her from gaining her inheritance. Even before Henry I's death, there was muted opposition to Matilda's candidacy as her father's heir. As early as 1128, several of Henry I's chief supporters considered their oaths to Matilda invalid since they were not consulted on the selection of her husband.[14] While Geoffrey of Anjou's patrimony was an attractive component of Henry I's continental territorial ambitions, he was far from a popular figure among the Anglo-Norman baronage. At the time of Henry I's death, in fact, Geoffrey was vigorously attempting to gain possession of those strategic castles in Normandy, part of Matilda's dowry, that Henry had refused to relinquish to him. Not surprisingly, relations between Henry I and his son-in-law were far from cordial when the king died. While reports on the state of Henry's relationship with Matilda at the time of his death were contradictory, she was not with her father when he died on December 1, 1135, at Lyons-la-Foret in Normandy.[15]

Matilda's residence in Anjou at the time of her father's death was a serious complication. It is curious that Anglo-Norman historians have never seriously questioned why Matilda made no attempt to immediately claim her inheritance in England. This was a major problem; not until the death of Henry III and the accession of Edward I in 1272 would the next king's accession be recognized in absentia. In 1135, in the time-honored habit of the Norman kings, Henry I's death initiated an interregnum that ended only when the next monarch was crowned. While the oaths had recognized Matilda's candidacy, they were hardly enough to place her on her father's throne. This Matilda had to do herself, by being physically present in London to make good her claim and be crowned in Westminster Abbey.

Matilda, however, remained in France, undoubtedly aware of what was necessary to claim her English inheritance. One possible explanation for why Matilda did not jump at the opportunity was that she had just become pregnant with her third child. Matilda's second pregnancy had nearly killed her; her third pregnancy may very well have physically immobilized her in those crucial weeks immediately following her father's death.[16] What is even more intriguing is her husband's failure to take any steps to further their recognition as Henry I's successors in England. Instead, Geoffrey immediately set his sights on the acquisition of Normandy.

While Matilda remained in France, her cousin, Stephen, Count of Blois, swiftly moved into the vacuum. On paper, Stephen looked like an ideal male successor to Henry I: a younger son of Henry I's sister Adele, Countess of Flanders, Stephen was handsome and dashing and had been conspicuously loyal to Henry I, who rewarded him generously. Nevertheless, Henry I never seriously considered Stephen a viable candidate. But once Henry I was dead, Stephen moved with lightning speed. Imitating the procedure that Henry I followed in 1100, Stephen bolted for London, while his brother Henry, bishop of Winchester, seized the royal treasury conveniently located in his diocesan seat.[17] After convincing the magnates and prelates present in London that Henry I had effected a deathbed change of mind concerning his successor, Stephen was crowned a mere three weeks following Henry I's death.

In contrast to Stephen's well-documented election to the English crown, the chroniclers are rather terse concerning Matilda's activities following her father's death. Robert of Torigny commented that Matilda simply remained in Anjou with her family, while Orderic Vitalis reported that Geoffrey sent her to Normandy to gain possession of the castles that were part of her dowry.[18] The chroniclers then made no mention of her activities until the fall of 1136, when she was reported coming to Geoffrey's aid at the siege of Le Sap, three months after she gave birth to her third and final son.[19]

It appears that Geoffrey and Matilda initially agreed that the conquest of Normandy was the most practical strategy for gaining her inheritance. This proved to be a sustained and difficult process. While Stephen also gained recognition as Duke of Normandy, he was never able to bring the duchy fully under his control. Stephen and Geoffrey, in fact signed a truce in 1137, but for the next seven years Geoffrey remained focused on Normandy's conquest, and was formally invested as duke in 1144. Geoffrey's success in gaining possession of Normandy was a conventional example of a husband taking control of his wife's feudal inheritance on behalf of his eldest son, Henry, whom he himself invested as duke in 1150, when Henry was seventeen.

Matilda's interest in the conquest of Normandy, however, waned considerably as she watched events unfold in England. By 1138, Stephen had fully revealed his kingly limitations; as he imprisoned bishops, and courted the church's antagonism, illegal castles were mushrooming all over England in response to the lack of a firm royal hand. In response, Matilda was resolved to offer herself as a viable alternative to Stephen. While there is no historical record of the agreement between Matilda and Geoffrey, it is clear that Geoffrey, probably reluctantly, acquiesced in Matilda's determination to gain her English inheritance, while refusing to assist her in this endeavor. In effect, Matilda and Geoffrey divided the pursuit of her inheritance into two distinct and autonomous zones of action, England and Normandy.

What is provocative about this decision is that Matilda had no choice but to leave her husband and three young sons in France.

Since Geoffrey wanted nothing to do with this enterprise, Matilda's chief military strategist was her illegitimate half-brother Robert, Earl of Gloucester, who had formally renounced his homage to Stephen in 1138. In September 1139, Matilda and Gloucester sailed to England, landing on the Sussex coast. As Gloucester made his way to Bristol castle, Matilda enjoyed the protection of her stepmother, dowager Queen Adeliza, in Arundel castle. In yet another example of disastrous decision-making, Stephen granted Matilda a safe-conduct to join Gloucester in Bristol, a move that inaugurated a period usually called "the anarchy," as Stephen and Matilda operated as rival sources of royal power, which rapidly deflated the expansive royal power that Henry I had wielded. Once in England, Matilda accepted the homage of a number of key baronial figures, such as Miles of Gloucester, Brian fitz Count, and, later, Geoffrey de Mandeville.

From the fall of 1139 until the spring of 1141, Matilda established herself as an alternative monarch in the southwest of England, minting coins, issuing charters, and granting patronage, issued with her imperial seal, which displayed her favorite representation of herself, as *Mathildis regina Romanorum*, crowned and seated upon the imperial throne.[20] Matilda's public representations in England made no acknowledgement of her position as Countess of Anjou, her current married status. Instead, she identified herself as the Empress Matilda, daughter of King Henry, her other, and more exalted, relationships to royal power and status. In the extant charters Matilda issued between autumn 1139 and spring 1141, she forged a public representation that was, to all intents, that of a single woman, relying on her hereditary position as her father's daughter and her first husband's widow, men who, because they were dead, were not in a position to restrain her in any way.

Matilda's career experienced an unanticipated turn of events in the spring of 1141. As the "anarchy" further destabilized central-ized royal authority, barons had already begun to construct castles and engage in petty wars without royal license. In one of these acts of baronial vandalism, Ranulf, Earl of Chester, besieged and invested Lincoln castle in January 1141. When Stephen attempted to lay siege to the castle, Ranulf took him prisoner and handed him over to Matilda, who kept the captive king in close confinement in Bristol castle.

For most of the spring and summer of 1141, Matilda was ef-fectively recognized as Stephen's successor. While a few charters mention Matilda as a queen, she never received an English coro-nation.[21] What contemporaries did recognize was that Matilda had taken possession of the kingly estate and office. But none of the chroniclers based in England made any mention of Geoffrey of Anjou or his eldest son Henry, implying that Matilda *alone* had succeeded Stephen as king.

But what to call a female king? In March 1141, a church council was held in Winchester, presided over by Henry of Blois, the bishop and papal legate. There, a large gathering of lords temporal and spiritual elected Matilda *Domina Anglorum*, "Lady of the English," and formally offered her Stephen's crown.[22] During this supreme moment, the pinnacle of her career, Matilda triumphed over her social position as a wife and mother as she presented herself as a female Roman imperator.

"Lady of the English," however, remained just one component of Matilda's representational style. In her charters and writs, the title *Imperatrix*, "Empress," always came first.[23] It seems certain that Matilda wanted to make sure that none of her subjects forgot she was a consecrated empress, the loftiest status to which any woman could aspire in twelfth-century Europe. Matilda then signified herself as *regis Henrici filia*, "daughter of King Henry." This designation, second in importance to empress, but still quite powerful, emphasized Matilda's position as her father's closest heir as well as her position as the mother of Henry I's next *male* heir.

The designation *Domina Anglorum*, which always came last, is also the most intriguing. The title has no connection to any male kinsmen at all; it was an explicit recognition of sovereign female lordship before Matilda's coronation. Matilda alone was in possession of kingly power, beyond any form of wardship over her freedom of action, including that of her husband, who remained in France, focused on subjugating Normandy. Conceptually, this was a problem. English queens had wielded effective political power for centuries, but what legitimized such actions was their relationship to male gendered power; queens could render assistance to their fathers, husbands, and sons, or rule in their place temporarily as regents.[24] But women were not supposed to pursue political power for themselves. Geoffrey of Anjou did not put his Norman campaign on hold to rush to London for a joint coronation, nor did he send young Henry, then aged eight, as a legitimizing presence. Had Matilda been crowned, she would have been crowned alone. The Lady of the English was a lady without a lord, even though she had a husband and three young sons back in France.

Matilda, however, was unable to create a working relationship with the Londoners and ultimately failed to receive a Westminster coronation. Contemporary chroniclers, nearly all of whom were monks displaying various levels of misogynistic tendencies, are quite clear on what went wrong.[25] As Matilda displayed to her subjects her ability to be as ruthless and forceful as her father, contemporaries sourly noted her shocking deviation from properly womanly behavior, particularly when she demanded money from the Londoners while refusing all requests to grant Stephen's son Eustace his father's lands before he became king. While Matilda had gained recognition as Lady of the English, contemporaries were really taken aback by her near total rejection of feminine attributes, which turned out to be a serious mistake.

Contemporaries, in fact, used Matilda's gender as a political weapon. One hostile anonymous chronicler, the author of the *Gesta Stephani*, refused to identify her as empress or Lady of the English, referring to her instead as "Countess of Anjou" and "Robert, Earl of Gloucester's sister," a slap in the face to Matilda's chief representational props to the power and legitimacy she claimed.[26] Other contemporaries castigated Matilda for her "arrogant demeanor," her "insufferable pride," and her "hard heart."[27]

At the same time, the *Gesta Stephani* heaped praise on Stephen's consort, also named Matilda, for playing the same role as the empress when she rallied loyalist forces, indicating that a woman could get away with unwomanly behavior as long as she did it for her lord and master.[28] This the empress Matilda was plainly not doing; her exercise of autonomous power resulted in contemporary ambivalence concerning how they wanted a sovereign female lord to behave.

The Londoners, however, were more than ambivalent and chased the empress out of the city at a crucial moment in time. Stephen had greatly favored their economic interests from the beginning of his reign. In contrast, Matilda's demand for stiff financial exactions from the city became her fatal tactical mistake. While clerics such as Henry of Blois had supported Matilda for her support for Cluniac-style reforms, and a number of barons looked forward to the eventual succession of Henry I's eldest grandson, London's favor was heavily influenced by economic considerations. Just before her ceremonial entry into the city at the end of June 1141, Matilda was forced to withdraw to Oxford in the face of an imminent armed attack.[29]

Following her timely escape from the angry clutches of the

Londoners, Matilda's glorious summer turned into a long winter of discontent. In October, Matilda's forces faced Stephen's loyalists for a showdown in Winchester. When the dust had settled, the empress Matilda was forced to beat a hasty retreat to Devizes, while the forces of Queen Matilda captured Robert of Gloucester, the empress's chief military advisor. As she and Queen Matilda traded Gloucester for King Stephen, recreating the "anarchy," which persisted until 1154, Matilda returned to the stalemate that existed before Stephen's capture. In 1148, following Gloucester's death, Matilda effectively bequeathed her claims to her eldest son Henry and returned to Normandy, fully reunited with her husband and sons for the first time since 1139.

It is highly unlikely that Matilda returned to any state of marital coverture. Geoffrey died in 1151, and three years later her eldest son succeeded Stephen as king in England. Following her return to the continent, Matilda dropped *Domina Anglorum* from her style but chose not to signify herself as dowager Duchess of Normandy, much less Countess of Anjou, an identity she had banished long ago. Instead, for the rest of her life, Matilda represented herself as *Imperatrix* and *regis Henrici filia*. Nevertheless, Matilda insinuated herself into the government of Normandy, where she functioned as a de facto justiciar until her death.

Only as a widow, and the mother of a king, could Matilda enjoy the exercise of political power without being lambasted by her contemporaries for transgressing the gendered bounds of female behavior. During her fleeting moment of success, Matilda constructed a model for representing female power that contemporary commentators had some difficulty comprehending within their understanding of appropriate gender roles for women. Casting herself as a female imperator and a worthy heir and successor to a powerful and much-feared king, Matilda put aside the "modest gait and bearing proper to the gentle sex" to present herself, in that glorious spring and summer of 1141, as an autonomous female lord, a historical task she undoubtedly considered much greater than either marriage or motherhood.[30]

Notes

1. The standard biography remains M. Chibnall, *The Empress Matilda: Queen Consort, Queen Mother, and Lady of the English* (Cambridge MA: Blackwell, 1991). For a recent study of Matilda's career, see C. Beem, *The Lioness Roared: The Problems of Female Rule in English History* (New York: Palgrave Macmillan, 2006), 25–62.

2. B. F. Reilly, *The Kingdom of Leon-Castilla under Queen Uracca* (Princeton: Princeton University Press, 1982); B. Hamilton, "Women in the Crusader States: The Queens of Jerusalem, 1100–1190," in *Medieval Women*, ed. D. Baker (Oxford: Studies in Church History, Subsidia I, 1978), 143–74; and S. Lambert, "Queen or Consort? Rulership and Politics in the Latin East, 1118–1128," in *Queens and Queenship in Medieval Europe*, ed. A. Duggan (Woodbridge, Suffolk: Boydell, 1997), 153–69.

3. E. Searle, "Women and the Legitimization of Succession of the Norman Conquest," *Anglo-Norman Studies* 3, ed. M. Chibnall (Woodbridge, Suffolk: Boydell, 1980), 159–70.

4. For a larger discussion of Matilda's career as Holy Roman empress, see Chibnall, *Empress Matilda*, 18–44.

5. K. Leyser, "The Anglo-Norman Succession, 1120–1126," *Anglo-Norman Studies* 8, ed. M. Chibnall (Woodbridge, Suffolk: Boydell, 1991), 224–35.

6. R. Bartlett, *England under the Norman and Angevin Kings, 1075–1225* (Oxford: Clarendon Press, 2000), 4–25.

7. C. Warren Hollister, *Henry I* (New Haven: Yale University Press, 2001), 323–25.

8. Contemporaries differ on the date of when these oaths were offered: William of Malmesbury dated the oaths to Christmas 1127, while John of Worcester reported a second oath in April 1128. See William of Malmesbury, *Historia Novella*, ed. E. King (Oxford: Clarendon Press, 1998), 3–5; John of Worcester, *The Chronicle of John of Worcester*, ed. P. McGurk (Oxford: Clarendon Press, 1998), 176–77.

9. K. R. Potter, ed., *Gesta Stephani* (Oxford: Clarendon Press, 1976), 135.

10. J. Gillingham, "Love, Marriage and Politics in the Twelfth Century," *Forum for Modern Language Studies* 25 (1989): 292–303.

11. J. Bradbury, *Stephen and Matilda: The Civil War, 1139–1154* (Stroud, Gloucester: Allen Sutton, 1996), 10; Hollister, *Henry I*, 323–25.

12. *Regesta Regum Anglo-Normannorum*, ed. C. Johnson and H. A. Cronne (Oxford: Clarendon Press, 1968), 2, no. 1691; *Regesta Regum Anglo-Normannorum*, ed. H. A. Cronne and R. H. C. Davis (Oxford: Clarendon Press, 1968), 3, nos. 20, 567.

13. P. Marchegay and A. Salmon, *Chroniques des Comtes d'Anjou* (Paris: 1856–71), 1:xv, note 1, cited in Chibnall, *Empress Matilda*, 70.

14. Malmesbury, *Historia Novella*, 10–11.

15. Malmesbury, *Historia Novella*, 13–14; Potter, ed., *Gesta Stephani*, 10–12.

16. Robert of Torigny described the near-death experience of Matilda's second pregnancy. See Elisabeth M. C. van Houts, ed., *Gesta Normannorum Ducam of William Jumieges, Orderic Vitalis, and Robert of Torigny* (Oxford: Clarendon Press, 1995), 2:246–47.

17. See note 15.

18. *Gesta Normannorum Ducam*, 2:264–65; *Orderic Vitalis; Historia Ecclesiastica*, ed. M. Chibnall (Oxford: Clarendon Press, 1998), 6:455.

19. Chibnall, *Empress Matilda*, 67.

20. W. de Gray Birch, *A Fasciculus of the Charters of Mathildis Empress of the Romans and An Account of her Great Seal* (London: Reprint from the *Journal of the British Archaeological Association*, 1875), 381.

21. *Regesta Regum Anglo-Normannorum*, 3, no. 343, sealed 3 March 1141.

22. William of Malmesbury provided the most detailed description of Matilda's investiture as Lady of the English. See *Historia Novella*, 88–89.

23. *Regesta Regum Anglo-Normannorum*, 3, nos. 20, 368, 391, 597, 628, 794.

24. For a study of Anglo-Saxon queenship, see P. Stafford, *Queen Emma and Queen Edith: Queenship and Women's Power in Eleventh Century England* (Cambridge MA: Blackwell, 1997).

25. For a historiographical discussion of twelfth-century monastic chroniclers, see Beem, *The Lioness Roared*, 27–30.

26. Potter, ed., *Gesta Stephani*, 85, 87, 97, 115.

27. Henry of Huntington, *The Chronicle of Henry Huntington*, ed. Thomas Forester (London: Henry Bohn, 1853), 280; *John of Worcester*, 297.

28. Potter, ed., *Gesta Stephani*, 123.

29. Malmesbury, *Historia Novella*, 56–57; Potter, ed., *Gesta Stephani*, 122–27.

30. Potter, ed., *Gesta Stephani*, 118–19.

2

Widow Princess or Neglected Queen?

Catherine of Aragon, Henry VIII, and English Public Opinion, 1533–1536

TIMOTHY G. ELSTON

On May 23, 1533, the archbishop of Canterbury, Thomas Cranmer, annulled Henry VIII's marriage to Catherine of Aragon. For Henry and his new wife, Anne Boleyn, it was as if the previous twenty-four years had never happened. For Catherine, Cranmer's decision on the annulment had the unique consequence of making her, for the second time, the widow of Prince Arthur, Henry's long-dead brother. To confirm that new position, Henry issued a proclamation on July 5, 1533, that stripped Catherine of the title of queen and required all subjects to address her henceforth as Princess Dowager of Wales. For Henry, his long ordeal had ended. His new wife was pregnant, and he now kept his sickly old wife out of sight, and thus, he hoped, out of the public's mind. But the reality of the situation was much more difficult for Henry to manage than a man of his immense ego could imagine. Henry had underestimated how his own behavior, public opinion, and Catherine's determination made her a cast-aside wife and queen, not the widowed princess he desired.

No doubt, most are familiar with Catherine's obstinate refusal to bow to Henry's will and accept the change in her title and marital position, but her refusal in no way changed her circumstances: under English law, Catherine was the widow of Arthur. As this essay demonstrates, however, Catherine pursued a conscious strategy of continuing to portray herself in the manner the English people had come to expect, whatever her husband chose to do. Catherine had a twenty-four-year reputation for piety and advocating for the people. After the annulment, in her "widowed" isolation, Catherine exploited the expectations of both her own Christian humanist training and those of an aristocratic English society that often treated widows harshly in order to reaffirm her status with the public and, in a small sense, to subvert Henry's proclamation.

To accomplish this, Catherine had to negotiate and, to some extent, negate contemporary expectations of widowhood. From the Christian humanist perspective, two differing assessments of widowhood appear in the early sixteenth century. Most familiar in England, and perhaps to Catherine, were the opinions of Juan Luis Vives in his *De Institutione Feminae Christianae*. Vives insisted on widows maintaining their chastity, and thus safeguarding their late husbands' reputations, by staying home, remaining aloof from worldly matters, and assiduously avoiding opportunities for the community to question their reputations.[1] In Vives's world, widows were especially vulnerable to charges of immorality owing to the supposed weaknesses of their characters as women. Yet as Barbara Todd has recently shown, Erasmus in his *De Vidua* argued that while maintaining a good reputation was essential for a woman, a virile woman, or virile widow, should still be involved in public activity, especially activity that provided the opportunity for service and demonstrated her abilities.[2] Thus for a virile widow responsible for maintaining her own reputation, publicly performing acts of humanitarian service would demonstrate her genuine Christian character.

17

Yet Catherine also had to balance this humanist view of her new position with the realities of sixteenth-century aristocratic life. Although upon the deaths of their husbands, their legal status changed from that of the "junior partner" in a marriage relationship to being women with their own legal rights, early modern aristocratic widows still faced great difficulties, including struggles over inheritance, jointure rights, and their ability to remain unmarried. Some widows, though they should have inherited and had their legal rights, often failed to receive these privileges because of more powerful and better politically connected male relatives.

Under the law, widows had every right to manage and maintain the real and moveable property in their possession. They could control all of the income from their inheritance or jointure, something previously only their husbands could do. This did not mean, however, that a widow would not have any difficulties in managing her own property or the property she held in trust for her children. Even if her husband had left specific directions concerning the distribution of the property, male relatives, in some cases sons and stepsons, often attempted to force widows to turn everything over to them.[3] One finds an example close to Catherine in Maria de Salinas de Willoughby, Catherine of Aragon's former lady-in-waiting and confidant, who, with the aid of powerful allies, successfully defended her right of inheritance from male relatives of her late husband.[4] Other widows were less fortunate.

There were, however, some women in this position who followed a path that Sara Mendelson and Patricia Crawford have called the independent aristocratic widow, a woman who had enough power and stamina to assert her own will in various situations. These women tended to manage their jointure and had no interest in remarrying. However, to maintain their standing in the community, they needed to increase their outward piety, or else risk damaging their reputation.[5] Thus, an independent widow could maintain her reputation by providing money for the poor or putting forth effort in some other way to benefit the less fortunate in her community.

Complicating the picture for Catherine was her royal status. The most recent royal example of how to treat a widow was Elizabeth Woodville, widow of Edward IV and Henry VII's mother-in-law. As Joel Rosenthal has noted, while Elizabeth's position in England was relatively safe after Henry VII's victory at Bosworth Field in 1485, that did not mean Henry would never consider her a threat to his well-being. During the Lambert Simnel uprising, in which Simnel claimed to be the Earl of Warwick and thus a Yorkist claimant to the English throne, Henry decided he could not trust his mother-in-law and sent her off to live in Bermondsey Abbey with a relatively small pension. There she lived the remainder of her life, complaining to the end of her "inability to leave bequests because she was bereft of worldly goods."[6]

Henry VII's treatment of Elizabeth Woodville in some ways served as a model for his son's treatment of Catherine. Henry VIII's decision to keep Catherine isolated and living on a relatively small pension limited her ability to threaten his position. By denying Catherine easy access to the dower she received according to the original marriage negotiations made before her 1501 marriage to Arthur, Henry behaved like a husband managing his wife's legal affairs. Ironically, by setting out to control her person, wealth, and influence, he inadvertently supported Catherine's claims that Henry was still her husband. Her refusal to bow to Henry's demands that she accept her position as Princess Dowager forced him to act in the manner of a more traditional dominant aristocratic husband.

Regardless of how the limitations he placed on Catherine might appear, of greater importance to Henry was his need to isolate her from the public and turn public opinion to his favor, which was a task that had proven quite difficult. Although Henry was able to control politics and the church to gain his divorce, he could not convince his subjects to transfer their long-standing allegiance from Catherine to Anne. According to the Imperial Ambassador Eustace Chapuys, Henry feared that Catherine might raise her standard in defense of herself and her daughter.[7] While this never happened, the distress many felt about the divorce would surely have given Henry pause.

Even before the annulment took place, Catherine had considerable support. The most spectacular example was that of a young nun from Kent, whose complaints, uttered as public prophecies, the local authorities could not ignore. By 1532, Elizabeth Barton, a twenty-six-year-old Benedictine nun from the convent of St. Sepulchre's in Canterbury, already had a history of visionary activity. In 1532, she became an outspoken opponent of the divorce and remarriage, gaining popularity especially among Catherine's supporters in the clergy, including the queen's favorite and most loyal community of Syon Abbey. Barton had a vision of Christ recrucified because of the King's adultery and of Anne Boleyn as a Jezebel whom dogs would eat.[8] Chapuys further reported that she had a revelation in which Henry lost his crown and his kingdom, and that she had seen the "particular place and spot destined for him in Hell."[9]

Consequently, the authorities arrested the "Holy Maid of Kent" and held her for questioning in hope of entrapping many others. Eventually, the names of Sir Thomas More and John Fisher, bishop of Rochester, along with many members of Syon Abbey, came out as possible supporters. Thomas Cromwell even investigated Catherine, but as Chapuys noted, she fortunately had had nothing to do with the nun.[10] Authorities took Barton and some other agitators on a brief tour to denounce her publicly as a fraud, and then in 1534 they executed her along with several others for treason.

If viewed as a single incident during the divorce and Catherine's years as a political widow, then Elizabeth Barton's voice could simply be dismissed as a young woman misled by powerful and religiously motivated sympathizers who used her pious reputation for their own means.[11] Yet, contemporary sources reveal discontent across the entire class spectrum and thus serve as evidence that Henry and his representatives had a great deal of difficulty in selling his concept of Catherine as widow. This was especially the case as long as the general populace believed there was a link between the divorce and religious reform, for they were reluctant to endorse either.

From among the governing class, an example comes through the letters of Martin Giustinian, the Venetian ambassador to France. He reported that the English ambassador, Sir John Wallop, had expressed his disappointment at the divorce, and praised Catherine's wisdom, innocence, and patience. He went on to state that the "Queen was beloved as if she had been of the blood royal of England." According to Giustinian, Wallop also believed that if the divorce took place, the King of England would soon be at war with the emperor and Scotland.[12] Since Wallop lasted in his post at least through 1537, his views apparently never made it to the king's ears.[13]

Yet the vast majority of examples of discontent concerning Catherine's new position and the rise of Anne came from the lower and middling classes. Craftsmen of the city of London, for example, were hostile toward the divorce and refused to show respect for Anne. Their behavior forced Henry to issue a proclamation warning them to dare not speak "otherwise than well of this new marriage and Queen Anne, and to prepare the entertainments and expenditures usually made for the Queen's coronation."[14]

At the same time as his difficulties with the behavior of the craftsmen, Henry also issued a command restricting preaching by the Mendicant orders, because at least one of them had encouraged his auditors to pray for "the King and Queen Katherine, and the Princess" but not for Queen Anne. According to Carlo Capello, who was a member of the Venetian Embassy, Henry's government even had to prohibit, under pain of death, anyone even publicly mentioning "Queen Katherine."[15]

While Catherine complained about her lack of funds and about the houses in which she lived, some of the common people also protested dissatisfaction with Henry's arrangements for her. On August 20, 1535, the high constable of South Brent arrested David Leonard, an Irishman, for saying, "God save king Henry and queen Katharine his wedded wife, and Anne his pleasure, for whom all England shall rue."[16] He was not alone in his complaints. Earlier in the year, authorities had arrested Margaret Chanseler for publicly stating that Anne was "a goggyll yed hoore," and then crying "'God Save queen Katharine' for she was a righteous Queen, and she trusted to see her Queen again."[17] Still another complaint in March 1535, this time by Guilliaum Cowschier of St. Omer's, called the king a "wretch, a caitiff, and not Christian man, having two wives and a concubine." The deposition further charged Cowschier with saying, "Pity it was of the King's life to forsake the noble blood of the Emperor and to take a poor knight's daughter."[18]

In June 1535, the Lincolnshire authorities arrested the hermit Hugh Lathbury, who claimed he had gone to Kimbolton, Catherine's last place of residence, visited with "Katharine the Queen of Fortune," and then journeyed on to Lincolnshire where he began looking for, and apparently found, local supporters of Catherine. Her supporters, he claimed, were such in number that she "would make ten men against the King's one." Witnesses claimed that Lathbury had also stated, "he trusteth that she will be hereafter Queen again."[19] It is somewhat ironic that Henry, in his attempt to isolate

Catherine in the midlands of England, ended up placing her where she might possibly have a good number of supporters.

A final example of broad support for Catherine among the middling classes is found in the story of John Scot, also a hermit, from Scotland. Scot was well known in northern England by 1532 and first came to the notice of English authorities after his release from prison by James V. The Scottish authorities had arrested, convicted, and then fined Scot, though for what exactly English sources do not tell. Scot could not pay the fine, so he took refuge in the chapel of Holyroodhouse and remained there for thirty to forty days without food or drink. James V, not believing Scot's claims of heavenly sustenance, had Scot "shut up" in a private room within Edinburgh castle. Once there, he had Scot tempted with bread and water, neither of which he would consume, for "32 days." The king then released Scot, who became a local holy hero after he claimed that the Virgin Mary had nourished him during his confinement and fast. After a tour of the Holy Land and Rome, Scot stopped off in London in 1534 on his way back to Scotland. According to the early seventeenth-century chronicler John Spottiswood, Henry's treatment of Catherine of Aragon horrified Scot. From the pulpit of Paul's Churchyard, he began preaching "against the divorce of King Henry from Katherine his queen, inveighing bitterly against him for his defection from the Roman See, and thereupon was thrust in prison, where he continued fifty days fasting."[20] Scot's time in prison apparently did him no harm, for in 1535, once again living in Scotland, he met with Peter Suavenius, Duke Christian of Denmark's ambassador, who found Scot to be rather enigmatic.[21]

As the evidence demonstrates, Catherine's support from the public came from all classes and both genders, and for a variety of reasons. While some scholars, such as Retha Warnicke, have placed a great deal of emphasis on the women who supported Catherine and argued that their backing may have reflected their fears concerning the ease with which Henry put Catherine away,[22] it is significant that men also objected for similar reasons. Further, while some complained merely because of religious concerns, several of the aforementioned examples of public support reflect long-standing respect and appreciation for Catherine as queen.

Nevertheless, Catherine could not depend just on her reputation or Henry's actions to keep her case alive. She also had to play as public a role as Henry's restraints would allow. While Elizabeth Woodville was only a supporting actor in the drama that unfolded at the end of the fifteenth century, during the sixteenth century, Catherine had played a starring role. Thus, after the annulment, circumstantial evidence suggests she continued in that vein by acting as a virile woman, circumventing some of her former husband's wishes.

Catherine's efforts to keep her name in the public's mind coincided well with her own desires to demonstrate her piety and support of the people. This is demonstrated by Catherine's possible influence on the lace-making industry in Bedfordshire and surrounding environs, and her attempt to keep the Maundy Thursday service in 1535.

Catherine's proficiency with a needle, specifically embroidery, a domestic art she learned under the tutelage of her mother, Isabella of Castile, was widely known and added to her reputation as a virtuous woman among her contemporaries and long after. Of her, John Taylor, the seventeenth century "Water Poet," wrote

> I Read that in the seauenth King Henries Raigne,
> Faire Katherine, Daughter to the Castile King,
> Came to England with a pompous traine
> Of Spanish Ladies, which she thence did bring.
> She to the eighth Henry married was,
> And afterwards diuorc'd, where virtuously
> (Although a Queene) yet shee her dayes did pas

In working with the Needle curiously,
As in the Tower, and places more beside,
Her excellent memorials may be seene:
Whereby the needles Praise is dignified
By her faire Ladyes, and her selfe, a Queene
Thus for her Paynes, here her reward is just,
Her workes proclaime her praise, though she be dust.[23]

It is, therefore, no great stretch to assume, based on circumstantial evidence, that the popularity of certain styles of lacework in areas of England where Catherine spent her exile from Henry's court can be credited to Catherine's influence. Fanny Bury Palliser, in her *History of English Lace*, wrote that during Plantagenet times Flemish lace was popular, while with the Tudors it was Spanish lace or Spanish stitch. Palliser argued that Catherine introduced this new stitch through Spanish fashion when she first arrived in England in 1501, and that Catherine had possibly influenced the development of the lace trade in Bedfordshire while she was at Ampthill through 1533.[24] Based on her observations of local tradition, Palliser suggested that Catherine imparted the art of lace making as a means of subsistence for the poor, who yearly celebrated the memory of Catherine's decision to burn all her lace and order new made while the industry was in a recession.[25] Further, Thomas Wright pointed to the existence in Northamptonshire of a "Queen Katharine Pattern" and a "Kat Stitch" used in Buckinghamshire as more evidence of Catharine of Aragon's influence in the region.[26] Wright has also noted that while the great holiday for English lace makers was Tanders (St. Andrew's Day, November 30), Northamptonshire, Buckinghamshire, and Bedfordshire celebrated Catterns (St. Catharine's Day, November 25). St. Catharine was the patron saint of spinners, and this change of date may have reflected the presence of Catherine of Aragon in the region and her possible influence on the industry.[27]

More recently, Joan Thirsk has noted that Catherine's links to the lace-making industry would also have been consistent with her willingness, encouraged by humanist teachings, to aid the poor. Thirsk states that there was "a rising tide of opinion in favor of finding work for the unemployed and the vagrant poor" throughout the sixteenth century.[28] Thus, Catherine's support of the lace industry, especially during her time of exile and widowhood, would have been in keeping with her own humanist beliefs, and have had the additional effect of securing her a positive place in the minds of the English people.

A second way in which Catherine served the poor, and her reputation, was through her annual ritual of observing Maundy Thursday, when she washed the feet of a few hand-selected poor women and afterward gave them a small purse with coins. In 1535, now living at Kimbolton and in worsening health, Catherine asked the men responsible for keeping her close confined, Sir Edmund Bedingfield and Sir Edward Chamberlain, for permission to observe her Maundy service, a practice she had observed in previous years. Owing to her health, Catherine offered to make her observance "in her chamber prevely," but if not there then "sche wyll attempt to doo yt in the sayd parysche chyrche." Cleverly, Catherine argued on two points. First, Maundy Thursday had been her tradition for years. Second, Maundy Thursday service was something that the "kynges graunt dame during her lyfe kepte" every year.[29] In this case, Catherine reminded Henry that his grandmother, Margaret Beaufort, Countess of Richmond, had kept her Maundy, and she had done so as a widow, which would seemingly support Henry's interpretation of Catherine's status. Yet, Catherine's move was also calculated to force Henry's hand, for if Henry refused to allow Catherine to observe her Maundy Thursday, then he would have acted more in keeping with the domineering aristocratic husband than the brother-in-law of an independent widow. For their part, Bedingfield and Chamberlain, all too aware of their orders, yet clearly moved, or possibly intimidated, decided to write to Thomas Cromwell, Henry's chief advisor, for assistance in the matter. Though Henry did grant her permission as long as she acted as the princess dowager and not queen, no record exists of Catherine performing the Maundy service.[30] It is likely that Catherine kept it, limits and all, simply because of her high degree of religiosity and her continued ability to show her suffering to the people, who saw her as queen regardless of Henry's proclamations.

Using these examples as indicative of Catherine's character, one can draw a few conclusions. First, Catherine used whatever means were within her disposal to challenge the restrictions placed on her by the king or his representatives to fulfill culturally acceptable actions for a woman of her status and virile reputation. Second, even though her pious actions resemble those of an independent virile widow, they were also in keeping with the character that the English people had come to expect. A third point must be made clear: regardless of what Henry believed or did, regardless of how the people saw her, no record exists of Catherine ever referring to herself as a widow. Instead, to her dying day, she saw herself as the one true wife of Henry VIII. Consequently, her actions, when performed to benefit the people, were the actions not of a widow princess, or even a widow queen, but were in her view the actions of *the* queen.

As history has shown, what the common person might have believed about Catherine meant little to Henry. Thus, at her death on January 7, 1536, he would have the last word concerning her status. Though Catherine had wanted a burial at a Franciscan convent, Henry chose to have her buried at the more obscure abbey of Peterborough. There, above her tomb, he had a stone placed which declared that the one who lay beneath had been the Princess Dowager of Wales, and nothing more. From Henry's standpoint, the case was now closed.

Yet from a common Englishwoman or man's viewpoint, what was Catherine's status at her death? During her last years, Catherine played equally the roles of neglected queen and isolated widow princess, and at times even her ex husband's actions clouded the issue. A king like Henry could legislate public behavior, but he could not require inward obedience. Thus, at the time of her death, Catherine of Aragon may have had the title of Princes Dowager or widow princess, but in the hearts and minds of many of the people of England, she was still apparently Catherine the queen. She did not necessarily maintain the public's esteem because of her continued defiance of Henry. She received the love and admiration of the common people for her years of service and philanthropy, and though these people were largely unable to provide any assistance in her last years, they did not forget her or her claim to the status of true queen. As one anonymous chronicler from the period wrote just after Catherine's death in 1536, "Then dyid queen Kataryn a boute twelfe tide, and was beryed in Peturborow Abbey."[31] Surely, our anonymous chronicler represents the adage "old habits die hard" and demonstrates that a king's desires enforced by law, and at times tyranny, could not change what the people, and at times Henry's own actions, knew to be true. Long live the Queen.

Notes

1. See J. L. Vives, *The Instruction of a Christen Woman*, trans. Richard Hyrde, ed. V. Beauchamp et al. (Urbana: University of Illinois Press, 2002), 163–78.

2. B. J. Todd, "The Virtuous Widow in Protestant England," in *Widowhood in Medieval and Early Modern Europe*, ed. S. Cavallo and L. Warner (London: Longman, 1999), 70–71. Also see R. Kelso, *Doctrine for the Lady of the Renaissance* (Urbana: University of Illinois, 1956), 126–33.

3. B. Harris, *English Aristocratic Women, 1450–1550: Marriage and Family, Property and Careers* (Oxford: Oxford University Press, 2002), 127, 149.

4. S. J. Gunn, *Charles Brandon, Duke of Suffolk* (Oxford: Blackwell, 1988), 95–96, 132; Harris, *English Aristocratic Women*, 113.

5. S. Mendelson and P. Crawford, *Women in Early Modern England, 1550–1720* (Oxford: Oxford University Press, 1998), 175.

6. J. Rosenthal, *Patriarchy and Families of Privilege in Fifteenth-century England* (Philadelphia: University of Pennsylvania Press, 1991), 181.

7. *Calendar of Letters, Despatches, and State Papers, Relating to the Negotiations Between England and Spain, Preserved in the Archives at Venice, Simancas, Besonco and Brusseles*, ed. G. A. Bergenroth et al. (London: Her Majesty's Stationery Office, 1862–1954), vol. 5, pt. 1, sec. 142, p. 430.

8. A. Fraser, *The Six Wives of Henry VIII* (London: Weidenfeld and Nicolson, 1992), 205.

9. *Calendar of Letters, Despatches, and State Papers, Relating to the Negotiations Between England and Spain*, 5.1.1149, 857.

10. *Calendar of Letters, Despatches, and State Papers, Relating to the Negotiations Between England and Spain*, 5.1.1149, 857.

11. D. Watt, *Secretaries of God: Women Prophets in Late Medieval and Early Modern England* (Woodbridge: D. S. Brewer, 1997), 54; A. Hamilton, *The Angel of Syon: The Life and Martyrdom of Blessed Richard Reynolds, Bridgettine Monk of Syon, Martyred at Tyburn, May 4, 1535* (Edinburgh: Sands and Co., 1905), 34–40.

12. *Calendar of State Papers and Manuscripts, Relating to English Affairs, Existing in the Archives and Collections of Venice: and in other Libraries of Northern Italy*, ed. R. Brown et al. (London: Her Majesty's Stationery Office, 1864), 4:871, April 15, 1533, Martin Giustinian to the Signory.

13. J. J. Scarisbrick, *Henry VIII* (Berkeley: University of California Press, 1968), 356. When Henry was in the market for a fourth wife, Wallop had presented him with the names of Francis I's daughter, Margaret, and with Marie de Guise. Marie eventually married James V of Scotland.

14. *Calendar of State Papers and Manuscripts, Relating to English Affairs, Existing in the Archives and Collections of Venice*, 4:878, April 27, 1533, Carlo Capello to the Signory.

15. *Calendar of State Papers and Manuscripts, Relating to English Affairs, Existing in the Archives and Collections of Venice*, 4:878, April 27, 1533, Carlo Capello to the Signory.

16. *Letters and Papers, Foreign and Domestic, of the Reign of Henry VIII*, ed. J. S. Brewer et al. (London: Her Majesty's Stationery Office, 1862–1932), vol. 9, p. 136.

17. *Letters and Papers, Foreign and Domestic, of the Reign of Henry VIII,* 8:196, February 11, 1535.

18. *Letters and Papers, Foreign and Domestic, of the Reign of Henry VIII,* 8:324, March 3, 1535. There are many more complaints against Anne and for Catherine, too numerous to list here.

19. *Letters and Papers, Foreign and Domestic, of the Reign of Henry VIII,* 8:809; D. Wilson, *A Tudor Tapestry: Men, Women and Society in Reformation England* (Pittsburgh: University of Pittsburgh Press, 1972), 48.

20. J. Somers and W. Scott, eds., *A Collection of Scarce and Valuable Tracts, on the most Interesting and Entertaining Subjects: But chiefly such as relate to the History and Constitution of these Kingdoms* (London, 1809), 6–7; *Letters and Papers, Foreign and Domestic, of the Reign of Henry VIII,* 5:1280, 6:140.

21. *Letters and Papers, Foreign and Domestic, of the Reign of Henry VIII,* 8:1178.

22. For example, see R. M. Warnicke, *The Rise and Fall of Anne Boleyn* (Cambridge: Cambridge University Press, 1989), 189.

23. John Taylor, *The Needles Excellency,* 2nd ed. (London: Printed for James Boler, 1631), n.p.; STC 23775.5.

24. Mrs. (Fanny) Bury Palliser, *The History of English Lace,* 4th ed., ed. M. Jourdain and A. Dryden (London: Sampson Low, Marston and Company, 1902; reprint East Ardsley, England: E. P. Publishing, 1976), 310.

25. Palliser, *History of English Lace,* 375–76.

26. T. Wright, *The Romance of the Lace Pillow* (Olney, England: H. H. Armstrong, 1919), 25–26, plates 3 and 5.

27. Wright, *Romance of the Lace Pillow,* 27.

28. J. Thirsk, "England's Provinces: Did They Serve or Drive Material London?" in *Material London,* ed. L. C. Orlin (Philadelphia: University of Pennsylvania Press, 2000), 102–4.

29. "Original Documents Relating to Queen Katharine of Aragon," *The Gentleman's Magazine,* New series, 42 (December 1854): 574. According to the Catholic propaganda put out after Catherine's death, Henry had forbidden Catherine from passing out alms because he was afraid of the influence she might have with the common people. Protestant propagandists, including William Latimer and John Foxe, preferred to impress upon their readers how much more Anne Boleyn gave away on Maundy Thursday. See also, Warnicke, *Anne Boleyn,* 149–50; and Fraser, *Six Wives of Henry VIII,* 214.

30. *Letters and Papers, Foreign and Domestic, of the Reign of Henry VIII,* 8:435. Retha Warnicke does not believe Catherine would have kept the 1535 Maundy because of the restrictions placed on her. See Warnicke, *Anne Boleyn,* 287n47.

31. "A London Chronicle during the Reigns of Henry VII and Henry VIII," in *The Camden Miscellany IV,* ed. C. Hopper (London: Camden Society, 1859), 10.

3

"Most godly heart fraight with al mercie"

Queens' Mercy during the Reigns of Mary I and Elizabeth I

SARAH DUNCAN

During and after her reign Protestant writers criticized Mary I of England as a Jezebel, a tyrant, and a woman without mercy. Modern historians have likewise criticized England's first ruling queen for being too merciful to political opponents and not merciful enough to religious dissenters. Mary's sister Elizabeth I would also struggle with questions of mercy: she was concerned to appear merciful and yet chastised for showing too much clemency. K. J. Kesselring has demonstrated that "each of the Tudor monarchs recognized the need to appear merciful" and "responded to the broad cultural demands that a legitimate ruler embody both justice and mercy."[1] Nevertheless, the perception and performance of mercy was of special importance for regnant queens, and could prove to be a pitfall.

Although mercy was a virtue traditionally associated with queens in their position as king's consort, the notion of the queen's mercy became complicated for both Mary I and Elizabeth I because they were the first female English rulers to wield the (heretofore kingly) sword of justice as well. They were subject, therefore, to concerns about the extent and degree to which they practiced clemency. In Mary's case, balancing these two roles became even more complex after her marriage to Philip. The importance of defining the queen's mercy continued in the reign of Elizabeth I. Attuned to the negative connotations of being labeled merciless as a result of the successful propaganda against Mary I, Elizabeth had to walk a fine line between appearing to be a queen without mercy and a queen too merciful, thus endangering her realm.

Before the reigns of the first two regnant queens of England the dispensation of the king's royal mercy could be influenced by, and was associated with, queen consorts, who exercised their intercessory power to sway the king to acts of clemency.[2] Over the course of the Middle Ages, English queenly power contracted from the public sphere to the private sphere, and, as John Carmi Parsons has put it, "the queen became ever more isolated from government, in the process emerging as an attractive intercessor for those apprehensive of officialdom."[3] According to Parsons, "The queen's prescribed isolation from her husband's public authority touches, too, on the tendency prevalent in male medieval writing to place in opposition not only male and female but the qualities associated with them. For a king's wife, this set up a complementarity of powers: he the intelligence, she the heart, or the king as law and the queen as mercy."[4] Coronation ritual and civic pageantry reinforced queens' intercessory role: queen consorts interceded for pardons at the time of their marriage or coronation, and even the queen's placement on the king's left side during the coronation ceremony associated her "with the virge of justice and equity he held in that hand, . . . [and] related her to such qualities as mercy that he could not delegate."[5] Civic pageantry compared queen consorts to the Virgin Mary: their role as mediator between the king and his subjects mirrored that of Mary's role as intercessor between God and Christians.[6]

By the sixteenth century the queen's intercessory role was well understood. During the Tudor period, one of the most famous queenly intercessions was made by Catherine of Aragon after Evil May Day, May 1, 1517, when several hundred Londoners rioted in the streets threatening the mayor of London and Cardinal Wolsey with death and, in the words of the Venetian ambassador, plotting "to cut to pieces all of the strangers in London." After Henry VIII demonstrated "very great vengeance" on the ringleaders, Queen Catherine interceded on behalf of the approximately four hundred still awaiting execution, and this "most serene and most compassionate Queen, with tears in her eyes and on her bended knees, obtained their pardon from his Majesty."[7] The official pardoning was then carried out in a public ceremony at Westminster Hall by the king as the prisoners, chained and in handcuffs, filed past him shouting "Mercy!"[8] As queen consort, Catherine exercised her ability to temper the king's justice with mercy.

As a queen in her own right, however, her daughter, Mary I, was attacked by her critics, both during and after her reign, as a woman without mercy, and a tyrant: in the words of Christopher Goodman, a "cruele Jesabel."[9] In John Foxe's *Actes and Monuments*, Foxe warned: "Thus have ye Mary now made a queen, and the sword of authority put into her hand, which she afterward did use," and he went on to detail "the bloody murdering of God's saints, with the particular processes and names of such good martyrs, both men and women, as, in this time of Queen Mary, were put to death."[10] Her supporters, however, attempted to cast her in a different light during her reign, emphasizing her feminine virtues, including her merciful nature. She was portrayed as possessing such qualities as mercy, piety, and chastity, for which women, including female rulers, received high praise.[11] John Proctor commended her for being "so gracious, so mercifull, so liberall, so iuste, and so louinge a

Princesse," and spoke of her "incomparable pacience and endless mercie."[12] John Christopherson recommended that his country-men follow Mary's virtuous example, advising them, among other things, to "be merciful as she is, be lowly and humble as she is, be charitable as she is, cast awaye malice as she doth, be ready to helpe the poore as she is ready."[13] Mary's supporters had also depicted her as merciful during Wyatt's rebellion in January 1554, "desirous rather to quiete thys tumulte by mercie, then by iustice of the sword to vanquishe, whose most godly heart fraight with al mercie & clemencie, abhorred from al effusion of bloude."[14] In this case, however, she was forced to take action. As Christopherson wrote, the "bodye of my countrye (which I do greatlye lamente) hathe bene lately sore troubled with the greuous sicknes of rebel-lion, and as yet perhappes hathe some seditiouse folkes in it"; the necessary remedies included the use of "force of armes when as no other meanes wil serue: as due execution of iustice vpon all such, as be offenders therin."[15]

Yet Mary was still portrayed as merciful even in the execution of justice, and after the rebellion was over, she played out a public act of mercy very similar to the one performed by her father Henry VIII after Evil May Day. It is very likely that Mary was aware of the events of Evil May Day and the role both her parents played in it. It is not clear whether anyone interceded with the queen for the prisoners in 1554, but Mary herself intervened on behalf of the imprisoned rebels and granted pardon to them in a public ceremony that showed a striking resemblance to the one performed by Henry VIII years before. It was reported that during this ceremony the prisoners were brought, "knelynge all with halters aboute their neckes before the queenes highnes at Whithalle; her grace mercifully pardoned to the numbre of 600 who immediatelye thereupon with great shoutes casting their halters up into the ayre cried: God save

your grace, God save your grace."[16] In addition, Proctor recounted
that "six of the Gentlemen that were offenders were pardoned, going to their execution, by the Queen's clemency, at Rochester."[17]
In March 1554, Mary pardoned eight prisoners accused of taking
part in the rebellion, against whom nothing could be proved: Ambassador Renard later reported that this was in accordance with
"an immemorial custom that the Kings of England should pardon
a few prisoners on Good Friday." Renard thought that the queen
had been too merciful and complained that "as she had been pleased
to show mercy, there was nothing left to me but to approve."[18] The
Venetian ambassador Giacomo Soranzo also held the opinion that
Mary was more often inclined to mercy than not, reporting on
August 18, 1554, that "Her Majesty's countenance indicates great
benignity and clemency, which are not belied by her conduct, for
although she has had many enemies, and though so many of them
were by law condemned to death, yet had the executions depended
solely on her Majesty's will, not one of them perhaps would have
been enforced."[19]

As yet without a consort, Mary likely acted as her own intercessor in addition to performing the public act of pardon, tempering
kingly judgment with queenly mercy. In doing so, she may have
been attempting to counter the accusations of her mercilessness as
well as the fears that she was too merciful. Both charges stemmed
from contemporaries' understanding of the constructs of traditional
queenship. By denouncing Mary as a cruel Jezebel, her opponents
depicted her as both an unnatural woman and queen. According to
Mary Villeponteaux, the queen's detractors portrayed both Mary I
and Jezebel as tyrants, "and because they are women their tyranny
is particularly abhorrent, since as women they should by nature
be merciful rather than cruel."[20] The accusation would have been

strengthened by the traditional identification of queens with acts of and petitions for mercy: Mary was thus also an unnatural queen.

Likewise, fears that Mary I acted too mercifully may have stemmed from concerns that she was indulging in her role as queenly mediator to the detriment of her country's safety. Certainly, her treatment of rebels in 1554 differed markedly from the "systematic policy of punishment" undertaken by her father, Henry VIII, in 1537 in the aftermath of the Pilgrimage of Grace.[21] As J. J. Scarisbrick has pointed out: "Few contemporaries would have expected Henry to deal humanely or magnanimously with the rebels and fewer still, probably, would have applauded him if he had done so. A prince who lacked a standing army and a police force, a society which had known so much civil commotion in the previous century, inevitably tended to look upon rebellion as heinous sin crying out to God for condign punishment."[22] Mary's acts of pardon after Wyatt's rebellion would have alarmed those who believed she ought to wield the sword of justice in the same manner as her father. The fact that her very public pardon of the rebels mirrored Henry VIII's munificent performance in 1517 after Evil May Day, therefore, may have been intended to play up the similarities between sovereign father and daughter. The role of a regnant queen was ambiguous, and the struggle to define her position was an ongoing proposition. Balancing her opposing roles as both (just) ruler and (merciful) queen appeared to be a necessity for a ruling queen, and Mary and her supporters saw the value of exploiting her ambiguous position by interpreting her role as one that incorporated both kingly and queenly natures.

Mary's supporters, for example, used the idea that the queen was merciful in dispensing justice to justify not only her actions taken against rebels but also against Protestant heretics. For example, in the allegorical tale *The Spider and the Flie* (1556), John Heywood portrayed Mary coming to the defense of the true religion, saving the helpless fly (Catholicism) from the spider (Protestantism) by sweeping the spider from the window with her broom and crushing it underfoot.[23] Represented as a simple housemaid, Mary was bound by duty to her master ("Christ, the head master principall") and her mistress ("mother hollie church catholicall") to kill the spider in spite of her merciful nature: "And: save custom of iustice: forst her therto, / Loth was she: execution on him to do." Her kingly sword of justice was transformed into a less-threatening weapon: "Her brome not sword of rigor, (doble edged blade) / But the branche of mercie: that milde maiden made."[24] The reference to Mary as a handmaid also emphasized the connection between the queen and the Virgin Mary, the "handmaid of the Lord," and in particular her intercessory role with God in saving men's bodies and souls. By extolling the (Virgin) Marian trait of mercy in the person of Mary I, Heywood could reframe what would later be seen as her most controversial policy—the burning of Protestant heretics—as an act of mercy:

> Whose sworde like a brome: that swepeth out filth cleane:
> Not a sword that fileth the house: by blodie meane,
> This mercifull maiden tooke in hand to sweepe,
> Her window: this realme. Not to kill, but to keepe:
> All in quiet.[25]

By transforming the sword into a maid's broom, Heywood feminized the masculine symbol, tempering justice with mercy. His identification of Mary with the Virgin Mary, moreover, took advantage of traditional associations of queens with the Queen of Heaven, reinforcing the image of Mary I as a merciful ruler.

Mary's dual-gendered role in dispensing queen's mercy as well as king's justice became more complicated, however, after her marriage to Prince Philip of Spain in July 1554. From the time that Mary announced her choice of a husband, Philip was feared as a potential conqueror and tyrant who would usurp power from Mary: an "uncro[w]ned king out of a straunge lande," whom "the Lorde will make his sworde and maul to beate down your townes and Cities, and to devoure the people therof."[26] The imagery of Philip as God's sword reinforced fears that England's king consort would resort to force to wrest England under his control. John Foxe would later exploit this image by stating that upon Philip's arrival in England, after disembarking at Southampton in July 1554, he unsheathed his sword and carried it "naked in his hand a good pretty way," in spite of the fact that none of the contemporary eyewitness accounts of the prince's arrival recorded this action.[27] Contemporary portraits of the royal pair depicted Philip, rather than Mary, holding a sword, denoting the king's justice, and after the return of England to Catholicism in December 1554, Pope Julius III rewarded Philip with the gift of a sword in a silver sheath that was to be wielded "solely against such as either openly profess themselves the enemies of the Catholic religion, or corrupt the purity of the faith, or transgress against morality and the laws." (To Mary, in contrast, he gifted a golden rose.)[28]

Ironically, however, it appears that in spite of fears that Philip would wield the kingly sword of authority after his marriage to Mary, his role as king consort mirrored that of former queen consorts of England: his power was confined to that of an intercessor. Most famously, he interceded with the queen for the princess Elizabeth, who would later acknowledge that "when she was in prison, [Philip] had shown her favour and helped to obtain her release."[29] In January 1555 it was reported that all prisoners condemned of treason remaining within the Tower of London were "delivered out of prison by the Queens Councell, which satt there at their delyverie, and had the Queens pardon," but it was understood that this was on Philip's recommendation (although it is impossible to imagine that Philip went down on bended knee to intercede for them).[30] Roger Ascham drafted several letters in Latin to the king in 1554 and 1555 on behalf of a number of petitioners who were requesting release from prison or the remission of fines incurred by their involvement in Wyatt's rebellion. One letter, from Elizabeth Tailboys, the wife of Sir Ambrose Dudley, thanked Philip for restoring her husband to liberty.[31] Edward Courtenay, the Earl of Devonshire, also applied to Philip for aid in restoring him to Mary's good graces. According to Giovanni Michieli, the Venetian ambassador to England, Courtenay wrote a letter to Philip, "being induced to take this step and confirmed in it, by the great graciousness and benignity which he understood the King exercised, by interceding for every one with the most Serene Queen, having sought and obtained the release of many persons."[32]

Philip clearly acted in these cases in the queen consort's role of intercessor with the monarch. What cannot be fully determined is how much influence Philip actually had on Mary's decisions. For example, it was reported that Sir Peter Carew had been pardoned by the queen as a result of Philip's intercession, "who confers any favour he can on any Englishman, however ill-disposed he may be, with a view to obtaining their services in the affairs of the kingdom."[33] It is also clear from this statement, moreover, that it was believed that Philip interceded for more reasons than to display mercy: other motives were involved. According to David Loades, "it had been noticed in 1555, and was noticed again in 1557, how the king secured the pardon and release of political prisoners who were also 'serviceable' men of war."[34] One example of Philip's ulterior intercessory motives can be found in the example of Lord John Bray, who had been arrested and imprisoned in May 1556 on suspicion of being involved in the Dudley conspiracy against Mary and her government, as well as wishing aloud that Elizabeth was on the throne. His wife, Lady Ann Bray, had attempted to gain an audience with the queen in June 1556 to plead for her husband's release from the Tower but had been unsuccessful. The queen was aware of Lady Bray's suit and although she refused to give her a private audience, she "gave her a gret praysse," and sent the message "that god sent ofte tymes to good women evell husbands" (it is perhaps somewhat significant when considering Mary's words that she had just been informed of yet another delay in Philip's plans to return to England).[35] Although Lady Bray's attempt to appeal directly to Mary failed, Lord Bray was finally pardoned the following May 1557, in time to join the army that accompanied Philip when he left England for the second time, to fight in the war against France.

Whether or not Philip had ulterior motives in helping to secure these pardons, his apparent ability to sway the queen's opinion could raise questions about the amount of power he actually held as consort. It was not always clear, for example, that it was Mary who was ultimately responsible for pardoning prisoners, rather than Philip himself. Although the prisoners in the Tower released in January 1555 "had the Queens pardon," it was reported that on January 25, during the religious ceremonies celebrating St. Paul's Day and amid general celebrations of the return of Catholicism, they publicly made obeisance to Philip rather than Mary: "At the foot of the steps to the Choir, as the King went up, kneeled the Gentlemen lately pardoned, offering him their service."[36] It thus may have appeared to many Londoners as if Philip alone were responsible for their freedom.

The fact that Philip did possess some power to influence the queen, even if it was confined to an intercessory role, fueled speculation, and even the belief that Philip, however circumscribed his powers as consort, was gradually assuming control of the throne. It was understood that consorts had the ability to sway their spouses: this was not necessarily seen as a grave problem when the ruler was male and the consort his wife. A husband's influence on his wife was believed to be considerably stronger than that of a wife on her husband, however, and therefore, even the slightest show of influence underlined the grave threat of a male consort's potential ability to seize control of the government through his marital relationship with his sovereign wife. It is not surprising that some Englishmen therefore understood Philip's power to be greater than it was in actuality. William Herbert, Earl of Pembroke, would thus write to the Earl of Shrewsbury in January 1556 that "the kings majesty hath appointed the Bishoppe of yorke Lord Chancelor, and my Lord Paget Lord Prevey Seale," in spite of the fact that only Mary had the power to appoint any man to English governmental positions.[37] As long as Philip remained consort, fears would remain that his influence over the queen could be transformed into full control of the government. Even when his power was limited to that of a strictly intercessory role, he remained a potential threat to English political autonomy.

Although questions about how much power Mary's king consort actually held and how much influence he had over the queen may never be answered to everyone's satisfaction, contemporary fears about the extent of Philip's intercessory powers came to an end with Mary's death in 1558. During Elizabeth's reign, however, questions about the extent and performance of the queen's mercy continued. Like her sister before her, Elizabeth I also experienced the difficulty of balancing queen's mercy with king's justice. From the beginning of her reign, direct contrasts were made between that "cruel Jezebel" Mary I and Elizabeth. John Foxe, for example, recounting

Sir Henry Bedingfeld's cruelty toward the princess Elizabeth during her imprisonment in 1554, emphasized Queen Elizabeth's mercy (and wit) toward Bedingfeld after she took the throne. She

> showed herself so far from revenge of injuries taken, that whereas other monarchs have often-times requited less offences with loss of life, she hath scarce impaired any piece of his liberty or estimation, save only that he was restrained from coming to court. And whereas some . . . of her estate would here have used the bloody sword, her majesty was contented with scarce a nipping word; only bidding him to repair home, and saying, "If we have any prisoner, whom we would have sharply and straitly kept, then we will send for you."[38]

Elizabeth was also criticized during her reign, however, for being too merciful, particularly toward Catholics. At least one Protestant preacher, Thomas Drant, would later criticize Elizabeth I for refusing to take the same steps against Catholics that Mary had taken against Protestants. In Drant's sermon before the queen in 1570, he argued that "no perfect Papist can be to any Christian Prince a good subiect. . . . Upon them therfore first, and principally let her draw out her sworde." It was possible, in his eyes, for Elizabeth to use the sword of justice and still be considered merciful: "But they will tell me, which they tell the prince commonly, that she hath a goodly amiable name for mildnesse, and that now to draw the sword in this sort were the losse of that commendation . . . [But] her Majestie punishing euen to the vttermost Gods enemies, shall neuerthelesse by Gods worde reteine the name of a milde, and mercifull prince. She may be iust & seuere, and yet she may be mercifull and mild."[39] Drant's words echoed the same ideas used by Mary's supporters to justify her actions against Protestants. Just as Mary's supporters argued that Mary wielded both justice and mercy in her treatment of Protestants, Drant believed Elizabeth, too, could successfully demonstrate a similar feat in her dealings with Catholic recusants.

Elizabeth herself was very aware of Mary's reputation for tyrannical cruelty and mercilessness and was concerned that the same could not be said of her. In a speech to a joint delegation of Lords and Commons, November 5, 1566, Elizabeth reminded them of her merciful nature, even as she took them to task for presuming to discuss the succession, understanding "that there was no malice in you . . . for we think and know you have just cause to love us, considering our mercifulness showed to all our subjects since our reign."[40] She also understood, however, that no matter what her actions during her reign, she could be accused of being both too merciful and merciless at the same time. In her "answer without answer" to the parliamentary petitions for the execution of Mary, Queen of Scots, in 1586, Elizabeth defended herself against both charges. She explained that her long deliberations over her response were not because she "sought thereby the more to be commended for clemency and gentleness of nature," and attested that any person who thought the same "doth me greater wrong than ever he can be able to recompense."[41] At the same time, she complained that if she condoned her cousin's death, she would be labeled a tyrant in spite of the fact that "I have pardoned many traitors and rebels . . . so that mine actions have not been such as should procure me the name of a tyrant."[42] Forcing her to acquiesce to Mary's execution would provoke charges of mercilessness: "I may therefore full well complain," she continued, "that any man should think me given to cruelty, whereof I am so guiltless and innocent as I should slander God if I say He gave me so vile a mind." She concluded: "Yea, I protest I am so far from it that for mine own life, I would not touch her."[43] In the mind of Elizabeth, therefore, mercy—or at least the appearance of mercy—was a necessary part of queenship: for a ruling queen, mercilessness was too easily associated with tyranny.

In her dual-gendered role, dispensing both queen's mercy and king's justice, Elizabeth I, like her sister Mary I before her, was held to a different standard than previous kings of England had been. Both regnant queens found themselves subject to criticism regardless of whether they erred on the side of harsh justice or munificent mercy. The belief that a merciless queen indicated her tyrannical nature (thus jeopardizing her subjects) and, conversely, the fear that the actions of a too-merciful queen predicated her inability or unwillingness to wield the kingly sword of justice (again, endangering her people), stemmed from insecurities about the very nature of gynecocracy in sixteenth-century England.

Although both Mary I and Elizabeth I dealt with the same concerns about the extent and degree to which they demonstrated mercy during their respective reigns, after death, those similarities ended. Mary was dubbed "Bloody Mary" for posterity as a result of the execution of almost three hundred Protestants by fire during her short rule, while in contrast, Elizabeth achieved a lasting reputation for mercy in spite of the fact that over the course of her reign she arguably was as "bloody," if not more so, than her older sister. In the aftermath of the Northern Rebellion in 1569, Elizabeth undertook what has been called an "orgy of revenge" and ordered seven hundred rebels to be executed by martial law.[44] Elizabeth praised the violent actions of Walter Devereux, Earl of Essex, in Ireland in 1573–74, which "had elements of a massacre," as providing a necessary service in bringing that "rude and barbarous nation to civility."[45] In addition, in the mid-1580s laws were passed allowing Catholics to be executed as traitors, including over one hundred priests.[46]

Although during her life Elizabeth was concerned that she be perceived as merciful and mild, not everyone subscribed to that image either during her reign or after her death. Writing about Queen Elizabeth in 1655, Margaret Cavendish charged that "though she seemed loth, yet she never failed to crush to death those that disturbed her."[47] Nevertheless, Elizabeth's reputation as a merciful queen endured, in contrast to that of Mary I. Part of the reason for the divergence in reputations of the two queens can be attributed to the anti-Marian propaganda that disparaged the first ruling Catholic queen of England in order to glorify the second ruling Protestant queen. In 1558 it was still possible for one of Mary's fiercest critics, Christopher Goodman, to admit in *How Superior Powers oght to be obeyd* (1558) that if the queen would simply convert to Protestantism all would be forgiven: "To be shorte, if she at the burninge of three hundreth Martyrs at the leste, coulde have bene satisfied and vntaynedly moued to confesse the true Christe and Messias, and repented her former rebellion in geuing contrarie commandement to all her dominions, charging them to receaue agayne the true religion and to expel all blasphemous idolatrie of the pestilent papists . . . then were she more to be borne with, and reuerenced as a Ruler (if it were lawfull for a woman to rule at all)."[48] Marcia Lee Matzger has pointed out, however, that "Elizabethan undertakings to disparage Mary's memory began almost immediately upon her death."[49] By 1570, the publication of the second edition of John Foxe's *Actes and Monuments*, more commonly known as *The Book of Martyrs*, served as "a perfect example of propagandist history," to fix the image of Bloody Queen Mary and her martyrs in the minds of Englishmen for generations to come.[50]

In addition, Elizabeth may have worked on her own behalf to control her reputation for mercy. Vulnerable to the same kinds of attacks on queenship, and more attuned to the need to control her image than Mary had been in the few short years she ruled,

Elizabeth saw the need to distance herself from the actions of her predecessor in order to differentiate her rule. Elizabeth, therefore, was both more forthcoming with her advisors, her parliaments, and her public in offering reasons for her actions; and she was also careful to always define herself as merciful throughout her reign, even when her acts dictated otherwise.[51] Benefiting from a long reign, as well as the fact that her successor, James I, did not need to wage the same propagandistic campaign against her memory, Elizabeth I had more control over her image than did Mary I. Mary's reputation, moreover, may have had as much to do with her gender as with her religion or her anti-Protestant campaign. Leah S. Marcus has pointed out that "despite the genuine violence which erupted during her reign, we may wonder to what extent her sinister epithet 'Bloody' may have stuck to her because she was an 'unruly' woman on the throne. None of the male rulers of the previous centuries of near constant warfare and slaughter, not even the 'bloody dog' Richard III, had been given such a persistent sobriquet."[52]

Notes

1. K. J. Kesselring, *Mercy and Authority in the Tudor State* (Cambridge: Cambridge University Press, 2003), 136–37.

2. See J. C. Parsons, "The Queen's Intercession in Thirteenth-century England," in *Power of the Weak: Studies on Medieval Women*, ed. J. Carpenter and S. B. MacLean (Urbana: University of Illinois Press, 1995), 147–77; L. L. Huneycutt, "Intercession and the High-Medieval Queen: The Esther Topos," in *Power of the Weak*, 126–46; P. Strohm, *Hochon's Arrow: The Social Imagination of Fourteenth-century Texts* (Princeton: Princeton University Press, 1992), esp. chapter 5, "Queens as Intercessors," 95–119. See also Kesselring, *Mercy and Authority*, 141–42.

3. Parsons, "Queen's Intercession," 154.

4. J. C. Parsons, "English Medieval Queenship," in *Women and Sovereignty*, ed. L. O. Fradenburg (Edinburgh: Edinburgh University Press, 1992), 69.

5. Parsons, "Queen's Intercession," 116.

6. J. N. King, *Tudor Royal Iconography: Literature and Art in an Age of Religious Crisis* (Princeton: Princeton University Press, 1989), 196–97.

7. *Calendar of State Papers and Manuscripts, Relating to English Affairs, Existing in the Archives and Collections of Venice: and in other Libraries of Northern Italy,* vol. 2, ed. R. Brown (London: Longman, Green, Longman, Roberts, and Green, 1864–1947), 385.

8. J. J. Scarisbrick, *Henry VIII* (Berkeley: University of California Press, 1969), 67.

9. Christopher Goodman, *How Superior Powers oght to be obeyd of their subicts* (Geneva: John Crispin, 1558), sig. Fviii(v).

10. John Foxe, *The Acts and Monuments of John Foxe: With a life of the martyrologist,* ed. Rev. George Townsend, vol. 6 (New York: AMS Press, 1965).

11. M. E. Wiesner, *Women and Gender in Early Modern Europe,* 2nd ed. (Cambridge University Press, 2000), 21.

12. John Proctor, *The Historie of Wyates rebellion; with the ordre and maner of resisting the same* (London: Robert Caly, 1554), sig. Lv, Lvii.

13. John Christopherson, *An exhortation to alle menne to take hede and beware of rebellion* (London: 1555), sig. Eevi(v).

14. Proctor, *Historie of Wyates rebellion,* sig. Gv(v).

15. Christopherson, *An exhortation to alle menne,* sig. Av.

16. Proctor, *Historie of Wyates rebellion,* sig. Kv(v).

17. Proctor, *Historie of Wyates rebellion,* sig. Kvi(v).

18. *Calendar of Letters, Despatches and State Papers Relating to Negotiations between England and Spain Preserved in the Archives at Simancas and Elsewhere,* ed. R. Tyler (London: Longman, Green, Longman, and Roberts, 1862), 12:175.

19. *Calendar of State Papers and Manuscripts, Relating to English Affairs, Existing in the Archives and Collections of Venice,* vol. 5, ed. R. Brown (London: Longman, Green, Longman, Roberts, and Green, 1864–1947), 533.

20. M. Villeponteaux, "To Be Jezebel: Mary, Elizabeth, and Early Modern Attitudes towards Woman's Rule" (paper presented at the South Central Renaissance Conference, Malibu CA, March 3–5, 2005).

21. A. Fletcher, *Tudor Rebellions,* 2nd ed. (London: Longman Group, 1973), 45.

22. Scarisbrick, *Henry VIII,* 343.

23. John Heywood, *The Spider and the Flie* (1556; New York: Spenser Society New Series no. 6, 1967), 453.

24. Heywood, *Spider and the Flie,* 452.

25. Heywood, *Spider and the Flie,* 453. According to J. N. King, Heywood's "transformation of a partisan epithet into the language of proverb—'the grene new bro[o]me swepith cleene'—constitutes an implicit defense of the Marian heretical prosecutions as actions of political necessity and mercy in defense of domestic tranquility" (*Tudor*

Iconography: Literature and Art in an Age of Religious Crisis [Princeton: Princeton University Press, 1989], 189). In *The displaying of the Protestants* (London, 1556), Miles Huggarde would characterize the Protestant burnings as "iuste punishementes" (127).

26. John Bale, *A Declaration of Edmonde Bonners Articles Concerning the Cleargye of Lo[n]don Dyocese Whereby That Excerable* [sic] *Antychriste, Is in His Rightecolours Reueled in the Yeare of Our Lord A. 1554. by Iohn Bale* (London: By Ihon Tysdall, for Frauncys Coldocke, 1561), f. 68; Goodman, *How Superior Powers oght to be obeyd*, sig. Iiii(v).

27. Foxe, *Actes and Monuments*, 6:555.

28. *Calendar of Letters, Despatches and State Papers Relating to Negotiations between England and Spain Preserved in the Archives at Simancas and Elsewhere*, 13:137.

29. "The Count of Feria's Dispatch," in *Camden Miscellany XXVIII*, ed. M. J. Rodriguez-Salgado and S. Adams, Camden Fourth Series (London: Royal Historical Society, 1984), 301–44. See also M. A. E. Wood, *Letters of Royal and Illustrious Ladies of Great Britain* (London: 1846), 294.

30. Charles Wriothesley, *A Chronicle of England during the Reigns of the Tudors, from AD 1485–1559* (New York: Johnson, 1965), 2:125.

31. *The Whole Works of Roger Ascham with a life of the author*, ed. Rev. Dr. Giles (London: 1865), 1:414–29.

32. *Calendar of State Papers and Manuscripts, Relating to English Affairs, Existing in the Archives and Collections of Venice*, vol. 6, pt. 1, ed. R. Brown (London: Longman, Green, Longman, Roberts, and Green, 1864–1947), 31.

33. *Calendar of State Papers: Domestic Series of the Reign of Mary I, 1553–1558, Preserved in the Public Record Office*, ed. C. S. Knighton (London: Public Record Office, 1998), 153.

34. D. M. Loades, *Mary Tudor: A Life* (Oxford: Blackwell, 1989), 279. After all, Philip made no attempt to intercede on behalf of those Protestants sentenced to burn in the fires of Smithfield, in spite of the fact that Renard had counseled that he curb the enthusiasm of the bishops, and his own confessor, Fray Alonso de Castro, preached a sermon before the court on February 10, 1555, in which he pleaded for the use of less violent methods. See Joseph Pérez, *L'Espagne de Philippe II* (Paris: Librairie Artheme Fayard, 1999), 42–43.

35. Talbot Papers, MS 3206 [Volume P], ff. 279–80, Lambeth Palace Library, London.

36. John Strype, *Ecclesiastical Memorials, relating chiefly to Religion . . . under King Henry VIII, King Edward VI, and Queen Mary I* (Oxford: Clarendon Press, 1822), 3:208.

37. Talbot Papers, MS 3194 [Volume C], f. 211, Lambeth Palace Library, London. D. M. Loades has pointed out that "with the exception of the promotion of Lord Paget to the office of lord privy seal, Philip had no demonstrable influence upon the personnel of either the government or the court" (*The Reign of Mary Tudor: Politics, Government and Religion in England 1553–1558*, 2nd ed. [London: Longman, 1991], 210).

38. Foxe, *Actes and Monuments*, 6:554.

39. Thomas Drant, *Two Sermons preached, . . . the other at the Court of Windsor the Sonday after twelfth day being the viiij of Ianuary, before in the yeare 1569* (London, [1570?]), sigs. K3–4, 17(v)–8.

40. Elizabeth I, *Collected Works*, ed. L. S. Marcus, J. Mueller, and M. B. Rose (Chicago: University of Chicago Press, 2000), 94.

41. Elizabeth I, *Collected Works*, 199.

42. Elizabeth I, *Collected Works*, 197.

43. Elizabeth I, *Collected Works*, 201–2.

44. Fletcher, *Tudor Rebellions*, 100. Fletcher points out that in fact, the maximum number of those executed was "no more than 450" (101).

45. C. Levin, *The Reign of Elizabeth I* (New York: Palgrave, 2002), 55.

46. Levin, *Reign of Elizabeth I*, 29. According to Kesselring, "in later Elizabethan England the courts sent, on average, between 600 and 700 people to their deaths every year" (*Mercy and Authority*, 200).

47. Quoted in Sara Mendelson, "Popular Perceptions of Elizabeth," in *Elizabeth I: Always Her Own Free Woman*, ed. C. Levin, J. E. Carney, and D. Barrett-Graves (Aldershot: Ashgate, 2003), 203.

48. Goodman, *How Superior Powers oght to be obeyd*, sig. i, ii.

49. M. L. Metzger, "Controversy and 'Correctness': English Chronicles and the Chroniclers, 1553–1568," *Sixteenth Century Journal* 27, no. 2 (1996): 442.

50. F. A. Yates, "Foxe as Propagandist", chapter 3 in *Ideas and Ideals in the North European Renaissance: Collected Essays* (London: Routledge & Kegan Paul, 1984), 3:30.

51. Additionally, Elizabeth and her government may have been more circumspect in their application of harsh measures against Catholics than Mary and her government were against Protestants. In 1585 the Catholic Edward Rishton made the charge against the Elizabethan government that "in the midst of this cruelty exercised upon all Catholics of every rank, in order to conceal at times in some measure from foreign princes, and even the Pope himself, the severity of the persecution, and gain for themselves the reputation of being moderate and merciful, they show their mercy so fraudulently, that while they are harassing, torturing, and killing one, the royal indulgence is often extended to another." From Edward Rishton's *Continuation of Nicolas Sanders, Rise*

and Growth of the Anglican Schism, quoted in R. L. Greaves, *Elizabeth I, Queen of England* (Lexington MA: D. C. Heath, 1974), 26.

52. L. S. Marcus, "Shakespeare's Comic Heroines, Elizabeth I, and the Political Uses of Androgyny," in *Women in the Middle Ages and the Renaissance: Literary and Historical Perspectives*, ed. M. B. Rose (Syracuse NY: Syracuse University Press, 1986), 147.

4

Princess Elizabeth Travels across Her Kingdom

In Life, in Text, and on Stage

CAROLE LEVIN

In May 1549, the fifteen-year-old Princess Elizabeth commissioned a portrait of herself for her younger half brother, Edward VI (see frontispiece). Several months earlier in late January, she had strongly expressed her desire to come to court to physically disprove a rumor that she was with child by Thomas Seymour, the widower of their stepmother Katherine Parr and the maternal uncle of the king. Seymour was soon to be executed, in part because of his alleged involvement with Elizabeth. Elizabeth wrote to Seymour's older brother Edward, Duke of Somerset and Lord Protector:

> Master Tyrwhit and others have told me that there goeth rumors abroad which be greatly both against mine honor and honesty, which above all other things I esteem, which be these: that I am in the Tower and with child by lord admiral. My lord, these are shameful slanders, for the which, besides the great desire I have to see the king's majesty, I shall most heartily desire your lordship that I may come to the court after your first determination, that I may show myself there as I am.

Elizabeth was not allowed at court so that she might show the powerful her innocent, unpregnant state. But this did not stop the young princess from making demands. She then demanded a proclamation of her innocence be sent out to prove that the Council refused to allow that "such rumours should be spread of any of the king's majesty's sisters (as I am, though unworthy)."[1] Even though such a proclamation was apparently sent forth to the counties, Elizabeth did not forget her goal of being received at court.

When later that year her brother requested a portrait of her, she was pleased at the opportunity. Along with the portrait, she sent a letter to let him know that she wished to come to court so that she could see him more often. "I shall most humbly beseech your majesty that when you shall look on my picture you will witsafe to think that as you have but the outward shadow of the body afore you, so my inward mind wisheth that the body itself were oftener in your presence." Later that year, Elizabeth got her wish: she was invited to spend Christmas at court with her brother. The Spanish ambassador noted that Elizabeth "was received with great pomp and triumph, and is continually with the King."[2] Over a year later, in January 1551, Elizabeth returned to court with a great retinue of gentlemen and ladies.

The young Elizabeth was very aware of the importance of controlling images of herself and of being on physical display. In the interaction with the Lord Protector and young king discussed earlier, she demonstrated that she knew how vital it was for her to be able to travel to court to show herself off *as she was*, and, failing that, to remind those in power and, even more important, the common people of her position as "king's majesty's sister." She recognized the need to make her claim to good character and to publicly demonstrate her honor and integrity. Elizabeth was also clever enough to use the portrait to compensate, at least in part, for the Lord

Protector's refusal to allow her to visit court that year. She used similar strategies of self-presentation at many other times in the reigns of both her half brother and half sister. Travel presented an especially opportune occasion for self-display, and Elizabeth repeatedly used this to her advantage.

After she became queen, Elizabeth's progresses were important in inspiring loyalty in her subjects; they also brought her much pleasure. But even before she took the throne, Elizabeth had a number of occasions to travel, moving from household to household, from household to court, and back again. Elizabeth's life during the reigns of her father, brother, and sister was difficult and dangerous, and many of these journeys were taken against her will and fraught with hazard and jeopardy. To appreciate the young Elizabeth's ability to turn difficult situations to her advantage, it is useful to examine her travels, especially during the reign of her sister Mary, and the ways that she made use of them to stir loyalty and sympathy. Elizabeth's travels—or travails—as she was princess, and the response of the people to them, may well have been one of the reasons she was aware of the importance of traveling on progress once she had become queen. In fact, her later progresses as queen owe much of their development to these earlier travels, which we may see as "protoprogresses": they were not officially progresses and they were often involuntary, but clearly the young Elizabeth learned much from them.

As queen, Elizabeth went on progress many times during her reign. Mary Hill Cole reports that Elizabeth went on twenty-three of what Cole considers formal progresses during her reign of over forty-four years. Elizabeth never traveled to certain outlying areas in England, such as Yorkshire, Cornwall, Devon, or to any place in Wales; she did, however, visit twenty-five of the fifty-three counties of her realm in trips that averaged between forty-eight and fifty-two days. During these progresses she made an average of twenty-three visits to various residences, each usually lasting only a few days.[3]

In this essay I discuss the princess Elizabeth's progresses in relationship to her (sometimes quite theatrical) self-portrayals during these movements. Elizabeth traveled by carriage, on horseback, and on foot, depending on the length and purpose of the journey. These modes presented different opportunities for interaction or self-display. I am especially concerned with certain specific travels to, from, and within the city of London: Elizabeth's trip to London to meet Mary when she had been proclaimed queen; her slow return to London from Ashridge after Thomas Wyatt's rebellion; her removal to the Tower of London; her travels from London to Woodstock and back; and her triumphant return to London as queen after Mary's death. As well as discussing the events themselves, I also examine how this travel was portrayed during and immediately after her lifetime, especially in John Foxe's *Acts and Monuments* (1563; expanded 1570), and then right after her death in Thomas Heywood's play *If You Know Not Me, You Know Nobody, Part I* (1605). The written and staged versions of these travels served as another method for the English to know their queen. These emotional appeals and the dangers that the young Elizabeth had experienced while these journeys were made encouraged loyalty. Such accounts both prefigured her later progresses as queen and paralleled and echoed them. These stories of the young Elizabeth's dangerous travels were also significant to the Protestant nation soon after her death in glorifying Elizabeth as a political/religious heroine. Elizabeth was particularly effective at creating close connections with her people. As Wallace MacCaffrey points out, she "could turn respect and awe for a distant sovereign into lively loyalty to a warm and vivid human being."[4]

Mary's Accession and Elizabeth's Travels

If Elizabeth felt at risk during the Seymour incident early in Edward's reign, her sense of danger only increased as her brother's reign was ending. John Dudley, Duke of Northumberland, had engineered a coup against Somerset in 1549 that eventually led to his death in January 1552. But as Edward's health deteriorated, Northumberland's future became more and more problematic, since Mary's accession would, at the very least, have ended his career. Elizabeth was obviously too independent-minded to be drawn into a plot with Northumberland, and in the uncertain spring of 1553 Northumberland's youngest surviving son, Guilford, married Edward's cousin, Lady Jane Grey, whom Edward named in his will as the next heir. Northumberland kept secret how truly close Edward was to dying and sent word to each of Edward's sisters that Edward's last wish was to die in his sister's arms; presumably, it did not matter which sister. This message was probably received the 4th or 5th of July. While Mary immediately took to the road, Elizabeth stayed put. Always more astute than Mary, Elizabeth knew that this was a time when not traveling—progressing—was the wisest decision. Elizabeth had already attempted to go to London to see her dying brother and had been turned back; she did not trust this newer message.

Whatever Mary or Elizabeth might have felt about the prospect of losing their brother, it also meant that according to the succession that Henry VIII had set forth, Mary was the next queen. Mary had immediately started toward the court when she was stopped on the way with the message that the summons was a trap. Edward was already dead; he had died July 6. Though the King's Council had publicly supported Northumberland and the change in the succession, many privately despised the plan. They were not alone; Northumberland's army melted away and Mary became queen without a battle. On July 19 Dudley's own Council proclaimed Mary the ruler of the realm, and the next day the Earl of Arundel and Lord Paget arrived at Framlingham Castle to present Queen Mary with a letter from the Council telling her that they had "proclaimed in your City of London your majesty to be our true natural sovereign liege lady and queen."[5] Jane's brief rule was over.

Ten days after the proclamation, Elizabeth came to London to await Mary's triumphant entry. Elizabeth and her retinue rode along Fleet Street to Somerset House, which she owned. Elizabeth was accompanied by her five hundred horsemen. A contemporary observer wrote, "The lady Elizabethes grace came the 29 of July to Somerset place, well accompanied with gentlemen, and others righte strongly."[6] All her close servants were dressed in Tudor green, with coats trimmed "whytt welvett saten taffaty" depending on their rank, according to the contemporary observer London citizen Henry Machyn.[7] Elizabeth was well aware of the significance of color. The use of the Tudor green could have been a way for Elizabeth to show her loyalty to the new queen; it was also a method to demonstrate that both Elizabeth and Mary came from the same royal stock, and for Elizabeth to make sure that instead of being a supporting player, she had stolen the show.

On July 31 Elizabeth rode out through Aldgate to meet Mary on the road and escort her into the city. Elizabeth had as many as a thousand people on horseback with her; Mary may have had as many as ten thousand. Elizabeth may have wondered how her older half sister and now queen would respond to her. While they shared a father, both had had a problematic relationship with him; moreover, their mothers had been bitter rivals. The sisters met at Wanstead, and Elizabeth and her entourage made their first homage to Mary as queen. Elizabeth may well have noted the effectiveness of Mary's enormous entourage and kept it in mind should she have the opportunity to have one of her own.[8] In the first euphoria of becoming queen, Mary greeted her younger sister with great affection and kissed every lady Elizabeth presented to her. On August 3, when Mary rode in state, Elizabeth was positioned in a place of honor immediately behind her sister, the queen. At public appearances Mary held Elizabeth's hand and gave her a place of honor at her side.[9]

Leaving Court Freely, Returning under Guard

This pleasant state of affairs did not last, however. By September Mary had become publicly suspicious of Elizabeth, even stating that they were not sisters at all but instead that Elizabeth was the daughter of Anne Boleyn and her musician Mark Smeaton, one of the five men executed for being Anne's lover and the one of meanest status. Such an insulting statement was clearly aimed at humiliating Elizabeth and undermining her claim to the throne. Still, Elizabeth had her proper place at Mary's coronation, which had been delayed until September 30 so Mary could use "uncontaminated" chrisom oil obtained from the Low Countries for the ceremony.[10] On the day before the coronation, during a splendid pageant through London, directly behind the gold-canopied litter that bore Mary herself, was a carriage trimmed in white and silver "and therein sat at the ende, with hir face forwarde, the lady Elizabeth; and at the other ende, with her backe forwarde, the lady Anne of Cleves."[11] Elizabeth wore a French dress of white and silver. For Mary's coronation procession from the Tower through the city of London, directly behind Mary's open litter was "the first chariot, richly covered, the horses richly trapped, conveying Princess Elizabeth and Anne of Cleves, appareled with crimson velvet."[12]

D. M. Loades argues that Mary could not believe that anyone could hold "genuine religious convictions which differed from her own," and deeply distrusted her younger sister.[13] At first Elizabeth boycotted the Catholic services at court, and the Spanish ambassador suggested to Mary that Elizabeth "is only clinging to the new religion out of policy, in order to win over and make use of its adepts in case she decided to plot."[14]

By the beginning of September, Elizabeth realized her allegiance to the new religion put her in too vulnerable a position so, "weeping," she begged Mary for instruction in the "true faith," and claimed conversion. Mary, however, was no doubt highly suspicious, especially since on September 8, the first day Elizabeth was to attend Mass, the princess asked to be excused because she felt ill. When the queen insisted on her presence, Elizabeth "complained loudly all the way to church that her stomach ached, wearing a suffering air."[15] A week later, Elizabeth did not attend mass. Mary was furious that Elizabeth was not a true convert to Catholicism and hated that according to Henry VIII's will, Elizabeth was the next heir. She proclaimed what a scandal and disgrace it would be to the kingdom if a heretic, hypocrite, and bastard such as Elizabeth were to be the next queen. Mary was convinced that Elizabeth too much "resembled her mother; and as her mother had caused great trouble in the kingdom, the Queen feared that Elizabeth might do the same."[16]

Mary began to give precedence ahead of Elizabeth to the Countess of Lenox and the Duchess of Suffolk, even though the latter was the mother of the condemned traitor Lady Jane Grey. In November 1553 Elizabeth could no longer tolerate the suspicious atmosphere of life at court and requested that she be allowed to leave so that she might reside at Ashridge, though she begged to see Mary before she left. The Spanish ambassador Simon Renard wrote to the emperor that "I had much difficulty in persuading the Queen to dissemble" in her meeting with her sister.[17] While Mary had taken Renard's advice and the meeting was pleasant, it no doubt filled Elizabeth with foreboding. Mary, on the advice of the Spanish ambassador, gave Elizabeth an expensive gift of sables as a parting gift; but what Elizabeth wanted more was the promise that if Mary ever heard something about Elizabeth that was to her discredit, Mary would agree to see her sister in person. She begged Mary not to put faith in treasonous stories about her without giving her a hearing. But Mary had long since ceased to trust Elizabeth.

Mary doubted her sister's sincerity even more after Thomas Wyatt led an abortive rebellion against her marriage to Philip of Spain in early 1554. Mary was convinced that Elizabeth had known about and encouraged the rebellion. Elizabeth's great danger and the travails that she had to endure at this time came to be engraved in the minds and hearts of her subjects in part because of how vividly Foxe described these events in his *Acts and Monuments*, an often-read text in Elizabethan and Jacobean England. Foxe was supremely effective at depicting the sufferings of "true" Christians during the history of England, especially the martyrdom of three hundred Protestants in the reign of Mary I. Besides the histories of those who were accused and executed for heresy, Foxe also asks his readers to consider the "extream misery, sickness, fear, and peril" that led Princess Elizabeth to despair of her life. Foxe portrays Elizabeth's travails by referring to her travels: how Elizabeth was "clapped in the Tower, and again tossed from thence, and from house to house, from prison to prison, from post to pillar."[18]

On January 29, Mary sent Sir Richard Southwell, Sir Edward Hastings, and Sir Thomas Cornwallis to Elizabeth demanding that the princess return to court and respond to the charges against her. While Mary's chancellor Stephen Gardiner and the Spanish ambassador Renard wanted Elizabeth sent directly to the Tower, Mary decided to first have her examined at court. Elizabeth, however, claimed that she was too ill to travel. To her benefit, all of these negotiations delayed the time before Elizabeth had to appear at court. Mary refused to accept Elizabeth's illness as a genuine excuse, and Hastings and Cornwallis made a return trip, this time accompanied by Lord William Howard and two doctors, Thomas Wendy and George Owen, who were told that unless travel would endanger her life, she must answer the queen's summons. The doctors examined Elizabeth and determined that though she was unwell, she could travel. Elizabeth said "that she wolde most willinglye, in as spedy a manner as she coulde for her sicknes, repayre to the queens highness with hir owne company and folks onely."[19] But she was not allowed to come with only her people—she came guarded by the queen's men. Foxe describes Mary's men as particularly harsh, not even caring whether Elizabeth could survive this trip. Foxe tells his readers that Elizabeth was "sick in her bed . . . very weak and feeble of body." Yet despite her illness, the men inform Elizabeth "our commission is such . . . we must needs bring you with us, either alive or dead."[20]

I would argue that Elizabeth was indeed unwell, but that she also used this condition to prolong the travel time. The entourage moved slowly, taking five days to cover the thirty-three miles to London. Foxe describes Elizabeth as she left Ashridge as "very faint and feeble," and often swooning. The first night they stopped at Redborne, and Elizabeth was guarded as she slept. "From thence to St. Alban's to sir Ralph Rowlet's house, where she tarried that night, both feeble in body and comfortless in mind." Each day's travel was a very short distance, and Foxe emphasizes how ill and distraught Elizabeth was.[21]

The Spanish ambassador wrote to the emperor about how slowly Elizabeth was traveling and presented his own interpretation of the reasons why: "The Lady Elizabeth, who is so unwell that she only travels two or three leagues a day, and has such a stricken conscience that she cannot stand on her feet and refuses meat or drink. It is taken for certain that she is with child."[22] Just as during the crisis for Elizabeth in Edward's reign rumors swirled about her that she was pregnant, now, at the most dangerous time for her in Mary's reign, the Spanish ambassador several times spread these rumors as well. But Elizabeth again took the opportunity of travel to show herself, ill but not with child, to the people.

Lady Jane Grey and her husband Guilford had been executed February 12, 1554, just as Elizabeth was summoned to London, and this news would have been horrifying for her. But even with that terror Elizabeth still understood the importance of how the people regarded her as she traveled through the capital. Foxe explains, "From that place she was conveyed to the court, where by the way came to meet her many gentlemen to accompany her highness, who were very sorry to see her in that case. But especially a great multitude of people were standing by the way, who then flocking about her litter, lamented and bewailed greatly her estate."[23] Certainly, the Londoners would have realized that Mary's court would have linked the Wyatt rebellion, Lady Jane Grey, and Elizabeth, putting the princess in great danger.

Elizabeth had been ordered to court where a frightening confrontation awaited, but her appearance also demonstrated how many people cared for her and the publicity her commanded presence had generated. The public response would have been some comfort to Elizabeth as well as allowing her to witness her own popularity, which was of critical importance to her. The slow pace of travel may also have allowed Elizabeth to elicit more sympathy and affection, and Elizabeth made sure that she was seen. Henry Machyn observed that her "grace rod in a charett opyn of boyth sides. . . . and so thrught Flestret unto the cowrt thrught the que[een's] garden, her grace behyng syke."[24] Even though Simon Renard was Elizabeth's enemy, he did not discount her impressive self-control and how well she showed herself while traveling:

> The Lady Elizabeth arrived yesterday, dressed all in white and followed by a great company of the Queen's people and her own. She had her litter opened to show herself to the people, and her pale face kept a proud, haughty expression in order to mask her vexation. The Queen would not see her and had her lodged in part of her house out of which neither she nor any of her suite can pass without crossing the guard, whilst only two gentlemen, six ladies and four servants were permitted to stay with her, the rest being quartered in the city of London.[25]

Elizabeth well understood the impact of color symbolism. When she had met her sister at the beginning of Mary's reign, Elizabeth had all her ladies dressed in the Tudor colors of green and white. No doubt Elizabeth deliberately dressed in white on this occasion so that when she drew back the curtains of her litter, she could show herself as someone who signified innocence and virtue. Once she was queen and especially when she was so visible on progress, Elizabeth remained aware of color, and the particular significance of the colors she wore on specific occasions. The monarch Elizabeth wore blue to demonstrate her connection to the Virgin Mary, or black and white as symbols of her virginity.

Removal to the Tower

After waiting nearly a month in her rooms at Whitehall while Mary and the Council dithered about what to do, Elizabeth was told she would be taken to the Tower. The princess was in great danger, and she knew it. Renard wanted Elizabeth thrown in the Tower and was convinced that if Mary did not execute Elizabeth when she had the chance, the situation would be even more perilous for

Mary and for Spain, since Elizabeth appeared as the lightning rod for all dissatisfaction with the current regime.

Elizabeth managed to gain twenty-four hours by convincing the Earl of Sussex to allow her to write to Mary, begging that her sister see her before the order was carried out. Mary refused, and the next day, Elizabeth was taken to the Tower by barge; Mary and her Council were afraid that there might be attempts to rescue Elizabeth if she were brought through the streets of London. They were no doubt aware of the crowds that had surrounded her litter when she had earlier been brought to court.

It was raining on Palm Sunday as Elizabeth was brought by barge to the gate which at that time was known as the "Traitor's Gate." According to a contemporary account, "She was taken in at the drawebridge. Yt is saide when she came in she saide to the warders and soldears, loking up to heaven: 'Ohe Lorde! I never thought to have come in here as prisoner; and I praie you all goude frendes and fellows, bere me wytnes, that I come yn no traytour, but as true a woman to the queens majesty as eny is noew lyving; and thereon will I take my deathe.'" She added that she was "but a weak woman."[26] This trip of Elizabeth's was one of the most renowned during her own lifetime because it was memorialized in *Acts and Monuments*. Foxe dramatically shows an Elizabeth who, once she had arrived at the Tower, did not want to disembark at Traitor's Gate. Finally, she stepped out of the barge, and, in front of a large group of servants and warders, Elizabeth used the occasion to proclaim her innocence: "Here lands as true a subject, being prisoner, as ever landed at these stairs; and before thee, O God! I speak it, having no other friends but thee alone."[27] Foxe describes an Elizabeth who even at this moment was aware of her public persona and the potential theatricality of the moment. Then, Foxe's Elizabeth paused for a moment outside the gate and sat on a stone wet from the rain. When one of her gentlemen ushers began to weep,

Elizabeth further used the moment to proclaim that there was no reason for anyone to weep for her since she was innocent. Foxe's widely known description of this moment portrays a courageous and astute Elizabeth who would use any opportunity possible to gain sympathy from those around her. Foxe's Elizabeth took a simple process and broke it into discrete and lengthy steps. Though there is disagreement about how accurately Foxe recorded Elizabeth's words and actions, Tom Freeman argues that in this scene Foxe's sources "were well-informed and, in some cases, eyewitnesses to the events described. . . . [Foxe's] research among the oral sources for Elizabeth's imprisonment was thorough and systematic."[28] In some ways more important than the accuracy is the fact that culturally, this was the image of Princess Elizabeth that the English people widely believed and admired.

Elizabeth was kept in the Tower for several months during the spring of 1554; she used every opportunity she could find to proclaim her innocence. For the first month, Elizabeth was kept in her room, but finally, after repeated requests, she was allowed to go outside "to walk in the Tower garden."[29] A boy, the son of Martin, the Keeper of the Wardrobe, occasionally brought flowers to Elizabeth when she walked. But officials feared that another prisoner in the tower was using the boy to send messages. The child was told he could no longer come and see Elizabeth. The next day, the little boy cried out to the princess, "Mistress, I can bring you no more flowers," and Elizabeth, Foxe writes, smiled at the boy understandingly.[30] Even her brief walks, mini-travels, had allowed her to gain sympathy that was perceived by those in power as too dangerous.

London to Woodstock and Back Again

At times Elizabeth was in such despair in the Tower that she considered asking Mary that she, like her mother, be executed by a

French swordsman. Finally Mary's Council determined to move Elizabeth from the Tower. On May 19 Sir Henry Bedingfield, called Benifield in Foxe, came to remove Elizabeth to Woodstock. Unaware of the situation, Elizabeth thought that they might be taking her to her execution, and demanded to know whether Lady Jane's scaffold had been taken down. Foxe describes an Elizabeth who feared, quite reasonably, that she might soon be killed. The first night they stayed at Richmond, a guard brought Elizabeth a dish of apples. Bedingfield ordered the man imprisoned. More terrifying for Elizabeth, Bedingfield sent her own servants away, which really frightened her about what was to happen. She asked for her gentleman usher and eloquently begged her people to pray for her: "For this night . . . I think to die." Again, given the immense popularity of *Acts and Monuments*, Elizabeth's subjects would have had this dramatic moment firmly placed in their minds. Soon after the queen's death, English people would also have had a visual portrayal of this moment when they attended Heywood's play, when the character Elizabeth fears her fate as she is being moved. She wonders, "What fearful terror doth assaile my heart? . . . to be plaine, this night I looke to die."[31]

Elizabeth did, of course, survive after she was removed from the Tower, and she was taken to Windsor and from there to one Mr. Dormer's house. Foxe explains how, when she arrived, many of the common people were waiting for her. They cheered for her, and some offered her gifts. This display of affection and support for Elizabeth greatly disturbed Sir Henry, and he "troubled the poor people very sore, for shewing their loving hearts." Bedingfield lambasted them as "rebels and traitors," using other "vile words."[32] When the entourage passed through villages, townsmen rang the bells to show their support for Princess Elizabeth. Foxe reports that Sir Henry was so enraged he sent his soldiers to arrest the bell ringers and put them in the stocks. The enthusiasm about Elizabeth's release from the Tower is corroborated by a much less sympathetic and more contemporary source. In May of 1554 the Spanish ambassador wrote to the emperor: "Last Saturday the Lady Elizabeth was taken out of the Tower and conducted to Richmond. Thence she has been conveyed to Woodstock, there to be kept until she is sent to Pomfret. Four hundred men accompanied her, and the people rejoiced at her departure, thinking she had been set at liberty. When she passed by the house of the Stillyard merchants they shot off three cannons as sign of joy, and the Queen and her Council were displeased about it."[33]

At Woodstock, Elizabeth was still kept very strictly; Foxe suggests it was especially stressful for the princess since one of the men at Woodstock, Paul Penny, was "a notorious ruffian and butcherly wretch," so that many were afraid he would kill Elizabeth. But then the political situation shifted. That autumn, Mary was convinced that she was pregnant. Mary's husband Philip of Spain persuaded his wife that "delivering the lady Elizabeth's grace out of prison" was a good idea, since if Mary died in childbirth, Philip feared the French influence of Mary's cousin, Mary Stuart, more than Protestant Elizabeth, the queen's sister.

Elizabeth was summoned to join them at Hampton Court for Christmas celebrations. Stephen Gardiner, Chancellor, Bishop of Winchester, and one of Mary's closest advisors, wanted a contrite Elizabeth who admitted her guilt. But even then Foxe presents a cruel Sir Henry in the way he treated the guarded Elizabeth on the trip from Woodstock, a trip that demonstrated clearly how difficult, even dangerous, travel was. As Elizabeth traveled, it was very windy, and her hood kept getting blown off her head. She asked if they could stop at someone's house while she refastened her hood and redid her hair; however, she "could not be suffered by Sir Henry

Benifield so to do, but was constrained under an hedge to trim her head as well as she could." The first night Elizabeth rested at Ricote, the second night in Buckinghamshire, and the third at an inn at Colnebrook. At Colnebrook, sixty former members of her household, who had not seen the princess for some months, came to the inn and were delighted to see Elizabeth, though they were not allowed to come close enough to her to speak with her, and Bedingfield commanded them to leave. The following day, Elizabeth arrived at Hampton Court but found herself still under guard. Gardiner and his colleagues told Elizabeth that if she were to be freed, she had to confess and throw herself on the queen's mercy. Elizabeth refused, saying that she "had as lief be in prison, with honesty, as to be abroad suspected of Her Majesty . . . that which I have said I will stand to." Elizabeth refused to confess to something of which she was not guilty. On her trip to Hampton Court Elizabeth had just seen how much she was loved by her people; that may well have given her the strength to maintain her innocence.[34]

After staying in close confinement for a week, Mary summoned Elizabeth at ten o'clock at night. The lateness of the hour must have made the summons even more frightening for Elizabeth, but the relationship between the sisters eased slightly. Elizabeth appeared publicly at the Christmas eve festivities and was seated at Mary's table during the banquet. On December 29 Elizabeth sat with their majesties in the royal gallery to watch the tournament, a long-delayed pageant to honor Mary's marriage to Philip. When Elizabeth returned to Woodstock after the celebrations, she was allowed to have some of her own people in her household.[35]

In April of 1555 Queen Mary was at Hampton Court awaiting the birth of the child she was so sure she would soon welcome. Mary was so convinced of the reality of her (false) pregnancy that she ordered processions and prayers that her child "might be a male child, well favoured and witty," and had a beautiful little cradle prepared, as well as dispatches announcing the birth.[36] At this emotional moment, Mary sent for Elizabeth, and on April 25 the princess was again brought to court as a prisoner of state. Elizabeth was lodged in an outbuilding but was later summoned to see Mary, who, pressured by her husband, grudgingly reconciled with her sister.

From Hatfield to the Crown

Mary also agreed to allow Elizabeth to reside at her own favorite residence, Hatfield House, though under the guardianship of Sir Thomas Pope. Hatfield was a more comfortable residence for Elizabeth, and she sometimes left Hatfield to visit Mary at court. Since Mary's pregnancy proved to be a phantom, it was more and more clear that Elizabeth would be the next ruler. Once that autumn as she returned to Hatfield House, people in London "great and small followed her through the city," the French ambassador M. de Noailles reported, and greeted her with acclamations and "vehement manifestations of affection."[37] Elizabeth, not wanting Mary's supporters to use her popularity against her, allowed some of the officers of her train to ride in front of her so she would not be so visible to the crowds and thus not so publicly acclaimed. Elizabeth visited court several other times as Mary's reign progressed, such as state visits to court in December 1556 and the spring of 1558.[38]

Though Elizabeth had been in fear of losing her life earlier in her sister's reign, toward the end of it as she waited at Hatfield House, she must have realized that despite the appalling odds, she would indeed become queen of England. Mary died on November 17, and the transition was smooth. Chancellor Heath went before Parliament to announce Mary's death and the accession of her sister. The news was solemnly proclaimed throughout London. At Hatfield, Elizabeth stated what she had clearly prepared to say, quoting the

118th Psalm: "A domino est istud, et est mirabile in oculus nostris" (This is God's doing and is marvelous in our eyes).[39]

Over the next few days Elizabeth stayed at Hatfield with her principal advisors. On November 22, she began her expedition to London, staying for six days at the Charterhouse near the Barbican just outside the city walls. There, she consulted with the Lord Mayor and city dignitaries who rode out to see her. Then Elizabeth entered London. She and her entourage rode through the Barbican and Cripplegate, along London Wall to Bishopsgate, and by Leadenhall Street, Gracechurch Street, and Fenchurch Street to Mark Lane and Tower Street to the Tower.[40] Everywhere she went, Elizabeth was loudly cheered; those who had loved her as Princess Elizabeth in her difficult journeys and days of disgrace could now celebrate her triumphant return to the city as queen.

Travel as Princess, Travel as Queen

As I have mentioned, *Acts and Monuments* widely disseminated the stories of Elizabeth's troubles during Mary I's reign. In addition, the 1586 edition of *Holinshed's Chronicles* recounted these stories again—almost word for word from Foxe, making them even more accessible. These authors' influence on the people's perception of Elizabeth did not end with her death. Heywood used them as sources for his very popular play about Elizabeth during Mary's reign, *If You Know Not Me, You Know Nobody, Part I*.[41] Such works depict Elizabeth in great danger in her sister's reign traveling through the kingdom. As a result, the image of the heroic young Elizabeth making her way across the country would have been well fixed in the minds and hearts of the Protestant English people. While Heywood emphasizes Elizabeth's impressive courage, he is also concerned with portraying her vulnerability and fear; the conflict between fortitude and fear creates effective dramatic tension. As Elizabeth is being moved to Woodstock in the play, there are crowds to greet her. "The towns-men of the country gathered here, To greete our Grace, hearing you past this way," one of her servants tells her. Just as Beningfeld is calling them traitors, they all call out "Now the Lord blesse thy sweete Grace." To protect the crowd from Beningfeld's wrath, Elizabeth tells them, "Pray for me in your harts, not with your tongues."[42] Heywood's play ends with Elizabeth as queen telling her company "And now to London Lords lead on the way."[43]

Once queen, Elizabeth never forgot what she had learned in self-preservation and self-presentation during her dangerous travels in the reign of her sister, or how valuable it was for her to be seen by subjects and to interact with them. She made the court, especially when at Whitehall, a public place where her subjects who had come from all over the country could see her in person. Her court moved often from house to house in a wide circle around the capital. As well as during her summer progresses, she showed herself often in London, becoming a familiar, if no less thrilling, figure through these frequent visits and processions.

Even meetings in London that were theoretically "private" in fact were often staged for public consumption and to show a far happier face than the ones she had shown during her sister's reign. In April 1566 Robert Dudley, Elizabeth's chief favorite and potential marriage partner, met with her in a beautifully staged rendezvous. Dudley, recently created Earl of Leicester, came to London with seven hundred lords, knights, and gentlemen. The queen's footmen as well as his own also accompanied him; they were gorgeously dressed "in theyr riche cotes." They marched from Temple Bar through the city down New Fish Street to London Bridge, then to Southwark and to Greenwich. Elizabeth came "secretly" by taking a small boat with two ladies in waiting with all three of them rowing. At the three Cranes in the Vintry, she entered a blue coach. Leicester and his entourage met her coach, Elizabeth emerged, and then she embraced Robert and "kissed hym thrise," everyone observing. Robert then rode in the coach with Elizabeth to Greenwich before he and his entourage departed one way and Elizabeth the other.[44] Why Elizabeth decided to do this is a question we might ponder. Was she balancing the pressure toward a marriage alliance with the Archduke Charles, which was strong at the time? Was this a token to Dudley to show he was still important to her though she had decided not to marry him? Was it a purposeful "treat" for her subjects that she delighted to provide every so often? Or was it simply that the young queen wanted to do something dramatic and romantic to have a good time? Regardless, this publicly staged "secret" meeting was probably far more thrilling for the people of London to see and hear about than it is today when we in Britain and the United States gobble up stories of the romantic meetings of movie stars. After her forced travels in Mary's reign, creating this trip must have delighted the queen.

Elizabeth had learned well the importance of showing herself to and having direct interaction with her subjects. This was a time long before such modern inventions as radio, television, and the Internet allowed people to see and hear their leader over long distances, and Elizabeth had early realized that loyalty came in part from this public presentation of self, particularly when she was at risk. While there was much in her life she could not control, especially during the dangers of the reigns of her siblings, she could make a point of presenting herself to the people and to control the strategy of this spectacle. The most salient example of this, as we saw, was her journey back to court from Ashridge after she had been accused of participation in the Thomas Wyatt rebellion of 1554. She kept the litter open so that she was not hidden away: people could see her, and she kept her expression, as one enemy stated, "proud." This recognition of her power and use of her public role was important to Elizabeth's success as queen. Clearly, she had carefully studied the art of self-presentation during the reign of her sister, and carefully planned what was worth emulating and what she should avoid.

Wallace MacCaffrey is correct in stating that by the time Elizabeth had become queen she had "acquired a public persona which shaped most of her intercourse with other human beings" and, as queen, used that public persona as she traveled through her capital city and her realm. Elizabeth fashioned this persona partly in the course of these journeys; she used it to become more real and intimate to her people. Her strategy was remarkably successful. As her early biographer William Camden put it, "Neither did the People ever embrace any other Prince with more willing and constant mind and affection with greater observance, more joyfull applause, and prayers reiterated, whensoever she went abroad, during the whole course of her Life, than they did her."[45]

Notes

Some of the issues discussed here are also addressed in my essay with Jo Carney, "Young Elizabeth in Peril: From Seventeenth Century Drama to Modern Movies," in *Elizabeth I: Always Her Own Free Woman*, ed. C. Levin, J. E. Carney, and D. Barrett-Graves (Aldershot: Ashgate, 2003), 215–37. Jo Carney has been a wonderful friend and colleague for many years, and I greatly appreciate her help with this project and many others. I wish to thank Natasha Luepke for her research aid, and I am especially grateful to Amy Gant for all her help with preparing this essay. I also greatly appreciate the help and support of Anya Riehl and Michele Osherow and the valuable advice of my coeditor, Robert Bucholz.

1. L. S. Marcus, J. Mueller, and M. B. Rose, eds., *Elizabeth I: Collected Works* (Chicago: University of Chicago Press, 2000), 24, 32–33.

2. A. Somerset, *Elizabeth I* (New York: St. Martin's Press, 1992), 28.

3. M. H. Cole, *The Portable Queen: Elizabeth I and the Politics of Ceremony* (Amherst: University of Massachusetts Press, 1999), 22–23.

4. W. MacCaffrey, *Elizabeth I* (London: Edward Arnold, 1993), 376.

5. British Library (hereafter BL)Lansdowne MS 3, fol. 26, cited in D. M. Loades, *Intrigue and Treason: The Tudor Court, 1547–1558* (Harlow: Pearson Education, 2004), 128.

6. J. G. Nichols, *The Chronicles of Queen Jane, and of Two Years of Queen Mary, and especially of the Rebellion of Sir Thomas Wyat, written by a resident in the Tower of London* (London: Camden Society, 1850), 13. The author is anonymous; from the text Nichols deduced that he was well born and well-educated.

7. J. G. Nichols, ed., *The Diary of Henry Machyn, Citizen and Merchant-Taylor of London, from 1550 to 1563* (London: Camden Society, 1848), 37. For more on Machyn, see G. G. Gibbs, "Marking the Days: Henry Machyn's Manuscript and the Mid-Tudor Era," in *The Church of Mary Tudor*, ed. E. Duffy and D. M. Loades (Aldershot: Ashgate, 2006), 281–308.

8. L. Montrose, *The Subject of Elizabeth: Authority, Gender, and Representation* (Chicago: University of Chicago Press, 2006), 44.

9. BL, Harley MS 419, fol. 1371, cited in T. S. Freeman, "'As True a Subiect being Prysoner': John Foxe's Notes on the Imprisonment of Princess Elizabeth, 1554–5," *English Historical Review* 118, no. 470 (2002): 107.

10. Loades, *Intrigue and Treason*, 137.

11. Nichols, *Chronicles of Queen Jane*, 28.

12. Agnes Strickland, *Lives of the Queens of England* (London: Henry Colburn, 1843), 6:67–70; William Camden, *The History of the most renouned and victorious Princess Elizabeth*, 3rd ed. (London: M. Flesher, 1688), 7; C. S. Knighton, ed., *State Papers of Mary I: Calendar of State Papers Domestic Series of the Reign of Mary I, 1553–1558, Preserved in the Public Record Office*, rev. ed. (London: Public Record Office, 1998), 10.

13. Loades, *Intrigue and Treason*, 129.

14. *Calendar of Letters, Despatches, and State Papers, Relating to the Negotiations between England and Spain, Preserved in the Archives at Simancas and Elsewhere*, vol. 11, *Edward VI and Mary, 1553*, ed. R. Tyler (London: Longman, Green, Longman, and Roberts, 1862–1954), 196.

15. *Calendar of Letters, Despatches, and State Papers, Relating to the Negotiations between England and Spain*, 11:221.

16. *Calendar of Letters, Despatches, and State Papers, Relating to the Negotiations between England and Spain*, 11:393.

17. *Calendar of Letters, Despatches, and State Papers, Relating to the Negotiations between England and Spain*, 11:418.

18. John Fox, *The Book of Martyrs: Containing an Account of the Suffering and Death of the Protestants in the Reign of Mary the First* (London: John Hart and John Lewis, 1734), 902. In this edition, Foxe's name is spelled without the customary "e."

19. Nichols, *Chronicles of Queen Jane*, 63.

20. Fox, *Book of Martyrs*, 902.

21. Fox, *Book of Martyrs*, 903.

22. *Calendar of Letters, Despatches, and State Papers, Relating to the Negotiations between England and Spain*, vol. 12, *Mary, January–July 1554*, 120.

23. Fox, *Book of Martyrs*, 903.

24. Nichols, *Diary of Henry Machyn*, 57.

25. *Calendar of Letters, Despatches, and State Papers, Relating to the Negotiations between England and Spain* 12:125.

26. Nichols, *Chronicles of Queen Jane*, 70–71.

27. Fox, *Book of Martyrs*, 904. For more on the significance of Foxe's description and how accurate it may be, see Freeman, "'As True a Subiect being Prysoner,'" 104–16, and J. King, "Fiction and Fact in Foxe's *Book of Marytrs*," in *John Foxe and the English Reformation*, ed. D. M. Loades (Aldershot: Scholar Press, 1997), 12–35.

28. Freeman, "'As True a Subiect being Prysoner,'" 108, 110.

29. *Calendar of Letters, Despatches, and State Papers, Relating to the Negotiations between England and Spain*, 12:221.

30. Fox, *Book of Martyrs*, 906.

31. Fox, *Book of Martyrs*, 906; Thomas Heywood, *If You Know Not Me You Know Nobody, Part I* (Oxford: Printed for the Malone Society by Oxford University Press, 1934), lines 974, 981.

32. Fox, *Book of Martyrs*, 907.

33. *Calendar of Letters, Despatches, and State Papers, Relating to the Negotiations between England and Spain*, 12:261.

34. Fox, *Book of Martyrs*, 909; Strickland, *Lives of the Queens of England*, 6:116.

35. Strickland, *Lives of the Queens of England*, 6:119–21.

36. I. Dunlop, *Palaces and Progresses of Elizabeth I* (New York: Taplinger, 1962), 96.

37. Quoted in Strickland, *Lives of the Queens of England*, 6:123.

38. For contemporary descriptions, see Nichols, *Diary of Henry Machyn*, 120, 166–67.

39. Robert Naunton and James Caulfield, *The Court of Queen Elizabeth* (London: G. Smeeton, 1814).

40. J. Ridley, *Elizabeth I: The Shrewdness of Virtue* (New York: Fromm International, 1989), 76.

41. This play was printed in eight editions between 1605 and 1639 and was one of Heywood's more popular plays. For more, see B. J. Baines, *Thomas Heywood* (Boston:

Twayne, 1984); T. Grant, "Drama Queen: Staging Elizabeth in *If You Know Not Me, You Know Nobody*," in *The Myth of Elizabeth*, ed. S. Doran and T. S. Freeman (Basingstoke: Palgrave Macmillan, 2003), 120–42; J. E. Howard, "Staging the Absent Woman: The Theatrical Evocation of Elizabeth Tudor in Heywood's *If You Know Not Me, You Know Nobody, Part I*," in *Women Players in England, 1500–1650: Beyond the All-Male Stage*, ed. P. A. Brown and P. Parolin (Burlington: Ashgate, 2005), 263–80; M. Bayer, "Staging Foxe at the Fortune and the Red Bull," *Renaissance and Reformation* 27 (2003): 61–94.

42. Heywood, *If You Know Not Me*, lines 850–51, 854, 859.

43. Heywood, *If You Know Not Me*, line 1569.

44. J. Gairdner, ed., *Three Fifteenth-Century Chronicles, with Historical Memoranda by John Stowe, the Antiquary, And Contemporary Notes of Occurrences written by him in the reign of Elizabeth* (Westminster: Camden Society, 1880). 137. Stowe describes Elizabeth's coming by boat as "secret," but we might wonder how secret it really was if he is reporting it. See also N. Jones, *The Birth of the Elizabethan Age: England in the 1560s* (Oxford: Blackwell, 1993), 119.

45. MacCaffrey, *Elizabeth I*, 376; Camden, *History of the most renouned and victorious Princess Elizabeth*, 12.

5

Marriage à la Mode, 1559

Elisabeth de Valois, Elizabeth I, and the Changing Practice of Dynastic Marriage

JOHN WATKINS

The 1559 peace settlement of Cateau-Cambrésis was the sixteenth century's most important treaty.[1] It brought three major
European dynasties into a complex dialogue about the continent's
destiny: the Hapsburgs of Spain, the Valois of France, and the
Tudors of England. Spain was arguably the big winner. The treaty
not only secured the claims of its king, Philip II, to Italy but, by
ending the war with France, helped it to build an immensely lucra-
tive transatlantic empire. Valois France, forced to negotiate in the
first place by a fiscal shortfall, gambled that the settlement would
allow it to stabilize its finances and its volatile ecclesiastical situation. The gamble failed. The French king, Henri II, was killed in
a tournament celebrating the treaty, and his realm erupted almost
immediately in religious civil war. Finally, Cateau-Cambrésis played
a significant role in English history. Since the Tudor queen Mary I
was married to Spain's Philip II, England fought in the later phases
of the Valois-Hapsburg conflict as a Spanish ally. In the process,
they lost Calais, the last remnant of an Anglo-French empire that
once extended from Ireland to the Pyrenees. Although England

negotiated for a return of the French coastal city to their control after eight years, they never got it back.

What I have just described is the standard textbook account of Cateau-Cambrésis and its three-point implication for the future of Europe: (1) an end to the contest between France and Spain over Italy; (2) the beginnings of French wars of religion; and (3) the end of England's territorial ambitions in France. As I have narrated it, and as dozens of scholars have narrated it before me, it is a classic chapter in diplomatic history: an account of high politics, the fate of nations, war, and the elusive dream of peace.

I want to reopen Cateau-Cambrésis, not simply because I believe there is more to be said about it, but because a reconsideration can offer a paradigm for reintegrating diplomatic history—currently an isolated subfield—into a broader, more comprehensive interrogation of the past.[2] As a scholarly community of medievalists and early modernists, we now have new questions and analytical perspectives to bring to archival materials that have not been touched in decades. For some time we have been examining how the histories of gender and sexuality intersect the political histories of individual nation states. Scholars like Phillipa Barry, Susan Doran, Susan Frye, Carole Levin, Anna Riehl, Linda Shenk, and Mihoko Suzuki have given us a better understanding of how Elizabeth's self-proclaimed identity as a woman with the "heart and stomach of a king" revolutionized English understandings of sovereignty.[3] It is time for us to consider the effect of gender on supernational and transnational political discourse as well. Scholars of comparative literature and comparative social and political history need to begin the same kind of intellectual collaborations that have allowed scholars of individual countries to rewrite the history of the nation state.

The peace of Cateau-Cambrésis provides a rich opportunity to begin this inquiry. Just as the treaty marked a watershed in the political history of western Europe, it also foregrounded a series of interrelated and often bewilderingly contradictory developments in the history of women. Their divergent experiences—as negotiators, as supporters, as critics, as brides—contributed at every step to the treaty's place in the evolving European state system. As the commissioners at Cateau-Cambrésis discussed the protocols for making peace among themselves and with the sovereigns that they represented, they participated in an array of competing discourses about sovereignty. At times, the proceedings make sense primarily in terms of an older understanding of the monarch as someone who effectively shares sovereignty with his or her fellow aristocrats.[4] At other times, the process primarily engages a more centralized notion of the monarch as the sole, absolute head of state. Finally, in the case of England, the peacemakers encountered an emergent constitutionalist discourse in which the monarch was imagined to be accountable to ministers and elected members of Parliament. Since these divergent models of sovereignty scripted divergent degrees of women's participation in the diplomatic process, making peace at Cateau-Cambrésis also meant balancing different understandings of the place of women in public life.

Cateau-Cambrésis: The Diplomatic Context

When Henri II and Philip II began their negotiations, the tradition of women's diplomatic agency scripted many of the roles undertaken by key figures on both sides of the Pyrenees and on both sides of the Channel. In fact, an unusually large number of women participated either as sovereigns, behind-the-scenes negotiators, or as potential brides. Every party assumed that a major Valois-Hapsburg settlement would need at least one high-profile marriage. At first, it seemed most likely that the heads of the rival households would marry off their heirs, Philip's son Don Carlos and Henri's eldest daughter, Elisabeth de Valois. A second marriage, between Henri's sister Marguerite de Valois and the Duke of Savoy might further advance the settlement.[5] But only a month after the formal negotiations opened in October 1558, the death of Philip's wife, Mary I of England, changed everything. What everyone assumed to be an offspring that would unite forever the houses of Tudor and Hapsburg turned out to be a false pregnancy. Mary was not pregnant: she had terminal ovarian cancer. Philip had never particularly liked Mary, but he did like the leverage in European politics that the marriage had given him, and her death threatened to diminish his power and prestige at a critical moment in Spanish history.[6]

Mary's tragedy was a timely reminder of how closely dynastic politics linked national destiny to human biology. Throughout Mary's reign, England had sympathized with Spanish interests. The final correspondence between Mary and her commissioners, for example, stresses their deference to Philip.[7] During the treaty negotiations, the English representatives literally sat with the Spaniards on one side of the table and glared at the French on the other side. But with a new queen on the throne, all bets were off. Mary's death and Elizabeth's accession meant that now two more players were on the dynastic marriage market, Elizabeth and Philip himself. To make things even more volatile, Elizabeth I made it clear early on that she was planning to rule as a Protestant.

By the end of 1558, too many eligible men and women were lined up on various sides of the Hapsburg, Valois, and now Tudor quarrel, and there were several possible configurations that could result. Philip and Henri might persist in the original plan to marry their heirs, Don Carlos and Elisabeth de Valois. But Spain could no longer count on England's support. What Philip saw as a new threat in the specter of an independent England, France saw as an advantage. Henri might have been willing to make peace with Spain in 1558, but old grudges died hard: as a child, Henri had been held hostage in Spain by Philip's father Charles V for over four years, and he hardly wanted to see Spain prosper. Nothing could have pleased Henri more than the disintegration of the Spanish-English alliance. There was only one sure way for Philip II to preserve the friendship between the Tudors and the Hapsburgs: Philip would have to marry Elizabeth I.[8]

On the other hand, if Elizabeth decided to move closer to Henri II, Philip might need to offset the threat of an Anglo-French alliance by marrying Elisabeth de Valois himself (marriage option number 4) and either leaving his son Don Carlos out in the cold or marrying him to Elisabeth's younger sister Marguerite, who was about six at the time.[9] Philip's Burgundian-Hapsburg ancestors had played the marriage game with such dazzling success that they created an empire that endured for seven hundred years. But Cateau-Cambrésis presented him with a set of choices and constraints that would have bewildered the most able strategist, even if one of the players had not been a woman as formidable as Elizabeth I. Europeans did not yet know much about the woman who would lead her people to triumph over Philip's Armada thirty years later, but they were about to learn.

In addition to the several potential brides—Elizabeth I, Elisabeth de Valois, Marguerite de Valois the elder (Henri II's sister), and Marguerite de Valois the younger (Henri II's daughter)—three other women figured in the politics of Cateau-Cambrésis: Henri II's queen, Catherine de' Medici; his mistress Diane de Poitiers; and the dowager Duchess Christine de Lorraine, the mother of the teenaged Duke of Lorraine, who had just wed Henri II's second daughter, Claude. Catherine de' Medici was one of Europe's most forceful, imaginative, and ultimately hated politicians, although her talents were not fully revealed until Henri's death a few months later in

1559. At this point in her career, a less formidable Catherine competed for influence over Henri with his mistress, Diane de Poitiers. Many took Cateau-Cambrésis to be yet another victory for Diane. Catherine—a scion of the Florentine Medici family who did not want to see France surrender its Italian claims to Spain—opposed the peace. Diane supported it, in part because of her alliance with one of the plan's architects and staunchest defenders, the Duke of Montmorency. A third woman, Christine of Denmark, the dowager Duchess of Lorraine, served as a principal mediator at the negotiations and even proposed the crucial compromise on Calais that all parties finally embraced. According to the Venetian ambassador Paolo Tiepolo, this most important treaty of the sixteenth century came about principally though her efforts.[10]

The political skills displayed by all three of these women were part of a premodern, aristocratic political culture that was falling victim in France and Spain alike to the concentration of power in the Crown. The process was moving more slowly in France, and would be slowed down further by the outbreak of civil wars led by rival aristocratic houses. Like the Hapsburgs and the Valois, the English Tudors systematically increased the powers of the Crown at the expense of provincial aristocrats. But the same years that witnessed the aggrandizement of Tudor rule also brought about an increasing encroachment of Parliament, and particularly the House of Commons, on such royal prerogatives as the right to set foreign policy. In England, the Crown was gaining and losing ground at the same time. That loss is what Whig historians traditionally hailed as the emergence of constitutional restraint on monarchy, and even the first glimmerings of modern elective democracy. But this is precisely the kind of commonplace that a new diplomatic history sensitive to issues like gender and sexuality invites us to reconsider. The emergence of a constitutionalist discourse was inseparable from a loss in the agency that at least some women had held in foreign affairs: until 1919, Parliament was all male. Both north and south of the Pyrenees, and on opposite sides of the Channel, the political conditions were eroding that once supported the enterprising diplomacy of a Christine de Lorraine. We need to bear this caveat in mind as we turn to the strikingly divergent careers of the two women whom Spain's Philip II considered marrying in 1559: Elizabeth Tudor of England and Elisabeth de Valois of France.

Elisabeth de Valois

Let's start with the dubious winner: Elisabeth de Valois, whose marriage to Philip inspired writers of tragic plays and operas for the next three centuries.[11] To be fair to Philip, the marriage was not nearly as disastrous as Saint-Réal, Schiller, and Verdi later portrayed it.[12] Reliable contemporary witnesses and Elisabeth's own correspondence suggest that the couple actually liked each other. There is no basis in fact for the legend that grew up shortly after Elisabeth's death that she and Philip's son Don Carlos were secretly in love. Don Carlos, whose mother had died four days after his birth, had already shown signs of serious mental instability.[13] But even if Elisabeth was not unhappy, her career manifests a distinct retreat from the public task of mediation toward the more passive responsibility of bearing offspring. Certainly any queen consort's primary duty was motherhood. But as I have already noted, women like Catherine de' Medici not only bore royal heirs but exerted considerable influence on royal policy. In the case of Elisabeth de Valois, almost everything we know about her involves her identity as a potential, and ultimately actual, mother. Ambassadors and other correspondents with the French court, for example, kept a constant eye on Elisabeth's health. There was worry on both sides of the Pyrenees about the apparent delay of puberty; several parties recommended folk remedies to alleviate the problem. Everyone was overjoyed when her first period began on August 11, 1561. We know an embarrassing number of details about her intimate life with Philip. It took her a long time to get pregnant, and this delay created even more anxiety than the initial delay in her menstruation. After her miscarriage in 1564, the relics of St. Eugene were brought from Saint-Denis to Toledo so that she might invoke his powers against barrenness. A year later, she gave birth to a daughter, Isabel Clara Eugenia, named for the fertility-enhancing saint. A second daughter, Catalina Michaela, followed a year later on October 6, 1567. One year later almost to the date, Elisabeth miscarried again, contracted postpartum fever, and died at the age of twenty-two.[14]

This biography, as I and scholars before me have narrated it, focuses almost exclusively on Elisabeth's body as a vehicle of dynastic perpetuation. As intimate as some of the details might strike us now, they are not particularly unusual. The onset of royal menstruations, for example, were openly celebrated in many European courts as an assurance of dynastic proliferation, and probably nothing was followed more closely than the course of royal pregnancies. What strikes me as noteworthy in this history is not so much what gets said as what does not. We have almost no information about Elisabeth's role in Spanish politics. Her mother, Catherine de' Medici, epitomized the power-wielding consort and, after her husband's death, emerged not only as the most powerful woman, but the most powerful person in France. Although some of her letters to Elisabeth after her marriage suggest that she wanted to groom her daughter to play a similar role in Spain, there is less business than one might expect in the letters between the Queen of Spain and her mother, the French regent.[15] Ambassadorial letters and dispatches leave the same impression. When Elisabeth was not confined or ill, she seems to have spent her days in typical aristocratic entertainments, especially gambling. The Spanish courtiers whispered that she was typically French in her tardiness in paying off her debts. She also spent a lot of time, and a lot of money, purchasing luxuries. A few sources suggest that Philip discussed politics with her, but he did not treat her as a significant consultant, and she did not pressure him to take particular courses of action. One Spanish historian has suggested that Elisabeth's incessant gambling was a compensation for her exclusion from state affairs.[16] Philip seems to have left her out of conversations that one might suspect were significantly within the queen's prerogative. She was not present, for example, during his discussions with the architects who planned either the renovation of the Alcázar palace or the building of El Escorial. Philip even seems to have planned Elisabeth's own suite of rooms without consulting her.[17]

Philip once ostensibly entrusted Elisabeth with an important diplomatic task: she technically presided over the 1565 Conference of Bayonne, a diplomatic exchange between France and Spain primarily over the perceived spread of Protestantism in France.[18] But as the conference unfolded, it testified to the nineteen-year-old Elisabeth's exclusion from rather than engagement with politics. Philip feared that Catherine was too lenient toward her Huguenot subjects; Catherine felt that some degree of toleration was the only way to avoid all-out civil war. In theory, this was precisely the kind of situation in which a foreign-born consort's abilities to mediate the conflicting interests of her adopted country and her country of origin could shine. Yet the conference was basically a showdown carried out in French between Catherine and Philip's de facto representative, the Duke of Alba. The contrast between Catherine's dominant role as queen regent of France and her daughter Elisabeth's marginalization as the queen consort of Spain could not be more striking. The conference culminated in a notoriously long and clandestine conversation between Catherine and Alba walking alone in a gallery out of the earshot of anyone else in attendance. To this day, no one knows the substance of that conversation.[19] What we do know is that Philip almost immediately pursued a policy of championing French reactionary aristocrats in their opposition to the more moderate positions of the French Crown, a strategy that ultimately exacerbated the French civil wars and drove a lasting wedge between France and Spain. By the time Elisabeth died a few years later, much of the hope first occasioned by her marriage to Philip II died with her.

Numerous factors undoubtedly contributed to Elisabeth de Valois' limited involvement in politics. She was ill during much of her life and experienced several difficult pregnancies, including the one that claimed her life. Perhaps above all, she did not live very long: we simply cannot know what role she would have played in Spanish and Franco-Spanish affairs if she had lived another three or four decades. Yet other European queens consort had played considerable roles in politics at very early ages, including Isabel of Bavaria and Margaret of Anjou. What seems to have mattered most in Elisabeth's career was Philip's determination to maintain as tight a grip as possible on every aspect of public life and Elisabeth's own submission to his authority. Nothing in the sources suggests that she was unhappy with her exclusion from politics. The domestic contentment that both Philip and Elisabeth seem to have enjoyed almost certainly depended on her lack of personal political ambition.

Elizabeth I

So what would have happened if Philip had married Elizabeth I, the woman who ruled England as a Virgin Queen for almost the next half century? Although we can never really answer this question, speculating about it might reveal a lot, not only about Philip and

Elizabeth, but also about our own historiographic assumptions. It is tempting to cast Elizabeth I as the big winner of Cateau-Cambrésis. Although she effectively surrendered England's last claim to French territory, she also extricated her country from the costs, confusion, and sheer horror of continental war. In rejecting her sister's vision of England locked in a tight Hapsburg embrace, she established the diplomatic basis for three decades of peace, prosperity, and the cultural and intellectual flowering that we now hail retrospectively as the Elizabethan age.

I am tempted to speak just as enthusiastically about Elizabeth's contributions to my particular subject of investigation, the intersections of the histories of diplomacy, sexuality, and gender. Truly original moments are rare in the history of negotiation, and even when revolutionary events occur, the diplomatic community is notoriously conservative in its response. But Elizabeth's decision to decline Philip's proposal of marriage, and her persistence in saying no to other suitors foreign and domestic for the next forty years, was a remarkable achievement whose significance for the history of European diplomacy has yet to be fully appreciated. Historians and literary scholars have written a lot about the effect of her decision not to marry on England's international position, the relationship between Crown and Parliament, religion, and the ultimate cast of Elizabethan culture. But they have not talked about it in the context of the history of diplomacy and of the negotiations and strategies through which early modern polities forged alliances.

The deliberate vagueness of that word, *polity*, rather than *rulers*, or *states*, or *nations*, underscores the originality of Elizabeth's contribution. By refusing to marry another head of state or any heir to another European throne, she turned her back on the dynastic motives that had dominated international relationships for centuries. When Philip II agreed to marry Elisabeth de Valois, and when Henri II agreed to let him, they were thinking primarily about the futures of their dynasties, the welfare of future Hapsburgs and Valois. When Elizabeth first refused Philip in 1559 and numerous illustrious suitors afterward, she may have been thinking about Protestantism, the advantages of another marriage down the road, or England. But, in contrast to her peer monarchs across the Channel, she was not placing a priority on future Tudors. At some point, she either renounced the dynastic vision that had so driven her father in his determination to produce a male heir or decided that it did not matter enough to compromise other policy objectives. In the eyes of most early modern heads of state, such a decision would have been inconceivable. The cost was enormous: Elizabeth's decision not to marry brought her dynasty to an abrupt close with her death in 1603.

Revisionist historians have asked us to reconsider the view that Elizabeth had committed herself to the single life as early as 1559. Some of the evidence on which that rested is clearly unreliable. We cannot assume, for example, that Elizabeth really told a parliamentary delegation in this crucial European year that she had already joined herself "in Marriage to an Husband, namely, the Kingdom of England." That speech was first attributed to her by her posthumous biographer William Camden, and nothing like it exists in Camden's reputed source, the Cecil papers.[20] Susan Doran has argued that Elizabeth took her marriage negotiations very seriously through 1581, and that on at least two occasions, she probably wanted to go through with them.[21]

While I generally agree with Doran and the other revisionists that, even though Elizabeth rejected Philip, she remained open to the possibility of marriage for the next several decades, the scholarly discussion has been framed too much in terms of two mutually exclusive positions: either Elizabeth always intended to be the Virgin

Queen, or she only fell into the role after all avenues to marriage failed. The first position is more biographically attractive because it upholds Elizabeth as a prototype for the strong woman who defies the constraints of patriarchal convention. The second position is more historiographically attractive—at least as history has been practiced within the Anglo-American academy—because of its apparent archival integrity. It rests not on any presuppositions about Elizabeth's character but on documentary evidence in all its messiness and indeterminacy.

But the revisionist position finally does not read that messiness closely enough. I want to qualify it by considering the exchanges between Elizabeth and the Spanish ambassador, Don Gomez Suarex de Figueroa, Count of Feria, at the height of the Cateau-Cambrésis negotiations. These discussions, which Feria reported in detailed letters to Philip II, suggest that Elizabeth at least considered remaining a virgin from the first months of her reign. Regardless of her actual feelings and intentions, she introduced that possibility into diplomatic exchanges as early as 1559, to startling effect.[22]

Philip II had every political reason to marry Elizabeth, and Feria worked hard to bring the marriage about. From a Spanish perspective, more was to be lost by not marrying Elizabeth I than was to be gained by marrying Elisabeth de Valois. Marriage to a sovereign gave one far more influence over her country's affairs than marriage to a princess. The Salic law barring succession through female lines, moreover, meant that neither Philip nor his heirs might one day inherit the French throne. But a son of Philip and Elizabeth could have claimed both countries—Spain and England—as his rightful patrimony. If England moved into the French sphere of influence, on the other hand, it would augment the power of his traditional enemy and jeopardize his title to the Low Countries by closing off the Channel to Spanish ships. Nevertheless, Philip also had reservations about marrying Elizabeth. A papal dispensation would need to clear the way for him to marry his deceased wife's sister, and above all, he feared that she would not renounce Protestantism.

Philip weighed the advantages and disadvantages of marrying Elizabeth before he gave Feria his reluctant permission to carry out negotiations in earnest. Once Feria broached the subject, it intersected other complex questions about England's religious settlement, Elizabeth's stance toward Calais, and Spanish threats that if Elizabeth did not marry Philip, the French would encourage Mary, Queen of Scots—currently married to the French heir—to press her claims to the English Crown. The conversations muddled on inconclusively for about two months. At first, Elizabeth primarily pressed religious differences, her own status as a "heretic" (Feria's word), and her conviction that the pope had no power to grant a dispensation allowing her to marry her sister's husband. But by late February, she became more emphatic. Instead of just refusing Philip, she started saying that she did not want to marry anyone. In a memorandum enumerating her reasons for not marrying Philip, Feria placed her general distaste for marriage at the head of the list: "That she had no desire to marry, as she had intimated from the first day." The next point followed logically from the first: "That she quite understood that this marriage would be advantageous to her honour and the preservation of both States, but that these ends could be attained by the maintenance of the good friendship with your Majesty, above all seeing the obligations she was under to maintain it, as she well knew."[23] Only then does Feria list the more specific objections to Philip on grounds of religion and his previous marriage to her sister.

Taken together, the first two points move from an expression of personal distaste—"she had no desire to marry"—to a boldly original insistence that good diplomatic ends might be achieved without an interdynastic marriage. This is quite a thing to say to a Hapsburg, the family whose success in negotiating such marriages was second to none. At this point in the two-month conversation, Feria conceded to Philip that even though he pretended "not to take her remarks as an answer at all . . . she [was] not likely to reply in any other kind."[24] Philip took her words as a decisive refusal. In a letter to Feria dated March 23, he not only accepts the finality of her decision but directly incorporates in his statement echoes of Elizabeth's own words:

> By your letters . . . I am informed of the Queen's decision about the marriage, and although I cannot help being sorry that the affair has not been arranged as I greatly desired, and the public weal demanded, yet as the Queen thinks it was not necessary and that with good friendship we shall attain the same object, I am content that it should be so. I advise you of this that you may inform the Queen from me, and at the same time repeat my offers of assistance and co-operation for the good government of her realm, and assure her that I will preserve the good friendship and brotherhood that I have hitherto maintained.[25]

Philip not only agreed that the discussion of marriage was over but joined Elizabeth in imagining a relationship between two polities sealed in the more abstract form of "friendship and brotherhood" rather than interdynastic marriage and a common progeny. He was not happy about it, and he doubted her claim that she had no intention of marrying. He later offered to assist with her eventual marriage, and he clearly had in mind a Hapsburg kinsman, one of the Austrian archdukes. Neither that marriage nor any other ever took place.[26] What did come out of this 1559 conversation was a workable Anglo-Spanish rapport that functioned quite well for two decades and only really unraveled with the outbreak of war in 1588, almost thirty years later. As any student of early modern Europe would certify, a thirty-year peace is quite an achievement.

Within its early modern context, the peace was all the more remarkable because Elizabeth and Philip achieved it despite the fact that previous Anglo-Spanish accords had been established through interdynastic marriages, of Catherine of Aragon to Henry VII's two sons and of Mary I to Philip. In not marrying, Elizabeth moved toward a more abstract foreign policy shielded from the accidents of biology and family psychodynamics. Such a policy was potentially more secure than one founded on interdynastic marriage, but as Philip worried, it was also potentially less secure. Elizabeth's language, paraphrased in Feria's memorandum and echoed in Philip's letter, is richly vague with respect to the conditions that guaranteed the agreement's observance by both parties. Elizabeth dismisses marriage on the ground that, in Feria's summary, "these ends could be attained by the maintenance of the good friendship with your Majesty, above all seeing the obligations she was under to maintain it." The phrase is more rhetorically than legally reassuring. The verbal stress falls twice on the notion of *maintaining* a good friendship, but the two uses of *maintain* also entail a logically slippery syllogism: "we will achieve our common purpose by maintaining a good friendship, which I am under an obligation to maintain." But what kind of obligation? To Philip? In that case, we have a tautology, since the obligation to maintain a friendship is part of what constitutes a friendship in the first place. Or is the obligation to herself or to her people? That possibility introduces further logical, legal, and political questions that might well have made Philip wonder just what this friendship was.

His bewilderment is understandable. With the wisdom of hindsight, we might be able to see Elizabeth's choice of friendship over marriage as part of a more general desacramentalization of English culture after the Reformation. I am not suggesting that religion was at the root of Elizabeth's conspicuous departure from the practice of interdynastic marriage, but that in her religious, diplomatic, and personal preferences, Elizabeth participated in a larger cultural shift toward abstraction and interiorization that would become the hallmarks of modern society. Eventually, this process would reinvest sovereignty itself in the collective will of a people rather than in the person of an anointed monarch.

I want to close these reflections on the originality of Elizabeth's contributions to Cateau-Cambrésis by considering the relationship between diplomatic originality and significance. Something can be original but fail to be influential or significant. Since interdynastic marriages remained a feature of European diplomacy well after Elizabeth's death, her commitment to virginity might seem to have had no lasting significance. France and Spain continued to seal their agreements through marriages well into the eighteenth century. Louis XIV's marriage to Maria Theresa, the daughter of Spain's Philip IV, was a mirror image of Cateau-Cambrésis, but this time with a Spanish princess, who also loved to play cards, going to France.[27] But in England, something changed: after Elizabeth, royal marriages became a frequent flashpoint between Crown and Parliament, and arguably between the Crown and the English nation, increasingly imagined as a bearer of sovereignty in itself that was distinct, and ultimately separable, from the monarch.[28] Complaints about the influence of foreign—typically Catholic—queens consort figured prominently in English constitutional crises throughout the next century and contributed to the execution of one king and the deposition of another.

No topic in early modern history is more fraught than the question of how far back we must trace the origins of the British civil war. I do not want to claim that Elizabeth's rejection of Philip II in 1559 started the country down the road to regicide. But I also want to be careful about depicting Elizabeth as an unambiguous winner of the marriage contest that unfolded at Cateau-Cambrésis. The more negotiation moved away from discussions about the fate of royal bodies and the destiny of royal blood, sovereignty itself became subject to a radical displacement from the kings and queens who traditionally bore it.

If Elizabeth's choice not to marry contributed in the *longue durée* to an erosion of monarchical authority, it also may have, again inadvertently, compromised the position of women both in diplomatic theory and practice. The Spanish and Venetians alike saw her rejection of Philip not as testimony to her independence but to the influence of her male advisors, with whom she, in effect, shared the government of her realm.[29] Over the next thirty years, other Europeans would echo their words in demystifying her celebrated answerability to her people as a subjection to powerful men: to Burghley, to the men of her council, to the men of Parliament, or to the merchants and landowners they represented. By the seventeenth century, English republicans like James Harrington would hail her as one of the few good monarchs that England ever had because her natural subservience to men meant that her reign had constituted a de facto republic.[30] Paradoxically, they argued that the only way to bring back the greatness of the Elizabethans would be to abandon monarchy. Elizabeth's repudiation of Philip, the Archdukes Charles and Ferdinand, the French Dukes of Anjou and Alençon, and numerous other suitors foreign and domestic thus worked its way into an antimonarchical discourse that eventually transformed affairs of state, once the sole prerogative of kings, and occasionally queens, into a prerogative of parliaments, departments of state, and prime ministers.

Culminating in the double wedding of Henri II's sister to the

Duke of Savoy and of his daughter Elisabeth to Philip II, the Cateau-
Cambrésis negotiations carried the medieval practice of interdynastic marriage to a kind of baroque excess. Within the immediate
sphere of French influence, other weddings that I have barely even
mentioned helped to rally support for Henri's controversial peace,
including the marriage of his younger daughter Claude to the teen-
age Duke of Lorraine; of his eldest son and heir Francis to Mary
Stuart, Queen of Scots, the niece of the powerful Guise brothers;
and of his illegitimate daughter Diane to the son of the Duke of
Montmorency. Everyone was marrying everyone else in an effort
to end hostilities abroad and to mitigate intra-aristocratic tensions
at home. But although such political marriages had been a feature
of the diplomatic practice for centuries, the sheer proliferation of
them around this particular treaty suggests that the practice may
have been reaching a crisis. There was something almost desper-
ate in Henri's efforts to resolve several domestic and international
conflicts through the intermarriage of belligerent parties. A diplomatic practice that had worked reasonably well in a period of
parceled sovereignty faced new challenges in a period of increased
monarchical centralization, religious schism on an international
scale, and the development of enormous transatlantic empires. As
rulers faced the conditions that we associate retrospectively with
the emergence of modernity, marriage diplomacy began to look
anachronistic, even quaintly feudal.

Notes

1. I am indebted to a substantial prior bibliography on Cateau-Cambrésis. See es-
pecially F. J. Baumgartner, *Henry II, King of France, 1547–1559* (Durham NC: Duke
University Press, 1988), 218–30; C. S. L. Davies, "England and the French War," in
The Mid-Tudor Polity, 1540–1560, ed. J. Loach and R. Tittler (London: Macmillan,
1980), 159–85; S. Doran, *England and Europe in the Sixteenth Century* (New York: St.
Martin's, 1999); J. H. Elliott, *Europe Divided, 1559–1598*, 2nd ed. (Oxford: Blackwell,

2000); D. M. Loades, *The Reign of Mary Tudor: Politics, Government, and Religion in England, 1553–1558* (New York: St. Martin's, 1979); R. J. Knecht, *The Rise and Fall of Renaissance France, 1483–1610*, 2nd ed. (Oxford: Blackwell, 2001), 230–45; W. T. MacCaffrey, *The Shaping of the Elizabethan Regime: Elizabethan Politics, 1558–1572* (Princeton: Princeton University Press, 1968), 46–49, 58; J. G. Russell, *Peacemaking in the Renaissance* (London: Duckworth, 1986), 133–223; R. B. Wernham, *The Making of Elizabethan Foreign Policy, 1558–1603* (Berkeley: University of California Press, 1980); R. B. Wernham, *Before the Armada: The Emergence of the English Nation, 1485–1588* (New York: Harcourt, Brace & World, 1966); R. B. Wernham, *After the Armada: Elizabethan England and the Struggle for Western Europe, 1588–1595* (Oxford: Clarendon Press, 1984).

2. Some recent scholars have started to reform the paradigms for the investigation of diplomatic history. See especially D. Frigo, ed., *Politics and Diplomacy in Early Modern Italy: The Structure of Diplomatic Practice, 1450–1800*, trans. A. Belton, Cambridge Studies in Italian History and Culture (Cambridge: Cambridge University Press, 2000). See also D. Biow, *Doctors, Ambassadors, Secretaries: Humanism and Professions in Renaissance Italy* (Chicago: University of Chicago Press, 2002), 101–52; C. Storrs, *War, Diplomacy and the Rise of Savoy, 1690–1720* (Cambridge: Cambridge University Press, 1999); A. E. Zanger, *Scenes from the Marriage of Louis XIV: Nuptial Fictions and the Making of Absolutist Power* (Stanford: Stanford University Press, 1997). See also the essays in the "Toward a New Diplomatic History of Early Modern Europe" special issue, *Journal of Medieval and Early Modern Studies* 38 (2008), ed. J. Watkins.

3. P. Berry, *Of Chastity and Power: Elizabethan Literature and the Unmarried Queen* (London: Routledge, 1989); S. Doran, *Monarchy and Matrimony: The Courtships of Elizabeth I* (New York: Routledge, 1996); S. Frye, *Elizabeth I: The Competition for Representation* (New York: Oxford University Press, 1993); C. Levin, *"The Heart and Stomach of a King": Elizabeth I and the Politics of Sex and Power* (Philadelphia: University of Pennsylvania Press, 1994); C. Levin, J. E. Carney, and D. Barrett-Graves, eds., *Elizabeth I: Always Her Own Free Woman* (Aldershot: Ashgate, 2003); L. Shenk, "Transforming Learned Authority into Royal Supremacy: Elizabeth I's Learned Persona in Her University Orations," in *Elizabeth I*, ed. C. Levin, J. E. Carney, and D. Barrett-Graves; A. Riehl, "'Shine like an Angel with thy starry crown': Queen Elizabeth the Angelic," chapter 9 in the present volume; M. Suzuki, *Subordinate Subjects: Gender, the Political Nation, and Literary Form in England, 1588–1688* (Burlington VT: Ashgate, 2003), 78–96. The scholarship on gender, sovereignty, and the rise of the nation-state is rich and vast. This list is representative rather than exhaustive.

4. For discussion of divergent models of European monarchy, see B. Barbiche, *Les institutions de la monarchie française à l'époque moderne: XVIe–XVIIIe siècle* (Paris:

Presses universitaires de France, 1999); J. Cornette, ed., *La monarchie entre renaissance et révolution, 1515–1792* (Paris: Seuil, 2000); J. R. Major, *From Renaissance Monarchy to Absolute Monarchy: French Kings, Nobles, and Estates* (Baltimore: Johns Hopkins University Press, 1994); C. Coleman and D. Starkey, eds., *Revolution Reassessed: Revisions in the History of Tudor Government and Administration* (Oxford: Clarendon Press, 1986); P. Collinson, "The Monarchical Republic of Queen Elizabeth I," *Bulletin of the John Rylands University Library of Manchester* 69 (1987): 394–424: G. R. Elton, *Studies in Tudor and Stuart Politics and Government* (Cambridge: Cambridge University Press, 1974–92); J. Guy, ed., *The Tudor Monarchy* (New York: Arnold, 1997); D. M. Loades, *Tudor Government: Structures of Authority in the Sixteenth Century* (Oxford: Blackwell, 1997); J. H. Elliott, "A Europe of Composite Monarchies," *Past and Present* 137 (1992): 48–71; M. J. Rodríguez-Salgado, *The Changing Face of Empire: Charles V, Philip II, and Habsburg Authority, 1551–1559* (Cambridge: Cambridge University Press, 1988).

5. The Venetian ambassadors to the French and Spanish courts left particularly fine accounts of speculations and rumors surrounding the conference. See *Calendar of State Papers and Manuscripts Relating to English Affairs, Existing in the Archives and Collections of Venice: and other Libraries of Northern Italy*, ed. R. Brown et al. 38 vols. (London, 1864–1947), 7:48–49, 61–62. Hereafter cited as *CSP Venetian*.

6. On Philip's relationship with Mary, see D. M. Loades, *Mary Tudor: A Life* (Oxford: Blackwell, 1989), 223–73; S. Nadal, *Las cuatro mujeres de Felipe II* (Barcelona: Editorial Juventud, 1971), 77–130.

7. *Calendar of State Papers, Foreign Series, of the Reign of Mary, 1553–58*, ed. W. B. Turnbull (London, 1861), 400–407.

8. *CSP Venetian*, 7:24–25.

9. *CSP Venetian*, 7:54.

10. *CSP Venetian*, 7:83. For further discussion of Christine's role at the conference, see *CSP Venetian*, 7:10–11, 20, 33, 38, 56; *CSP Foreign Series, Reign of Mary*, 402; see also J. Cartwright, *Christina of Denmark* (New York: E. P. Dutton, 1913), 428–49.

11. I am indebted throughout to previous scholarship on Elisabeth de Valois. See especially A. de Amezúa y Mayo, *Isabel de Valois, reina de España*, 3 vols. (Madrid, Gráficas Ultra, 1949); Nadal, *Las cuatro mujeres*, 133–208; A. Martinez Llamas, *Isabel de Valois, reina de España: Una historia de amor y enfermedad* (Madrid: Ediciones Temas de Hoy, 1996).

12. The Abbé de Saint-Réal popularized the story of a passionate love between Don Carlos and Elisabeth de Valois in *L'histoire de Don Carlos* (1691), a novel that had an enormous influence on such later works as Friedrich Schiller's play *Dom Carlos* (1787) and Giuseppe Verdi's opera *Don Carlo* (1867).

13. For further discussion of Don Carlos's mental state, see G. Parker, *Philip II*, 4th ed. (Chicago: Carus, 2002), 87–95.

14. Llamas, *Isabel de Valois*, 81–90, 135–38, 169–77.

15. See Catherine de' Medici, *Lettres de Catherine de Medici*, ed. Gustave Baguenault de Puchesse, 10 vols. (Paris: Imprimerie nationale, 1880–1909), 2:209, 232, 269, 293, 298, 330, 408; 3:12; 10:107–10, 114, 120, 126–27, 150.

16. Llamas, *Isabel de Valois*, 101.

17. Llamas, *Isabel de Valois*, 109–10; Nadal, *Las cuatro mujeres*, 166–67.

18. Amezúa y Mayo devotes much of his biography to this conference (*Isabel de Valois, reina de España*, 2:193–332). He includes in his appendix the primary extant source, the Duke of Alba's dispatches to Philip II. Publishing in the early years of the Franco regime, Amezúa y Mayo follows Alba in seeing Isabel's reserve and complete obedience to Philip and cooperation with his male advisors as a testimony to her complete hispanization.

19. Nadal, *Las cuatro mujeres*, 176–82.

20. See J. N. King, "Queen Elizabeth I: Representations of the Virgin Queen," *Renaissance Quarterly* 43 (1990): 30–74; Doran, *Monarchy and Matrimony*, 1–3; Levin, *Heart and Stomach of a King*, 39–65.

21. This is the principal thesis of Doran's *Marriage and Matrimony*.

22. For earlier treatments of the Philip II marriage negotiations, see Doran, *Monarchy and Matrimony*, 21–26; Levin, *Heart and Stomach of a King*, 48–54.

23. *Calendar of Letters and State Papers Relating to English Affairs, Preserved Principally in the Archives of Simancas*, ed. M. A. S. Hume (London, 1892), 1:35. Hereafter cited as CSP *Spanish/Elizabeth*.

24. CSP *Spanish/Elizabeth*, 1:35.

25. CSP *Spanish/Elizabeth*, 1:40.

26. Doran, *Monarchy and Matrimony*, 26–30, 73–98.

27. Zanger, *Scenes from the Marriage of Louis XIV*.

28. See especially Thomas Cogswell's discussion of the controversy over the future Charles I's efforts to marry a Spanish princess in *The Blessed Revolution: English Politics and the Coming of War, 1621–1624* (Cambridge: Cambridge University Press, 1989).

29. CSP *Venetian*, 7:28; CSP *Spanish/Elizabeth* 1:25, 35, 38.

30. J. Harrington, *The Art of Law-giving in III Books* (London, 1659), 17. For further discussion, see J. Watkins, *Representing Elizabeth in Stuart England* (Cambridge: Cambridge University Press, 2002), 97–107.

6

Queen Solomon

An International Elizabeth I in 1569

LINDA S. SHENK

As the Protestant Queen Elizabeth I and the Catholic Mary, Queen of Scots, reigned over their kingdoms in the 1560s, each watched the other with an ever-nervous eye. Not only were they rival monarchs (in religion and in claim to the English throne) but they were also queens who had to negotiate the deep-seated criticisms leveled against female rule. According to centuries of misogynistic thought, a woman in power violated natural and divine law: women were emotionally unstable, intellectually deficient, and morally corrupt. In 1567, Mary's own Protestant counselors manipulated these stereotypes to justify rebellion, and Mary was led into confinement amid shouts of "Burn the whore!" When Mary fled Scotland and placed herself in English custody the following year, Elizabeth and her nation suddenly had the rival under their control—a situation that made Elizabeth and England powerful . . . and vulnerable.

Mary's overthrow substantiated anxieties regarding female rule, which, in turn, destabilized Elizabeth's own sovereignty and laid England open to the threat of foreign invasion, particularly from

Catholic France and Spain. To England's advantage, however, Protestant Europe looked increasingly to England for leadership, and even Scotland's new regent (and Protestant) government gave England supervision over its practices. At a crossroads, England prepared for both war and international predominance. Missives from top officials ratcheted up security at all ports; tracts were published to call English subjects to rally behind Crown and country; and most important for this study, Elizabeth was portrayed as a Protestant, learned queen—specifically as a new Solomon—in the prayer book *Christian Prayers and Meditations*, published in 1569 by the famous Protestant printer John Day.

Throughout this prayer book, Elizabeth is repeatedly likened to King Solomon: in the frontispiece; in prayers written for her subjects to use in worship; and in a concluding section that presents Elizabeth as a wise queen who is skilled in key European languages (Italian, French, Spanish), the biblical language of Greek, and the international lingua franca, Latin. Although we have no autograph copy of these prayers to prove Elizabeth's authorship, the editors of the work, Leah S. Marcus, Janel Mueller, and Mary Beth Rose, have noted that the foreign-language prayers contain many of Elizabeth's idiosyncrasies of composition, which adds to the likelihood that she was indeed the author.[1] Even if Elizabeth did not write the final section of prayers, however, she clearly authorized this text: her royal coat of arms appears on the inside of both covers, and she was given a presentation copy, which is housed in the Lambeth Palace Library.[2] In addition to the foreign-language pieces, a few vernacular prayers, also written in her royal voice, appear in earlier sections of the volume. These first sections contain prayers written for her subjects to use as part of their private devotions. Because many of the English prayers also appear in the prayer book Henry Bull compiled in 1569 (*Christian Prayers and Holy Meditations*), it is almost certain that Elizabeth did not write them. By including some of Elizabeth's prayers within the same volume as devotional texts written for her subjects, Day's *Christian Prayers and Meditations* presents Elizabeth as a true Solomon. She is both at prayer and leading the prayers of her nation. Choosing to depict Elizabeth as a Solomon in 1569 was a powerful and highly strategic act: it was designed to refute the inadequacies of Elizabeth's authority as an unmarried queen and to portray her and her nation as stable, unified, and poised to assume leadership of Europe's providentially sanctioned Protestant Church.

Elizabeth was associated with Solomon frequently over the course of her reign; however, scholars have devoted only cursory attention to her connection with this persona, focusing more on her other biblical roles as Susanna, Esther, Judith, David, Joshua, Hezekiah, and Deborah. Studies by Margaret Aston, Susan Doran, John N. King, A. N. McLaren, Michele Osherow, Donald Stump, and Alexandra Walsham have made rich contributions to our understanding of how these figures provided crucial providential support for Elizabeth and her subjects to defend female rule while at the same time placing limitations on the queen's sovereignty.[3] Significantly, though, these biblical figures possessed authority over a single group of people, whereas Solomon—the builder of the temple and the wisest, wealthiest king in the region—had achieved decidedly *international* status. Given wisdom directly by God, Solomon possessed an exclusive access to divine wisdom that served as the foundation for his pointedly public authority as both monarch and ecclesiastical leader. He was a just judge, prudent king, sage author of scripture, and divinely selected builder of God's temple. As such a multicompetent figure, he became a model for the nations, attaining an international acclaim that prompted dignitaries and other rulers (such as the Queen of Sheba) to travel great distances to learn from him and to marvel at his governance. When Elizabeth assumes the image of Solomon, she in turn infuses her sovereignty with international stature and grounds this authority in wisdom. She becomes the educated, divinely endorsed Christian king—the monarchic ideal that civic philosophers such as Desiderius Erasmus had celebrated throughout the sixteenth century.

Elizabeth was not a king, however, but a queen. Examining Elizabeth's representation as Solomon in *Christian Prayers* reveals the complexity of associating her with this Old Testament ruler. Because of Solomon's singularity in wisdom and divine election, rulers for centuries had equated themselves with Solomon in a long tradition that extended back to Constantine and continued into the sixteenth century with Henry VIII and now Elizabeth herself. Solomon bows to no earthly power (such as a pope), and this characteristic informs Elizabeth's representations as Solomon in the 1565 pageant *Sapientia Solomonis* and in her own prayer book *Precationes priuatae. Regiae E. R.* (1563). Such unbridled authority, however, ran contrary to the image of a limited monarchy that civic philosophers typically employed to describe Elizabeth's sovereignty. These men (John Aylmer, Thomas Smith, and Laurence Humphrey, among others) repeatedly emphasized that Elizabeth did not reign alone but rather with the assistance of Parliament, the Privy Council, her clerics, her nobility, and her judges.[4] Surrounding the female monarch with counseling (male) subjects created a mixed monarchy that made female rule palatable.

Elizabeth's image as Solomon in *Christian Prayers* reflects the dueling principles of crowning a female monarch with public, even international, authority and needing to constrict that power because of her gender. In this devotional text, therefore, Elizabeth emerges not as a King Solomon but rather as a *Queen* Solomon. She rules within a political collective of guiding male advisors (appropriate for a mixed ruler), and she demonstrates public authority from the position of private, female humility. This complex image of Elizabeth in *Christian Prayers* arises, I propose, precisely because of the international scope of England's political situation in 1569—a situation that made it particularly expedient for both Elizabeth *and* her counselors to depict Elizabeth ruling within a powerful collective at the helm of a unified nation. Historians such as Wallace MacCaffrey have described how Elizabeth and her statesmen worked in tandem in this period.[5] Elizabeth's Solomonic image in *Christian Prayers* reflects this harmony and may even be a product of collaboration between counselors and queen.[6] Whatever the origins of its authorship, this prayer book participated in England's international strategy to present a strong face to other nations—a strength that supported the Crown's choice to take a diplomatic approach to handling both the threat and the power the nation experienced in 1569.[7]

In fact, Elizabeth's image as a Queen Solomon in *Christian Prayers* marks an early stage in what would become a trend of representing Elizabeth as a learned queen in times of international crisis. In the 1580s, Elizabeth's learned (often Solomonic) persona was invoked repeatedly when England wanted to assert a Protestant, even military, strength in the face of Catholic threat.[8] Examining Elizabeth's image as a Queen Solomon in *Christian Prayers* provides a crucial and early example of how Elizabeth and her subjects devised a powerful international, yet still gendered, image to support Elizabeth's and England's right to become the champions of the Protestant European community. It also opens up the relatively underexplored territory of royal representation: Elizabeth's association with the highly political identity of the learned monarch—an identity that would serve Elizabeth and her subjects well in bolstering the image of the English Crown long after 1569.[9]

A Queen Solomon Superior in Protestant Virtue

England's ability to assert international authority rested substantially on the perceived strength of its leadership. As Stephen Alford has noted in his work on William Cecil, England's security was intimately connected to the image of Elizabeth's stability. Thus, Elizabeth needed to be portrayed as a monarch who avoided the vices of her sex—a priority all the more pressing in 1569 because it was Mary Stuart's perceived failure at female rule that gave Elizabeth and England the opportunity to assume international preeminence.[10] To separate Elizabeth from the passionate Mary, *Christian Prayers* draws on the conventional connection between learning, moral virtue, and reason. Even more specifically, Elizabeth possesses pointedly Solomonic wisdom with a clearly Protestant and feminine hue: she is a vessel of divine wisdom because she is a mouthpiece for scripture. Tying Elizabeth's wisdom to the Bible emphasizes her Protestant devotion while simultaneously countering the stereotype that a woman asserting her own authority is immodest. *Christian Prayers* transforms the public, divinely elevated Solomon into the privately praying queen whose biblically focused faith assures her superiority over the lusty Scottish Mary.

The image of Elizabeth in the frontispiece of the volume demonstrates, in miniature, the delicate balance of asserting Elizabeth's virtue as an appropriate leader yet subsuming this authority under feminine, Christian submission (see fig. 6.1.) Elizabeth is depicted in solitary prayer with Solomon's words from 2 Chronicles 6:14 printed in Latin as a caption underneath: *Domine Deus Israel, non est similis tui Deus in caelo & in terra qui pacta custodis & misericordiam cum seruis tuis, qui ambulant coram te in toto corde suo.* (In the 1568 Bishops' Bible, this verse in English reads: "O Lorde God of Israel, there is no God like thee in heauen and earth,

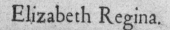

Fig. 6.1. Elizabeth in prayer, frontispiece from *Christian Prayers and Meditations* by John Day (1569). Reproduced by permission of the Huntington Library, San Marino CA (RB 60973).

which kepest couenaunt & shewest mercie vnto thy seruauntes that walke before thee with al their heartes.")[11] In addressing God with Solomon's description of submissive hearts, Elizabeth exudes an emotional devotion that has a particularly intimate tone because she is visually portrayed in the frontispiece both at prayer and in a small, private chapel. This combination of image and caption presents Elizabeth as a figure who has lovingly given over her personal faith to God's will. The presence of her imperial crown resting on the prie-dieu implies that she has also placed her regal status under God's direction—compliance that matches her contemporaneous and strongly gendered depiction in 1570 as "under Christ" in the historiated C of John Foxe's popularly titled *Book of Martyrs* (a text also published by Day).[12] The context of the actual passage from 2 Chronicles, however, is far from private. These words begin Solomon's prayer before the masses when he dedicates the temple, an event that could be considered his greatest moment as a religious leader. In the frontispiece, the gap between the biblical context and the visual image creates competing impressions of Elizabeth that acknowledge the hesitancy involved in bestowing ecclesiastical and international leadership on a female monarch. Although Elizabeth is depicted as a theocratic ruler (underscored also by the combined presence of the sword and book in the image[13]), her role as the providential leader of European Protestantism occurs within the gendered frame of private, feminine compliancy to divine direction.

Elizabeth's intimate relationship with the divine becomes clear in the queen's own prayers: she claims a daughterly bond with God. This relationship further identifies her with Solomon, because this king (like Christ) was a "son of David"—a familial image also used on the title page with its tree of Jesse extending through King David and Solomon and leading to Christ. As God's daughter, Elizabeth possesses wholesome virtue that distances her from the source of

Mary's alleged downfall: the lusts of the flesh. This emphasis begins in the second royal prayer—written, significantly, in Mary's first language of French: "As for my body and my soul, mayst Thou be my Protector, strengthening me against all the temptations of the devil and of the flesh" (145).[14] Then, in the second Italian prayer, Elizabeth asks that the divine image within her be kept "pure and untainted by any carnal affection"(153).[15] Free from physical temptations, she removes herself from not only the primary weakness of her gender but also the weakness that purportedly prompted Mary to murder her second husband. As a Queen Solomon, Elizabeth is a queen of the mind, not of the flesh.

Mary's alleged passionate desire for James Hepburn, Earl of Bothwell, was a mainstay of Elizabeth's claim of superiority over the Scottish queen. It is no wonder that England had worked with the Scottish regency government to capitalize on Mary's reputation as lusty. The Scottish government provided the "evidence" that cemented Mary's reputation as concupiscent when it brought forth the Casket letters—an act that caused an international sensation. These eight letters, written in French and allegedly in Mary's own hand, included bald statements of immodest affections. Casket letter 2 was particularly damning, for in it, "Mary" gushes forth what the English commissioners described in their report as her "inordinate love" for Bothwell.[16] The content of the letters sullied Mary's character by "proving" her lust, and their rambling style and disjointed structure confirmed the stereotype that a woman's rhetoric is as unbridled as her passion. As a recent biographer Retha M. Warnicke has pointed out, Mary was brought down through her sexuality and her literacy.[17]

As Mary's situation demonstrated, a woman's rhetorical skill could place her in a public and therefore precarious position. In response, Elizabeth's own learning in *Christian Prayers* is framed

within submission to divine authority and depicted as solely dependent on God's wisdom. In the penultimate Greek prayer, Elizabeth
portrays herself as a mere vessel for divine knowledge: "And since
there is no private wisdom in me, trusting in which I might continue
to govern well in such a realm, fill my breast with the intelligence
and wisdom of the Holy Spirit" (162).[18] This strategy matches the
high frequency with which her wisdom is tied closely to the Bible—a
strategy that works well with her gender *and* her Protestantism. The
two sections that preface Elizabeth's prayers in foreign languages
showcase this focus. First appears what is essentially a biblical
commonplace book that contains "sentences" taken from scripture that address various princely topics (Aa1r–Gg3r). Next follows
Solomon's prayer to God from the apocryphal Book of Wisdom
written as if Elizabeth is the speaker (Gg3v–4v). This prayer contains few modifications; however, the changes are in keeping with
Elizabeth's gender and the limited sovereignty she has as a Queen
Solomon. Through Solomon's words, the reader hears Elizabeth
express intellectual weakness ("to weake for the vnderstandying
of thy judgementes and lawes") and her need for divine wisdom.
Elizabeth's version omits, quite significantly, Solomon's articulation
of anointed royal power (verse 7) and his authority as the builder
of the Temple (verse 8).[19]

Elizabeth's scriptural wisdom couples her superiority in virtue
with religious superiority as a Protestant queen. The very wording
and format of the prayer book depict a Protestant agenda that undermines Catholic principles. In addition to the repeated references
to Christ as sole mediator and intercessor, many of the prayers begin
with a short scriptural passage in the vernacular that serves as a
model for the meditation that follows. Appropriately, this format is
used specifically for the prayers in Spanish and Italian—languages
of primarily Catholic nations. Elizabeth's position as a champion

of God's "true" Church is further emphasized because two of these passages are written by or modeled after Solomon. (A third passage, from Psalms 32, is attributed to him; however, this psalm is actually associated with David, not Solomon.) The second Spanish prayer even opens with the passage from 1 Kings in which Solomon prays to God for wise judgment, which Elizabeth, in turn, echoes in her accompanying prayer: "I, Thy maidservant, may have a wise heart that can discern between the good and the bad. And in this manner may justice be administered in this Thy kingdom" (156).[20]

The format of coupling a scriptural verse with a prayer not only roots Elizabeth's wisdom in the Protestant priority of *sola scriptura* but also establishes the religious practice that she shares with her fellow Protestant believers. Placing a passage with a prayer harkens back to the format used earlier in the meditations for the lay worshipper. This harmony between queen and subject is emphasized repeatedly throughout the text: Elizabeth is a figure of temperate, humble virtue wisely leading from within a collective of scripturally focused Protestant believers. In fact, the opening sections of the text do not trumpet Elizabeth or her authority at all. Rather, they contain sequences of prayers specifically for the lay worshipper. Elizabeth's royal voice emerges out of this chorus only sporadically at first and always in a way that demonstrates the compatibility of her words with those of her praying subjects. The first section of prayers, for example, includes devotions for prescribed times, such as morning or evening, for times of thanksgiving, and during periods of sickness (an approach Elizabeth adopts in her French prayers).[21] Nested within the prayers to be said during times of illness, however, appears one of Elizabeth's prayers that had been originally published in *Precationes priuatae. Regiae E. R.* (1563). Although its current translation into English retains Elizabeth as the speaker, the heading for the prayer lists it simply as "In time of sicknes" (κ2v). Without any royal fanfare, Elizabeth's voice comes in quietly, diminishing any distinction between her voice and those of the surrounding prayers. Such harmony between queen and subjects matches one of the few alterations in the wording of the prayer. In 1563, Elizabeth makes a solitary plea for her continued health on behalf of the nation. In 1569, a completely new sentence has her people join in the request. "Wherfore as well I as thy people committed vnto me bowing the knees of our hartes before thy maiestie, do humbly besech thee most gratious Sauiour, in thy judgement to remember thy mercy" (L1r) and save her from dangerous illness. Inspiring such concern, Elizabeth is depicted as the beloved governor supported by a nation of devoted subjects.

The Superiority of England's Solomonic Collective

This national unity through adoration played a primary role in how England conveyed its strength and political superiority to the international community. Less than two months after Mary was placed under house arrest, the Crown presented just such a demonstration for the Spanish ambassador, Guzmán de Silva. In describing the event to King Philip in a letter dated July 10, 1568, the ambassador wrote that Elizabeth "was received everywhere with great acclamations and signs of joy, as is customary in this country; whereat she was extremely pleased and told me so, giving me to understand how beloved she was by her subjects and how highly she esteemed this, together with the fact they were peaceful and contented whilst her neighbors on all sides are in such trouble."[22] For Elizabeth and her counselors, emphasizing England's strength through royal devotion was crucial. England had just begun talks with the Scottish regency government about mediating in Scottish affairs. These discussions would eventually lead to quasi-legal proceedings beginning in October to examine Mary's involvement in her second husband's murder. Such clear assertion of control over Mary threatened to invoke the ire of Spain and France. In December that year, the threat remained: Francis Walsingham reported information that suggested not just foreign attack but specifically that France and Spain were combining forces against England, its queen, and its Protestant religion.[23]

The legal investigation into the Scottish queen's affairs began a series of international situations in which England asserted its right to assume leadership—first to oversee affairs in Scotland, then to assist Protestant groups within nations embroiled in civil unrest, and finally to stamp out the enemies of God's church. With each successive assertion, the international stakes were higher. Playing a supportive role in this agenda, *Christian Prayers* portrays England as possessing a superior government with its Queen Solomon ruling within a powerful collective—not only of devoted lay worshippers but now also of wise counselors, clerics, and judges. With the strength of a mixed monarchy, Elizabeth becomes part of a conglomerate Solomon.

England's strongest authority in the international arena was over Scotland. In October 1568, Elizabeth appointed a group of commissioners to judge Mary's right to return to the Scottish throne based on her level of involvement, if any, in murder. Scottish representatives from the young King James VI's regency government as well as Mary's supporters appeared before the English commissioners during a three-month period. Not only did these proceedings make England's political superiority over the Scottish government officially and publicly visible, but they also placed Elizabeth in the role of judge. Elizabeth's judicial authority resonates in the repeated references to Solomon in *Christian Prayers* where the king seeks God's wisdom for the ability to discern between good and evil. England needed to present its and Elizabeth's role as judge very circumspectly because calling the affair a "trial" opened the possibility that a divinely anointed monarch was subject to earthly strictures. Mary herself acknowledged this dilemma. According to her commissioners, she stated that she would not "recognize her self to be Subjecte to any Judge in Earthe."[24] In the initial instructions to her commissioners, Elizabeth avoids the word *judge*, describing her role as "Umpire and principal Arbitrer."[25] Elizabeth lost some of her squeamishness when Mary and her commissioners stopped cooperating in December; Elizabeth threatened with the reminder of "our Judgement."[26] The first-person plural carries with it the strength of the Crown as a collective. The Crown becomes a larger entity that encompasses more than just Elizabeth's physical body.

In keeping with this strategy of employing a corporate image, Elizabeth's associations with Solomon in her prayers often place her within a network of authoritative subjects. Her first allusion to Solomon's request for divine judgment comes alongside this notion of a unified body of male advisors and judges:

> Thou wilt give to Thy maidservant and to thy menservants an understanding heart to judge Thy people and to distinguish between good from evil, so that we may not be unprofitable or, worse, pernicious in a vocation so holy as this. Give us also prudent, wise, and virtuous councillors, driving far from us all ambitious, malignant, wily, and hypocritical ones. Give us for judges true men who hate greediness and who shun acceptation of persons, so that my people may be governed [*soit gouverné*] in all equity and righteousness, the virtuous sustained [*soustenus*] in their justice and innocence, the wicked punished and chastised [*punis & chastiez*]. (147)[27]

Unlike Solomon who alone received God's ability to judge, Elizabeth includes "menservants" in her echo of 1 Kings 3:9. Though she does not identify these men specifically, later she mentions counselors and judges. Her request for others to gain divine perspective also eliminates her exclusive access to divine wisdom. Elizabeth now shares Solomon's authority with her male counseling subjects. This shift from aligning Elizabeth solely with Solomon to creating a predominantly male, corporate entity that possesses Solomon's wisdom directly addresses the anxieties of giving a queen this Old Testament king's authority.

These anxieties were justified. Elizabeth's use of Solomon in her 1563 prayer book, *Precationes priuatae. Regiae E. R.*, makes clear why. In 1563, Elizabeth had used a self-comparison to Solomon to assume an aggressively absolutist position—directly countering the image of a mixed sovereignty her subjects typically created.[28] In *Precationes*, Elizabeth subtly included references to Solomon that built progressively to a direct rejection of earthly guidance. First, she portrayed herself as taught by God and then echoed Solomon's words (without acknowledging the source). Later, she openly likened herself to this king before capitalizing on the implications of these connections: she had God's wisdom; therefore, she needed no earthly assistance. In this climactic moment, Elizabeth declares: "And besides, that I may know what is acceptable to Thee alone, vouchsafe that I wish, dare, and can perform it without paying respect to any earthly persons or things."[29] Significantly, this same prayer is included in English in *Christian Prayers*, and the difference between the prayer as it appears in 1569 and a literal translation of the Latin from the original 1563 version drives home the difference between the two representations of Elizabeth as Solomon. The translation in 1569 erases the rejection of advice: "finally without regard of persons, w'out accompt of worldly respectes take in hand, execute, and performe that which I shall know to please thee alone" (p3v–4r). The 1569 version softens Elizabeth's absolutist assertion by obscuring her agency: it delays acknowledging the queen as the subject, placing the "I" at the end of the sentence and by applying "earthly" only to "respects." Conversely, in the Latin (see note 28), the nominative case makes Elizabeth's agency clear with each verb. The Latin also allows for the possibility that "earthly" modifies both "persons and things" (*personarum aut rerum mundanarum*).

Elizabeth's Solomonic image in *Christian Prayers* places the queen within the appropriately guiding "earthly persons and things" that are more befitting the queen of a limited monarchy, and such differences between the two prayer books support the possibility that *Christian Prayers* was a co-production between the queen and her counseling subjects. In fact, the notion of the Crown as a broad entity is further emphasized in the same French prayer discussed earlier when, once the idea of counselors and judges is introduced, the passage shifts to passive voice (*soit gouuerné*), which leaves vague the agents of judgment and even government itself. This ambiguity extends the rights of governance far beyond Elizabeth's person by removing a "feeble woman" as the linchpin for such power. This indirection strengthens England's image as a strong governing collective.

Surrounded by a network of figures who govern with her, Elizabeth facilitates the power of a mixed sovereignty. The final French prayer includes the additional notion that this group is unified under divine supervision. Elizabeth and counselors are depicted conducting the business of the realm with God in their midst: "we Thy humble maidservant and Thy menservants, being assembled here [*estans icy assemblez*] in Thy presence to treat and advise about the business which concerns the holy vocation to which Thou hast called us by thy grace" (150).[30] This prayer emphasizes queen and counselor unified not only in godliness but also in political purpose. The sense of gathering is made poignantly immediate by the use of the present participle, which gives the impression that these words are being spoken during a conciliar session. This event becomes more precisely located in time—at the beginning of the session—when, a few sentences later, Elizabeth layers in the future and subjunctive tenses: "we may [*puissions*] with prudence and wisdom treat of the things that now will be [*seront*] propounded" and then "Furthermore, keep [*tienne*] Thou Thy hand in all our deliberations"(151).[31] Unlike Elizabeth's rejection of counsel in *Precationes, Christian Prayers* depicts her within a mixed sovereignty actively engaged in making political decisions. This dynamic image intensifies the notion of England as a corporate sovereignty that functions as nimbly as it does harmoniously—an image of collective power that takes the vulnerability of having an unmarried queen on the throne and turns it into an asset.

While putting forward this face of religious, powerful unity, Elizabeth and her counselors still felt the threat of attack on both the international and domestic fronts. Despite such bravado, tensions within England were building as Mary's arrest rallied Catholic support from the northern earls. This support would escalate to rebellion in November 1569. Participating in this climate of conspiracy, the new Spanish ambassador Guerau de Spes was plotting with some of these nobles as well as other international figures—so much so that on April 2, 1569, he complains to Philip that all letters (including his) leaving the country must now pass through Cecil's hands.[32] On May 23, de Spes says that England is worried about Spain declaring war.[33] That summer, Cecil wrote *A necessary consideration*, in which he depicts England as internationally isolated: it "so standeth alone upon the gard of it self, as never it did at any tyme before by the memory of any recordes or storyes." Cecil then adds a phrase that provides the remedy: "in which matter is to be noted that ther is no contrey with which it may be more proffitably knitt than with scotland and next to it with some leage of the princes protestantes of the Empire."[34] The answer to England's perilous position was to build Protestant alliances. As Stephen Alford has noted, in 1569 England increasingly identified itself in Protestant opposition to Mary, Queen of Scots, and her allies.[35] With this overtly Protestant position, the image of Solomon establishes England as a superior nation that is divinely blessed with tranquility (because it nourishes God's true church) and, like Solomon's kingdom, great wealth.

The integration of Protestantism, money, and international ascendancy was a particularly public issue for England in 1569. Not only had England given Scotland's regent, the Earl of Moray, a loan in January to solidify that relationship but also, less than a month earlier, England had captured five ships sent from Antwerp to deliver money to the Duke of Alva's Spanish forces in the Low Countries. These encounters with Spain may lurk behind a Solomonic boast in a Spanish prayer that expresses England's superiority as a peaceful—and wealthy—nation. Elizabeth asks that God "mayst be glorified in constituting me as head and governess of Thy wealthiest kingdom in these most unhappy times in which Thy Church, Thy only spouse, is in so great a manner oppressed by the tyranny of Satan and his ministers" (156).[36] England had become a bit wealthier at Spain's expense, and any act to weaken Alva's war efforts was doubly useful. It diminished England's fear that Alva would turn his eye next on England, and it gave relief to the Protestant forces that Alva was trying to crush.

Peaceful Champions of God's Church in a Chaotic Europe

England's association with wealth and assistance encouraged Protestant forces in the Low Countries and France to turn increasingly to England for aid—an act that further justified England's right to international leadership. In October 1568, de Spes already suspected that Elizabeth was building a Protestant powerbase abroad by giving money to the Protestant William of Orange in the Low Countries and preparing to do the same for the Prince of Condé, leader of the Huguenots.[37] Expressing interest in more financial ties, Henry Killigrew wrote Cecil from Hamburg in May 1569 to suggest: "If the Quenes Majestie agree to send Mony, I thinke the League will follow." He then affirmed Elizabeth's international image of strength: "the Quynes Majeste be more feared and honored this Day of all Contrys, what Religion soever they be of, then ever any of her Majestie's Predecessors before her was."[38]

Though the reference to England as wealthy in the Spanish prayer is an isolated instance, the foreign-language prayers repeatedly bolster Elizabeth's and England's political strength by emphasizing the tremendous upheaval happening across the Channel. In the second Latin prayer, Elizabeth asks God to keep her nation "exempt from the internal and domestic tumults by which a good part of the Christian world is now disturbed" (160).[39] By alluding to the strife in France and in the Low Countries, she links the superiority of her peaceful, divinely endorsed governance to her ability to rescue other nations. God has personally given her kingdom peace, unlike "other kingdoms being in horrible confusion—and that Thou hast sent to me the bowels of Thy Son Jesus Christ to give them refuge in their afflictions, give me the grace to be a true nourisher and nurse of Thy people according to the word of Thy prophet Isaiah, to have true compassion, as much on those who are here as on all others" (149).[40] Indeed, England had become a haven for Protestant refugees—proof of its stability and strength to attract and harbor these fellow believers. As the Spanish ambassador de Silva observed with frustration in July 1568, England was pretending to turn a blind eye to the transport of weapons and funds from England to the Low Countries.[41] Less than a year later, his successor, de Spes, complained of the high number of Flemish merchants who had settled in England and who were worshipping, like the French, in their own congregations.[42] The presence of such congregations suggests that a large number of Protestant refugees had found sanctuary in a stable England.

Out of this image of peaceful English superiority arises Elizabeth as a leader who cares not only for her own country but also for "all others." Repeatedly, she presents an aggressive Protestant agenda that extends well beyond English shores. In the second Italian prayer, she vows her commitment to "uprooting every wicked seed of impiety, to spread, plant, and root Thy holy Gospel in every heart, increasing *throughout this Thy earthly kingdom*, that heavenly one of Jesus Christ" (154; my emphasis).[43] Within this articulation of religious imperialism lies Elizabeth's Protestant focus on planting the gospel. Similarly in the first Spanish prayer, she echoes Romans 1:16, stating that her enemies "hate me so because I put all my hope in Thee alone, because I am not ashamed of the Gospel of Thy most loving Son; much rather, I have been honored as one who surely holds the Gospel to be Thy power for giving salvation to all those who believe"(155).[44] The particular scriptural echo further supports Elizabeth's focus on *sola scriptura* and role as leader of the Church because this passage (in Latin) also appeared beneath her image on the title page of the first edition of the Bishops' Bible (officially titled *The Holie Bible*) published the previous year. In fact, not only did this edition emphasize Elizabeth's rightful leadership of the Church as a learned queen but also, as Elizabeth Evenden suggests, Archbishop Matthew Parker himself probably intended Elizabeth to have this edition and *Christian Prayers and Meditations* as companion texts.[45]

These concluding moments situate Elizabeth in a unique connection to God that resembles her depiction in the frontispiece but now with an aggressively singular leading role. In the final prayer, which is in the biblical language of Greek, Elizabeth becomes the sole, chosen figure who leads the Church, promising "to protect freely willed religion, to destroy superstitious fear by working freely to promote divine service, and to spy out the worship of idols; further, to gain release from the enemies of religion as well as those who hate me—Antichrists, Pope lovers, atheists, and all persons who fail to obey Thee and me" (163).[46] Gone are the judges and counselors. Alone, this strong articulation of singular authority equating obedience to God with obedience to Elizabeth would support her divinely anointed status. The same elevating language of obedience, however, echoes from the first Greek prayer—the only foreign-language prayer written in the voice of Elizabeth's subjects. This prayer as said by her people limits Elizabeth's sovereignty by making Protestantism the condition on which she has both her authority (even as Solomon) and their obedience. These supplicants first link her to Solomon by requesting that she receive divine wisdom: "illumine her soul with the light of Thine unbounded wisdom" (161).[47] Then the language shifts to the other facet of providential rhetoric that scholars such as McLaren have examined in detail— that Elizabeth will retain this providential status only as long as she follows God's will: "remembering always that the sovereign rule is not hers, but that governance of the whole kingdom has been given to her as heir to the kingdom, or rather as servant, by Thee as sovereign, on condition that she revere Thee absolutely, defend the virtuous, and seek vengeance on the wicked and lawless" (161).[48] The biblical Solomon received divine wisdom "with no strings attached"; he even spent the last part of his reign still in power yet indulging in concupiscence.[49] Elizabeth will also enjoy the obedience of her subjects, but they emphasize that her sovereignty comes with certain conditions: they will lovingly follow her *only as long as* she abides by divine wisdom.

In the final prayer of the volume, Elizabeth's Solomonic voice booms, demonstrating the forcefully Protestant stance that her subjects stipulate in the previous prayer. Through the juxtaposition of these final devotions, England and Elizabeth fuse under Elizabeth's royal image. Here, Elizabeth articulates the notions of Protestant strength, unity, and superiority that her counseling subjects were also projecting to maximize England's international advantage in 1569. Elizabeth's image as a Queen Solomon provides at least the appearance, if not the reality, that she is participating directly in the diplomatic agenda of her nation—not through a traditionally feminine dynastic agency but through a policy-oriented persona. As John Watkins observes elsewhere in this collection, scholars have treated diplomacy as an exclusively male enterprise, relegating women to the role of mere physical pawns in the game of political matchmaking. He demonstrates how changes in the European political climate in this period led to an increase in diplomatic literacy and expanded women's participation in international affairs. Reminiscent of Frances Yates's work on Elizabeth as the imperial virgin Astraea, this study has revealed how Elizabeth's learned status imbues her with a transnational and singular sovereignty that, in this case, dovetails with the nation's diplomatic practice.[50] As scholars of Elizabeth, we have focused too closely on her compositions in English, and now, as Paul Franssen has noted, we need to study this queen "in *all* her languages"[51]—an examination that will situate her more specifically and emphatically within the larger picture of international politics.

Examining Elizabeth's persona as a Queen Solomon suggests her contribution to England's diplomatic agenda in 1569 and, indeed, I will suggest, beyond that year. Her royal image as a learned queen would be invoked with vigor in the 1580s, particularly after her final marriage negotiations with the Duke of Alençon terminated in treaty rather than nuptials. With that diplomatic resolution to what started as a dynastic alliance, England was clearly on the path to finish the Elizabethan years with an unmarried queen on the throne. To augment the nation's defenses (with tensions building yet again regarding Mary, Queen of Scots), Elizabeth would frequently be celebrated as an educated ruler in praise pointedly juxtaposed with images of international intimidation and England's military prowess. Maurice Kyffin, for example, would extol Elizabeth as "Tutor to Frends and Terror vnto Foes" in his 1587 *The Blessednes of Brytaine*[52]—a text that Kyffin both fills with descriptions of England's military readiness for war and dedicates to Robert Devereux, Earl of Essex, Elizabeth's new master of the horse. Kyffin's text will be one of many to represent Elizabeth as a Protestant learned queen. In essence, England's philosopher-queen wields the pen that will help justify her subjects in brandishing God's sword.

Notes

1. Elizabeth I, *Collected Works*, ed. L. S. Marcus, J. M. Mueller, and M. B. Rose (Chicago: University of Chicago Press, 2000), 143–44n1. Unless otherwise specified, all translations of Elizabeth's prayers come from this edition, and citations are hereafter provided in the text. The original foreign-language passages (as found in *Christian Prayers and Meditations in English[,] French, Italian, Spanish, Greeke, and Latine* [London: John Daye, 1569])are provided in corresponding endnotes with a parenthetical citation from the original 1569 text. Citations for passages that appear in English in *Christian Prayers* are provided in the text.

2. Steven W. May considers Elizabeth's prayers as more private texts that Elizabeth did not want circulated. His description of the context surrounding her prayers in the 1590s sheds important light on these later demonstrations ("Queen Elizabeth Prays for the Living and the Dead," in *Elizabeth I and the Culture of Writing*, ed. P. Beal and G. Ioppolo [London: British Library, 2007], 203–6). In the 1560s, however, Elizabeth authorized the publication of *Christian Prayers and Meditations* as well as an earlier royal prayer book *Precationes priuatae. Regiae E. R.* (1563)—authorized texts that suggest to me that she wanted at least these prayers disseminated.

3. See M. Aston, *The King as Bedpost: Reformation and Iconography in a Tudor*

Group Portrait (Cambridge: Cambridge University Press, 1993); S. Doran, "Virginity, Divinity and Power: The Portraits of Elizabeth I," in *The Myth of Elizabeth*, ed. S. Doran and T. S. Freeman (Basingstoke: Palgrave Macmillan, 2003), 171–99; J. N. King, "The Godly Woman in Elizabethan Iconography," *Renaissance Quarterly* 38, no. 1 (1985): 41–84; A. N. McLaren, *Political Culture in the Reign of Elizabeth I: Queen and Commonwealth, 1558–1585* (Cambridge: Cambridge University Press, 1999); M. Osherow, "'Give Ear O Princes': Deborah, Elizabeth and the Right Word," *Explorations in Renaissance Culture* 30, no. 1 (2004): 111–19; D. Stump, "Abandoning the Old Testament: Shifting Paradigms for Elizabeth, 1578–82," *Explorations in Renaissance Culture* 30, no. 1 (2004): 89–109; and A. Walsham, "A Very Deborah? The Myth of Elizabeth I as a Providential Monarch," in *The Myth of Elizabeth*, ed. S. Doran and T. S. Freeman, 143–68. In addition, Susan Doran is currently working on an essay about Elizabeth as Solomon. She presented her preliminary research on this topic at the Sixteenth Century Studies Conference in Minneapolis, Minnesota, in October 2007, and her focus in her conference paper, titled "Elizabeth and the Biblical King," centered on comparisons of Elizabeth with Solomon and David in the latter half of her reign.

4. For example, John Aylmer describes Elizabeth as a "mixte ruler" and not "a mere monarche" (*An Harborovve for Faithfvll and Trevve Svbiectes, Agaynst the Late Blovvne Blaste, Concerning the Gouernment of VVemen.* [Strasbourg, 1559], 114r).

5. W. MacCaffrey, *Elizabeth I* (New York: Edward Arnold, 1993).

6. This scenario is especially feasible because of the known connection between Day and William Cecil. See E. Evenden and T. S. Freeman, "John Foxe, John Day and the Printing of the 'Book of Martyrs,'" in *Lives in Print: Biography and the Book Trade From the Middle Ages to the Twenty-First Century*, ed. R. Myers, M. Harris, and G. Mandelbrote (New Castle DE: Oak Knoll Press, 2002), 23–54.

7. Primarily through Cecil's instigation, Elizabeth's Council chose diplomatic negotiations over the dynastic solution of having Mary wed the English Duke of Norfolk.

8. I discuss this trend in my book project, currently titled "Learned Queen: The Imperial Image of Elizabeth I." I devote a chapter to examining how numerous writers in the 1580s explicitly yoked Elizabeth's learned persona to images of national defense.

9. A few studies that examine the political implications of Elizabeth's learning include L. Benkert, "Translation as Image-Making: Elizabeth I's Translation of Boethius's Consolation of Philosophy," *Early Modern Literary Studies* 6, no. 3 (2001) 2:1–20; J. M. Green, "Queen Elizabeth's Latin Reply to the Polish Ambassador," *Sixteenth Century Journal* 31 (2000): 987–1008; S. W. May and A. L. Prescott, "The French Verses of Elizabeth I," *English Literary Renaissance* 24, no. 1 (1994): 9–43; J. E. Phillips, "Elizabeth I as a Latin Poet: An Epigram on Paul Melissus," *Renaissance News* 16, no. 4 (1963): 289–98; K. Sharpe, *Remapping Early Modern England: The Culture*

of Seventeenth-century Politics (Cambridge: Cambridge University Press, 2000); and L. Shenk (see note 7). In addition, several studies are forthcoming. Aysha Pollnitz is working on a manuscript that examines the politics of educating Tudor and Stuart princes, and Charles Beem demonstrates how Edward VI's educated persona was a crucial element in the young king's royal identity in "The Minority of Edward VI: 31 January 1547–6 July 1553," in *The Royal Minorities of Medieval and Early Modern England* (New York: Palgrave, 2008).

10. I describe Mary's failure as "perceived" because I do not wish to perpetuate the image of Mary as passion-blind and incapable of rule. See R. M. Warnicke's nuanced biography, *Mary Queen of Scots* (New York: Routledge, 2006).

11. Matthew Parker, *The Holie Bible* [*The Bishops' Bible*] (London: Richard Iugge, 1568), R3r.

12. Elizabeth Evenden observes that this depiction of Elizabeth using the open prayer book on the prie-dieu contrasts sharply with the way Day typically portrays Tudor *kings* interacting with religious texts. Evenden notes that Day depicts them either distributing or receiving books—an act that underscores their much more supportive role in promoting published works (*Patents, Pictures and Patronage: John Day and the Tudor Book Trade* [Aldershot: Ashgate, 2008], 115–16. I am grateful to Evenden for sharing this work with me in manuscript).

13. See J. N. King, *Tudor Royal Iconography: Literature and Art in an Age of Religious Crisis* (Princeton: Princeton University Press, 1989), 56–57, regarding the theocratic image of the sword and book. It is also significant that the crucifix that Elizabeth kept in her own private chapel is not depicted on the altar in the frontispiece.

14. "Que selon mon corps & mon ame tu sois mon protecteur, me fortifiant contre toutes les tentations du diable, & de la chair" (Hh2v).

15. "[P]ura & sincera d'ogni affetto carnale" (Ll4v).

16. J. Anderson, *Collections Relating to the History of Mary Queen of Scotland*, vol. 4, pt. 2. (London: James Bettenham, 1728), 150.

17. Warnicke, *Mary Queen of Scots*, 176–77.

18. Καὶ μὴν ἐπειδη οὐδεμὶα φρόνησις ἰδία παρ' ἐμοῦ οὖσα τυγγάνει, ἐφ' ἣ πεποιθυῖα τοιαύτην ἀρχὴν ἱκανῶς ἰθύνουσα διατελοῖμι, τῆς συνέσεως καὶ σοφίας τοῦ ἁγίου πνεύματος τὸ στῆθος ἐμὸν ἔμπλυθε (Pp4v; 148). For the Greek, I found it helpful to consult the modern font in Elizabeth I, *Autograph Compositions and Foreign Language Originals*, ed. J. M. Mueller and L. S. Marcus (Chicago: University of Chicago Press, 2003). After the citation for the Greek in *Christian Prayers*, I provide the page number for the corresponding passage in this edition.

19. The link between Solomon's request and feminine weakness also arises in one of Elizabeth's English prayers early in the text (a prayer originally published in Latin in

Precationes). Elizabeth recalls that "the wisest king Salomon plainly confesseth him self vnable to gouerne his kingdome without thy [God's] helpe & assistance: how much lesse shall I thy handmaide, being by kinde a weake woman, haue sufficient abilitie to rule these thy kingdomes of England and Ireland" (*Christian Prayers*, p2v–3r).

20. "[P]ara que yo tu sierua tenga coraçon entendido que pueda discernir entre lo bueno y lo malo: y desta manera sea en este tu Reyno administrada iusticia, sea lo bueno aprouado y remunerado: y por el contrario lo malo condenado y castigado" (NN2r–v).

21. Although most of these prayers are also found in Bull's *Christian Prayers and Holy Meditations*, the prayers written in Elizabeth's voice do not appear in Bull's volume.

22. *Calendar of State Papers Relating to English Affairs, Prepared Principally in the Archives of Simancas*, vol. 2, *Elizabeth, 1568–1579*, ed. A. S. Hume (London: Her Majesty's Stationery Office, 1894), 51.

23. *Calendar of State Papers, Domestic Series, of the Reign of Edward VI, Mary, Elizabeth, 1547–1580*, ed. R. Lemon (London: Longmans, 1856), 1:324.

24. Anderson, *Collections Relating to the History*, 49.

25. Anderson, *Collections Relating to the History*, 19. Elizabeth's commissioners also reject the language of judging, indicating that they "do not meane to proceade judicially, as Judges, or in judiciall Place; but as Commissioners" (S. Haynes, ed., *A Collection of State Papers Relating to Affairs from the Years 1542–1570 left by William Cecil Lord Burghley* [London: William Bowyer, 1740], 491).

26. Anderson, *Collections Relating to the History*, 183.

27. "[T]u donneras à ta seruante et à tes seruiteurs vn coeur entendu pour iuger ton peuple, & pour discerner le bien d'entre le mal, à fin que nous ne soyons point in-utiles, ou mesme pernicieux en vne vocation si sainte. Donne nous aussi des Conseillers prudens sages & vertueux, chassant loing de nous, tous ambitieux, malins, cauteleux, & hypocrites. Donne des Iuges, hommes veritables haissans auarice, & fuyans l'acception des personnes, à fin que mon peuple soit gouuerné en toute equité & droiture, les bons sustenus en leur Iustice & innocence, les iniques punis & chastiez" (Ii2v–3r).

28. I provide a detailed analysis of this 1563 prayer book in my current book project, "Learned Queen: The Imperial Image of Elizabeth I."

29. "[D]enique quod vni tibi acceptum esse nouerim, id sine vllo personarum aut rerum mundanarum respectu suscipere, exequi, perficere velim, audeam, atque possim" (E7v–8r); Elizabeth I, *Collected Works*, 143.

30. "Nous ton humble seruante & tes seruiteurs estans icy assemblez en ta presence, pour traiter & aduiser aux affaires qui concernent la vocation sainte à laquelle tu nous as appellez par ta grace" (Kk4r).

31. A few sentences later, "Nous puissions auec prudence & sagesse traiter les choses

qui maintenant seront proposées" (κκ4v), and then, "D'auantage que tu tienne tellement la main à toute nos deliberations" (ʟʟ1r).

32. *Calendar of State Papers Relating to English Affairs, Prepared Principally in the Archives of Simancas*, 2:138.

33. *Calendar of State Papers Relating to English Affairs, Prepared Principally in the Archives of Simancas*, 2:155.

34. Quoted in S. Alford, *The Early Elizabethan Polity: William Cecil and the British Succession Crisis* (Cambridge: Cambridge University Press, 1998), 194.

35. Alford, *Early Elizabethan Polity*, 190.

36. "[S]eas glorificado constituyendo me por cabeça y gouernadora deste tu opulentissimo Reyno en estos tan infelicissimos tiempos, en que tu yglesia vnica esposa tuya es en tan gran manera oprimida de la tyrania de Satanas y de sus ministros" (ɴɴ2r).

37. *Calendar of State Papers Relating to English Affairs, Prepared Principally in the Archives of Simancas*, 2:76.

38. Haynes, *Collection of State Papers*, 516.

39. "[A]b intestines & domesticis tumultibus, quibus bona iam orbis Christiani pars quatitur, immunes nos prolege" (ᴘᴘ1r).

40. "[E]stans les autres Royaumes en horribles confusions, & que tu m'as enuoyé les entrailles de ton filz Iesus Christ, pour leur donner refuge en leurs oppressions; fay moy la grace d'estre vraye nourrissiere & tutrice des tiens selon la parolle de ton Prophete Isaye, pour auoir vne vraye compassion tant de ceux qui sont icy, que de tous autres" (κκ1v). In Elizabeth's document to her commissioners about the proceedings with Mary, she also couples this blessing with Protestant enlightenment, claiming England's responsibility to be of international aid because of "the Dispensation of his Gospell in our Countries, and next there to indevour our self by all good Means to use this Opportunity of our peaceable Reigne, to the reliefe and ayde of our Neighbours, being destitute of Peace and afflicted with evill Warrs" (Anderson, *Collections Relating to the History*, 4).

41. *Calendar of State Papers Relating to English Affairs, Prepared Principally in the Archives of Simancas*, 2:53–54.

42. *Calendar of State Papers Relating to English Affairs, Prepared Principally in the Archives of Simancas*, 2:140.

43. "[S]piantando ogni maluagio seme d'empietà, spargere, seminare, & radicare il tuo santo Euangelio in tutti i cuori, aggrandendo per tutto questo regno tuo terreno, quel celeste di Giesu Cristo" (ᴍᴍ1r–v).

44. "Tenian me vn tal odio, porque yo ponia en ti solo toda mi esperança, porque yo no me auergonçaua del Euangelio de tu amantissimo Hijo" (ᴍᴍ4r).

45. Evenden, *Patents, Pictures and Patronage*, 105–8.

46. θρησκείαν ἀσπίζειν θελοθρησκείαν, δεισιδαιμονίαν καθ' ἐθελοργίαν ἀφανίζειν, λατρείαν

ἐγκεντρίζειν, εἰδωλολατρείαν κατασκόπτειν προσέτι τοὺς ἐχθροὺς τῆς θεοσεβείας ἀπολύειν, καὶ τοὺς ἐμὲ μισοῦντας, καὶ ἀντιχρίστους, καὶ παπιφίλους, καὶ ἄθεους, καὶ πάντας, τοὺς σου καὶ ἔμου παρακοόυντας (Qq1v; 149).

47. καὶ ψυχὴν ἀυτῆς φώτιζε τῇ ἀυγῇ τῆς ἀπειράτου σοφίας σῆς (Pp3r; 147). For A. N. McLaren's focused discussion of Elizabeth and providentialism, see her essay "Prophecy and Providentialism in the Reign of Elizabeth I," in *Prophecy: The Power of Inspired Language in History 1300–2000*, ed. B. Taithe and T. Thornton (Thrupp, Stroud, Gloucestershire: Sutton, 1997), 31–50.

48. μιμνήσκουσα ἀιεὶ ὀυκ ἀυτῇ τὴν ἀρχὴν ἀυτοκράτειραν εἶναι, ἀλλὰ ὡς διαδόχῳ ἤ μᾶλλον διακόνῳ τὴν ἐπιμέλειαν ὅλης πολητείας παρά σου παντοκράτορος δοθεῖσαν, ἐφ' ᾧτε καὶ σε σέβειν εἰλήκρινῶς, καὶ τῶν ἀγαθῶν ὑπερασπίζειν, κακούς τε καὶ ἀνόμους τιμορεῖν (Pp3r; 147).

49. For the negative tradition of Solomon, see W. Tate, "Solomon, Gender, and Empire in Marlowe's Doctor Faustus," *SEL: Studies in English Literature, 1500–1900* 37, no. 2 (1997): 257–76.

50. F. A. Yates, *Astraea: The Imperial Theme in the Sixteenth Century* (London: Routledge & K. Paul, 1975).

51. P. Franssen, "Gloriana's Allies: The Virgin Queen and the Low Countries," in *Queen Elizabeth I: Past and Present*, ed. C. Jansohn (Münster, Germany: LIT, 2004), 193.

52. M. Kyffin, *The Blessednes of Brytaine* (London, 1587), A3v.

7

The Virgin and the Widow

The Political Finesse of Elizabeth I and Catherine de' Medici

ELAINE KRUSE

In his 1558 tract *The First Blast of the Trumpet against the Monstrous Regiment of Women*, the Scottish reformer John Knox raged against women rulers, decrying their authority over men. His targets were Catholics: Mary Tudor of England; Mary Stuart, Queen of Scots; and her mother, Mary of Guise, regent in Scotland. But his timing was off. Within a few months, Lady Fortune had brought two other women to the fore: Elizabeth Tudor, the new Protestant queen of England, and Catherine de' Medici, widowed in July 1559 and now queen mother of France. For the next thirty years these two politically adept, powerful women would guide their kingdoms' destinies. One a virgin, the other a widow, they would correspond with each other, exchange diplomats, and play at the marriage game while skirting the pitfalls of religious rancor and territorial aggrandizement.[1]

Elizabeth was born in 1533, the same year Catherine de' Medici married Henri II of France when both were fourteen. Elizabeth came to the throne of England in November 1558 upon the death of her half sister, Mary Tudor. Catherine became queen of France in 1547 but would have little influence until her husband died from a splintered lance in his eye during a tournament in 1559. Her sons would succeed to the throne: Francis II (1559–60); Charles IX (1560–74); and Henri III (1574–89). Catherine was shunted aside during Francis II's rule by his wife's uncles, the Guises, but once Charles came to the throne, at age ten, she managed to have herself named queen regent to guide her young son through the early years of his reign. This domination of her sons, whether official or unofficial, would continue until her death in 1589. Thus, the virgin and the widow would face each other across the channel, managing to maintain peaceful relations through diplomacy though they would never meet.

Both Catherine and Elizabeth grew up motherless. Catherine's mother died in childbirth, her father several weeks later. Elizabeth's mother was executed before she was three by a father who saw her rarely before his death when she was thirteen. Catherine had no siblings; Elizabeth had a half brother, Edward VI, four years younger than she, who came to the throne when he was nine and was dead by fifteen; and a half sister Mary, twenty years her senior, who reigned from the age of thirty-seven to her death at forty-two. In the fractious politics of religion and power, Elizabeth was close to neither and probably realized from her early teens onward that her own rule would be dependent on the deaths of her siblings.[2] And so, Elizabeth as a ruler was as alone as Catherine, the king's widow. Francis Bacon wrote: "Those that continue unmarried have their glory entire and proper to themselves. In her case was more especially so; inasmuch as she had no helps to lean upon in government, except such as she had herself provided; no own brother, no uncle, no kinsman of the royal family, to share her cares and support her authority."[3] Having chosen not to marry, Elizabeth, the last of her family, ruled alone, without family support but also without family interference.

Catherine was even more isolated as an Italian in the French court. She cleverly courted the goodwill of her father-in-law, Francis I, who helped her to maintain her status through the ten years of barrenness of her early marriage.[4] She then gave birth to ten children, seven of whom lived to adulthood. Her sons became the focus of her attention and the basis of her power after her husband's untimely death. Catherine had the additional burden of her husband publicly maintaining his beloved mistress, Diane de Poitiers. Once Catherine was a widow, she took center stage and never relinquished it, even when her sons were ruling in their own stead.[5]

The courtesy the two queens showed one another betrayed their instinctive political sense. Lena Orlin points out that Elizabeth created a sibling trope for her relationships with foreign rulers.[6] Certainly, that was true for both Catherine and Elizabeth in their correspondence. At the time of Henri II's untimely death, Elizabeth wrote her condolences. Catherine replied to "The Most High and Excellent Princess, our true friend, good sister and cousin," offering thanks for her "wise and kind words of consolation."[7] Catherine continued to address Elizabeth in this fashion, employing the rhetorical forms laid out in the *ars dictaminis*. For example, in a letter in February 1573 thanking Elizabeth for serving as godmother for the infant daughter of Charles IX, she addressed her as "very high, very excellent and very powerful princess, our very dear and very good sister." But Catherine took on the role of surrogate mother during the marriage negotiations between Elizabeth and her youngest son, the Duke d'Alençon, in 1578: "Now my good daughter—I pray you pardon me herein if in place of sister I say what I have so desired."[8] And on November 9, 1578, Catherine repeated her desire "to be a mother to you." In 1584 when Alençon died, Elizabeth wrote of "the wound that my heart suffered," one greater than Catherine's "which I assure myself cannot exceed mine." She reiterated the mother-daughter relationship: "you will find me the faithfullest daughter and sister that ever Princes had," assuring that she was "as if I were your natural daughter."[9] Despite this assurance on Elizabeth's part, the widow and the virgin had limited contact once the marriage game had ended. Elizabeth may have used the term *mother* for Catherine, but given the mother's superiority in the mother-daughter relationship, it is unlikely that she would have relished this advantage. Elizabeth herself had attempted the mother role with Mary Stuart with no notable success, and so reverted to the "stepmother" role. In 1569 Elizabeth told La Mothe-Fénelon, the French ambassador, "that she had taken great pains to be more than a good mother to the Queen of Scots," but, in language approaching that of fairy tales, admits that "she who uses and plots against her mother, deserves to have nothing other than a wicked stepmother."[10]

The positing of a marriage alliance served both women well in maintaining peaceful relations between their two countries, despite numerous potential conflicts. Both queens played the game for some seventeen years, each with her own agenda. Catherine worked diligently to match her children with other royal houses: Francis II wed Mary Stuart; Elisabeth married Philip II of Spain; Claude married Charles, Duke of Lorraine; Charles IX married Elizabeth of Austria; and Marguerite married Henri of Navarre, later Henri IV. Meanwhile Elizabeth responded to the pressures from her people to pursue matrimony, first with the Archduke Charles of Austria and then with Catherine's sons. As early as 1564 Catherine expressed interest in a marriage between thirty-one-year-old Elizabeth and her fifteen-year-old son Charles IX. Elizabeth thought the boy too young, and when the talks fell through, no one was offended. In 1570 the possibility of a match with Henri of Anjou, Catherine's favorite son, was broached. The arguments against the match on the one hand were Henri's age, religion, and nationality, and the fact that he was heir to the French throne after his brother Charles, who was known to be frail. On the other hand, security issues could not be discounted. Since Mary Stuart, sister-in-law to the French kings, had fled to England after her deposition from the Scottish throne in May 1568, the Norfolk plan to marry her and the Ridolfi plot had revealed that the conspiracies based on Mary's claim to the English throne could not be ignored. Elizabeth's marriage to a Valois prince would undercut the machinations of Mary's Guise uncles in France.[11] Discussions continued secretly for a time, with Catherine insisting that her son be allowed free exercise of his religion. Even though there seemed to be public support for the match, it fell through in 1572 when Henri insisted on holding public masses. In point of fact, Elizabeth never really seemed intent on marrying Anjou.

Now Alençon's name came forward. Elizabeth's ambassador Thomas Smith wrote to William Cecil, Lord Burghley: "If marriage do like, Alençon is as rich in lands and moveables as Anjou . . . Alençon is not so tall or fair as his brother, but . . . he is not so obstinate, papeistical, and restive like a mule as his brother is. As for getting of children . . . they seem to assure him that he is more apt than the other."[12] As she had done in the past, Elizabeth insisted that she see the prince in person before consenting to the marriage. Catherine wrote to her ambassador, Monsieur de La Mothe-Fénelon, "Thanks be to God, he has no deformities; on the contrary, he has a handsome build."[13] Catherine made no reference to the rumored scars of smallpox. Later in the same letter Catherine expressed the true meaning of these negotiations: "[The Queen] is so prudent, so wise [that she would not marry based on] the beauty of a face, but for the good of her concerns . . . [The marriage would] unify and restore a perfect friendship."[14] And in fact, both women used these marriage negotiations for that very purpose: to maintain good relations and to avoid war.

Elizabeth and Catherine both faced enormous domestic and foreign difficulties. Elizabeth inherited a foreign policy based on failed English ventures on the continent, including a £300,000 debt and war weariness. Both she and Catherine had to deal with kingdoms divided over religion. When Francis II ruled, his wife Mary Stuart and her Guise uncles maintained the "Auld Alliance" of Scotland and France, inherently dangerous to England. But when Francis died, Catherine sent Mary back to Scotland within eight months. Elizabeth feared Mary might make a claim for the English throne. Neither Elizabeth nor Catherine trusted the Guise ambitions. Then, when Mary Stuart was deposed and fled to England in 1568, Elizabeth recognized her as a potential rallying point for the Catholics and detained her. As Norfolk's plan to marry Mary Stuart and the Ridolfi plot unfolded, Elizabeth desperately needed to hold off any foreign intervention by Catholic powers. The marriage negotiations with Henri of Anjou, though unsuccessful, provided a talking point leading to an Anglo-French alliance. The Treaty of Blois in April 1572 marked the apogee of their policy, providing for mutual defense, giving Elizabeth a free hand to support James VI of Scotland against his mother's followers, and leaving Mary Stuart out in the cold.[15] Negotiations resumed for a match with Alençon; peace seemed assured at home and abroad.

Only four months later the *entente cordiale* was for a time devastated by the news of the Saint Bartholomew's Day massacre of August 24, 1572. Over 3,000 Huguenots were murdered while at the marriage festivities of Catherine's daughter Marguerite to Henri of Navarre, the Protestant next in line to the throne after Catherine's sons. Then the killings spread outside Paris, leading to thousands more deaths. Elizabeth's ambassador, Francis Walsingham, witnessed the carnage, as did Philip Sidney, Walsingham's future son-in-law, who was only seventeen at the time. They would neither forget nor forgive the slaughter of fellow Protestants and detested Catholics from then on. In a letter La Mothe-Fénelon described Elizabeth's reaction. She approached him, looking sad and severe, then took him over to a window and asked if it were true. He told her it was an accident; that the king and regent had befriended the admiral and the Protestants, but that their ingratitude led them to plot against their natural prince.[16] Elizabeth was horrified. As the killings continued, Elizabeth declared that the massacres could not be justified and protested that there should have been trials before any executions. In her letter of diplomatic instructions to Walsingham, she ranted: "but when more was added unto it, that women, children, maids, young infants and sucking babes, were at the same time murdered and cast into the river; and that liberty of execution was given to the vilest and basest . . . this increased our grief and sorrow in our good Brother's behalf that he should suffer himself to be led by such inhuman Councillors."[17] Thus, when a proposed meeting of the two queens and Alençon was agreed on by the king, Charles IX, Elizabeth turned it down.[18] Nevertheless, Elizabeth resisted the suggestions of her advisers to send men to assist the beleaguered Protestants at La Rochelle, choosing rather to maintain neutrality.

The personal again became political. Charles IX's wife, Elizabeth of Austria, gave birth to a daughter, Isabella, on October 27, 1572. Catherine immediately asked Elizabeth to be the godmother, and she accepted "gladly" ("*de bonne coeur*").[19] Elizabeth was godmother to over fifty infants during her lifetime, but they were primarily Protestants. Given her anger over the murder of her religious compatriots and the religious difference between Elizabeth and Catherine's family, Elizabeth's willingness to send a representative to the baptism is clear evidence of a diplomatic gesture overriding personal distaste. Catherine gushed gratitude to Elizabeth in a letter of February 1573, saying the baptism "will confirm and assure all the more the good favor and mutual understanding between the two crowns of France and England."[20] The goodwill exhibited by Elizabeth in serving as godmother to the French royal infant made possible a new rapprochement after the ugliness of the massacre.

Already on September 11 Catherine had suggested to La Mothe-Fénelon that he revive the idea of the marriage with Alençon. Shortly after the baptism, she reiterated that he push for negotiations.[21] In the same letters Catherine indicated her concern about "Scottish problems" and La Rochelle, which was under siege. This pattern would continue as the negotiations resumed. Walsingham reported to Cecil on April 1 that he had made clear the queen's conditions: no marriage without seeing him first and that the would-be husband must profess the same religion. Catherine replied that (1) she and the king could not consent to the duke going to England without an assurance the marriage would take place; (2) Alençon could not change his religion *"tout d'un coup"* and that it was not honorable that she not allow him to exercise his religion. He replied that Queen Elizabeth forbade any other religion in her kingdom, and Catherine asked only that Alençon be allowed a secret observance of his religion. Then Walsingham, no friend of Catherine, told her that if she did not protect the oppressed (meaning La Rochelle), she would be the cause of the ruin of her kingdom. Catherine hotly replied that this was not true and that the French could intervene on the part of Mary, Queen of Scots.[22] Shortly after, Elizabeth granted Walsingham's request to return to England. Recognizing the influence Walsingham would have in shaping perceptions of France in England, Catherine tried to mend fences by sending his wife and daughter beautiful silk cloth "as gratitude for the hope of a marriage."[23]

When Charles IX died in 1574 and was succeeded by his fanatical brother Henri III, Elizabeth feared that the Anglo-French entente would be broken. But Henri took a long time returning from Poland, where he had been elected king, and Catherine ruled in his stead. When he did finally take his new crown, Henri proved to be far more tractable than expected.

Serious marriage negotiations between Elizabeth and Alençon revived in 1578 when Elizabeth was faced with another crisis. Rebels in the Netherlands had revolted against Spanish hegemony. On the one hand, if Elizabeth assisted the rebels, she might not succeed and meanwhile she would alienate the Spanish. On the other hand, Spanish control of the Netherlands would threaten English sovereignty. Alençon had responded to the cries for help from the Catholic deputies; if his intervention were successful, the French might gain influence or territory. Marriage to Alençon would protect England from French aggression.

Catherine, unwilling to see her son adventuring in Flanders, began a personal correspondence with Elizabeth once again, utilizing every term of endearment in her vocabulary: "your good sister and cousin, and the most affectionate you have ever had."[24] In a letter of November 9, 1578, she informed Elizabeth she was sending Jean de Simier to England, hoping "before I die of seeing one of the children of the king my lord who was so fond of you."[25] Elizabeth was won over by Simier, whom she affectionately called her "ape." William Camden described Simier as "a choice courtier, a man thoroughly versed in love fancies, pleasant conceits, and court dalliance."[26] Simier managed to have what Susan Doran has described as "regular, lengthy and intimate interviews" with Elizabeth for two months, culminating in Elizabeth giving him a miniature portrait as a love token for the duke.[27] Robert Dudley was so alarmed that he suggested that Simier had used magic to cause Elizabeth to fall in love with Alençon.[28] Alençon did come to England on August 17, 1579, for a short, secret visit. Elizabeth seemed quite taken with him and nicknamed him her "frog." However, she had underestimated the hostility of the English people to such a match.

Elizabeth found herself subjected to letters, tracts, and speeches denouncing the plan. The most offensive attack came in the form of a pamphlet by John Stubbs, *The Discoverie of a gaping gulf whereinto England is like to be swallowed by another French marriage, if the Lord forbid not the banes, by letting her Majesty see the sin and punishment thereof.*[29] Stubbs viciously attacked the French royal family:

> Here is, therefore, an imp of the crown of France to marry with
> the crowned nymph of England. . . . France is a house of cruelty,
> especially against Christians a principal prop of the tottering house
> of Anti-Christ. . . . The long and cruel persecutions in France,
> the exquisite torments, and infinite numbers there put to death
> do witness how worthy that throne is to be reckoned for one
> horn of that persecuting beast. . . . This man is a son of Henry
> the Second, whose family, ever since he married with Catherine
> of Italy, is fatal, as it were, to resist the Gospel.[30]

But what truly angered Elizabeth was his contention that she would be dominated by her husband, thus leading to a return to Catholicism and French control of England. He also suggested that the French hoped that she would die in childbirth, since she was so old, and then they could rule England. Stubbs and his associates were arrested and tried, and Stubbs and his printer, Page, were sentenced to have their right hands cut off. William Camden, who was present, reported that the crowd watching this spectacle were silent, out of horror or pity or "else out of hatred of the marriage, which most men presaged would be the overthrow of religion."[31] Elizabeth issued a proclamation banning the book, and the clergy were ordered to speak against it.

Rather than ending the controversy, such actions only fanned the flames. Susan Doran contends that Stubbs's objections were identical to those in Elizabeth's Council: religion, nationality, Elizabeth's age and thus vulnerability, and the dangers of marrying "the brother of childless France."[32] Philip Sidney wrote against the marriage, but this was only circulated in manuscript. Nevertheless, Elizabeth was very angry, and Sidney was not welcome at court at that time. Although Stubbs's words were clearly Puritan and insulting to Elizabeth as a female ruler, his position had struck home. Elizabeth dissolved in tears when she told her Council that she really wanted to marry Alençon and everyone except Cecil and Sussex opposed it. Despite Elizabeth's decision to go ahead with the marriage plans, she left an escape clause that she must first win her people over.

By this time Catherine and Henri had cooled to the idea of Alençon marrying a woman likely to be childless (she was forty-eight when he returned to England in 1581). In October 1581 Alençon came to England, this time to ask Elizabeth for financial assistance for his war in the Low Countries. On November 22 Elizabeth kissed Alençon on the mouth and gave him a ring as a pledge, saying "the Duke of Alençon shall be my husband." Although he seems to have taken her seriously, Elizabeth, according to the sources, came to hate "the idea of marriage every day more."[33] Finally, in order to get him to leave, she promised to lend him £60,000. His adventure did not go well, and he returned to France. He died on June 10, 1584.

Elizabeth had the last, and cruelest, lines in this marriage charade. She wrote to Catherine:

> Madam,
>
> If the extremity of my misfortune had not equaled my grief for his sake, and had not rendered me unequal to touch with a pen the wound that my heart suffered, it would not be possible that I

had so greatly forgotten to visit you with the fellowship of regret that I afford you, which I assure myself cannot exceed mine; for although you were his mother, yet there remains to you several other children. But for myself, I find no consolation if it be not death, which I hope will make us soon to meet. Madam, if you could see the image of my heart you would there see the picture of a body without a soul.[34]

This letter reinforces that Catherine and Elizabeth both used the marriage game as a form of diplomacy. Such remarks to a mother who had by this time lost three sons and four daughters suggest a "body without a soul." Elizabeth reiterated the mother-daughter relationship she hoped to maintain, indicating between the lines what they had both lost: their tool to maintain peace.

Years after both women were dead, Francis Bacon claimed that when Elizabeth's secretary was writing instructions to the ambassador to Catherine, he planned to insert the following clause: "That they two were the only pair of female princes, from whom, for experience and arts of government, there was no less expected than from the greatest kings." He claimed that Elizabeth "utterly disliked the comparison" and commanded that it be expunged, saying "that she practiced other principles and arts of government than the queen-mother did."[35] Elizabeth thus distinguished herself from Catherine, whose reputation as the "wicked Italian Queen" had been nurtured by propaganda ever since the Saint Bartholomew's Day massacre, a view shared by her counselors Philip Sidney and Francis Walsingham. It suggests that despite the verbiage of politically correct correspondence, Elizabeth saw herself as an upright monarch and Catherine as a duplicitous Machiavellian.[36]

Nevertheless, these two women were supreme diplomats and the finest of princes. Together they managed to maintain thirty years of peace between England and France, from 1559 to 1589, when

Catherine died. Elizabeth, the virgin, disdained the old means of dynasticism, yet she and Catherine, the widow, pretended all those years that they were pursuing an interdynastic marriage. The truth was that Elizabeth as the virgin queen could play her role of the intended and Catherine as the ambitious widow could play the role of the mother seeking a dynasty. Together they were able to stave off ruinous war, saving their energies for ruling as female princes in an age dominated by men.

Notes

1. On Elizabeth, see C. Levin, *"The Heart and Stomach of a King": Elizabeth I and the Politics of Sex and Power* (Philadelphia: University of Pennsylvania Press, 1994). Numerous biographies have been written of both queens, but much of the earlier writing on Catherine de' Medici repeated the Black Legend. For a more balanced biography of Catherine, see R. J. Knecht, *Catherine de' Medici* (London: Longman, 1998). On the marriage negotiations, see S. Doran, *Monarchy and Matrimony: The Courtships of Elizabeth I* (London: Routledge, 1998).

2. C. Levin, "Sister-Subject/Sister Queen: Elizabeth I among her Siblings," in *Sibling Relations and Gender in the Early Modern World: Sisters, Brothers, and Others*, ed. N. J. Miller and N. Yavneh (London: Ashgate, 2006), 77–88.

3. Sir Francis Bacon, *Biography in Happy Memory of Elizabeth Queen of England; or, A Collection of the Felicities of Queen Elizabeth*, in *Works of Francis Bacon, Lord Chancellor of England*, ed. B. Montague, vol. 1 (Philadelphia: M. Murphy, 1876), 379.

4. K. Crawford, *Perilous Performances: Gender and Regency in Early Modern France* (Cambridge: Harvard University Press, 2004), 27–29.

5. S. Doran, "Elizabeth I and Catherine de Medici," unpublished paper, by courtesy of the author, 2006.

6. L. C. Orlin, "The Fictional Families of Elizabeth I," in *Political Rhetoric, Power and Renaissance Women*, ed. C. Levin and P. A. Sullivan (Albany: SUNY Press, 1995), 85–110.

7. *Lettres de Catherine de' Medicis*, ed. Hectare de la Ferriere (Paris: Imprimerie National, 1880), 1:125, September 11, 1559. Translations of the letters are by Susan Doran.

8. *Calendar of State Papers, Foreign Series, of the Reign of Elizabeth*, ed. Joseph Stevenson et al. (London: Longman, Green, Reader, and Dyer, 1865–1950), 13:4–5, June 8, 1578.

9. *Lettres de Catherine de' Medicis*, 6:113, November 9, 1578; Elizabeth I, *Collected Works*, ed. L. S. Marcus, J. Mueller, and M. B. Rose (Chicago: University of Chicago Press, 2000), 260–61.

10 *Correspondance diplomatique de Bertrand de Salignac de la Mothe-Fénelon*, vol. 2 in *Récueil des Dépeches, Rapports, Instructions et Mémoires des Ambassadeurs de France* (Paris & London: 1840), 169.

11. Doran, *Monarchy and Matrimony*, 101–3.

12. *Calendar of State Papers, Foreign Series, of the Reign of Elizabeth*, 10:14.

13. *Lettres de Catherine de' Medicis*, 4:190, March 30, 1573.

14. *Lettres de Catherine de' Medicis*, 4:191–92, March 30, 1573.

15. S. Doran, *Elizabeth I and Foreign Policy: 1558–1603* (London: Routledge, 2000), 20, 31.

16. *Correspondance diplomatique de Bertrand de Salignac de la Mothe-Fénelon*, vol. 5 (1572–1573):122–23.

17. Elizabeth I, *Letters of Queen Elizabeth*, ed. G. B. Harrison (New York: Funk & Wagnalls, 1968), December 1572, 116.

18. Elizabeth I, *Letters of Queen Elizabeth*, September 29, 1572, 143.

19. Elizabeth I, *Letters of Queen Elizabeth*, November 3, 1572, 195.

20. *Lettres de Catherine de' Medicis*, 4:165, February 9, 1573.

21. *Lettres de Catherine de' Medicis*, 4:168, 176, February 16 and March 1, 1573.

22. *Lettres de Catherine de' Medicis*, 4:193, March 30, 1573.

23. *Lettres de Catherine de' Medicis*, 4:211, April 29, 1573.

24. *Lettres de Catherine de' Medicis*, 6:35–36, August or September 1578.

25. *Calendar of State Papers, Foreign Series, of the Reign of Elizabeth*, November 9, 1578, 273.

26. William Camden, *The History of the Most Renowned and Victorious Princess Elizabeth, late Queen of England*, 4th ed. (London: M. Flesher, 1688), 227.

27. Doran, *Monarchy and Matrimony*, 154–55.

28. Noted in Levin, *Heart and Stomach of a King*, 61.

29. John Stubbs, *The Discoverie of a gaping gulf whereinto England is like to be swallowed by another French marriage, if the Lord forbid not the banes, by letting her Majesty see the sin and punishment thereof* (London: Printed for H. Singleton for W. Page, 1579).

30. Stubbs, *Discoverie of a gaping gulf*, 21–22.

31. Camden, *History of the Most Renowned and Victorious Princess*, 270.

32. Doran, *Monarchy and Matrimony*, 164.

33. *Calendar of State Papers Relating to English Affairs Preserved in, Originally*

Belonging to, the Archives of Simancas, ed. M. A. S. Hume (London: Her Majesty's Stationery Office, 1892–99), 3:226, 243, 348; Camden, *History of the Most Renowned and Victorious Princess*, 268.

34. Elizabeth I, *Letters of Queen Elizabeth*, July 1584, 163.

35. Bacon, *Biography in Happy Memory of Elizabeth Queen of England*, 400–401.

36. On the Black Legend, see N. M. Sutherland, *Catherine de Medici and the Ancien Regime* (London: Historical Association, 1966); R. Kingdon, *Myths about the St. Bartholomew's Day Massacres, 1572–1576* (Cambridge MA: Harvard University Press, 1988); E. Kruse, "The Blood-Stained Hands of Catherine de Médicis," in *Political Rhetoric, Power, and Renaissance Women*, ed. C. Levin and P. A. Sullivan (Albany: SUNY Press, 1995), 139–55.

8

Crafting Queens

Early Modern Readings of Esther

MICHELE OSHEROW

The Old Testament's Queen Esther, heroine of the biblical book that bears her name, was an extremely popular figure in early modern England. Her story appears on canvases, papers, and silks. Sixteenth- and seventeenth-century Protestant ministers and those attending to female behavior considered Esther the embodiment of feminine virtue and praised her beauty and obedience. In 1582 Thomas Bentley remarked that Esther, "Though . . . a royal queene, yet was obedient unto . . . her poore kinsman . . . and did in everything after his counsel and advise."[1] Similarly, Thomas Heywood claimed that none is "better, more obedient than [Esther]."[2] While the duty Esther demonstrates is palpable, she also assumes an unmistakable authority in her narrative—a narrative that ends with the deaths of thousands at the hands of the Jews. There are moments when Esther would seem to uphold the silence and obedience prescribed for early modern women, but it becomes clear that the display of these virtues conceals Esther's larger, more severe purposes. The early modern practice of cloaking Esther in obedience is a reaction, I believe, to the threat contained within her story; interpretations, retellings, and reimaginings of Esther reveal a grappling with early modern concepts of female authority and the performance of femininity. Esther's virtue depends upon artifice. Her clever deceptions benefit her people and enable her to undermine the male authority she is engaged to serve.

The book of Esther begins with an apparent loss of feminine authority when Queen Vashti is banished from Persia. In the earliest verses it is feminine performance—or the refusal of performance—that propels the story: Vashti disobeys the drunken King Ahasuerus's command to appear before him and his advisors.[3] Vashti's modesty seems appropriate for a queen and is commended in some early modern readings, but her refusal shakes the foundations of Persian patriarchy.[4] The queen is exiled in order that—and the Bible could not be more clear—"euerie man shulde beare rule in his owne house."[5]

Esther is introduced in her narrative as a solution to the problem of a disobedient wife. Her arrival on the scene fulfills the king's sexual and social needs, but her presence at court requires a series of feminine displays that facilitate deception. Esther will appear in a royal beauty pageant, the preparations for which last nearly one year. She is costumed, doused with scent and oils, and surrenders herself entirely to the hands of the court eunuch.[6] Early modern readers delighted in Esther's "makeover" and used it to justify their own cosmetic indulgences.[7] "We may read that queen *Esther* made use of sweet perfumes . . . and . . . whatsoever was then in fashion," writes Hannah Woolley, "and this was in her so far from a sin, that it had been almost a sin in her not to have done it."[8] The narrative makes clear Esther's willingness to follow instruction. This may be considered a show of obedience, but more important, it facilitates disguise. She drops her Hebrew name and follows her cousin Mordecai's advice to conceal her Jewish identity.[9]

Esther's disguise will prove her greatest asset in overcoming her enemy, and it is a cunning practice for which the Bible prepares us. Esther and her cousin are identified immediately in the narrative as descendants of the Tribe of Benjamin.[10] Of all Israel's tribes, the Benjaminites have a most suspicious history. In the Hebrew Bible they are associated with lechery and trickery—a biblical reading that extends back to the early modern period. John Mayer delicately observes that Benjaminites used "their left hands as their right"[11]; and he reminds his audience of the biblical injunction "Curseth bee hee that giveth his daughter to *Benjamin* to wife."[12] In the story of Esther, the heroine's link to the Tribe of Benjamin signals an approaching deceit. It also helps to explain the apparently unholy purpose that prompts Esther's arrival at the palace. Before Esther's royal selection, the king amuses himself by deflowering virgins, and the narrative details the routine: "In the evening [the virgin] went, and on the morrow shee returned into the second house . . . which kept the concubines: shee came into the king no more, except . . . that she were called by name."[13] Esther's behavior was troubling to members of the early Protestant Church. Mayer asks, "Was *Ester* so godly a woman brought in to the king as an whore? . . . how happened it, that shee consented?"[14] Renaissance theologians differ in their justifications, though some conclude that Esther was taken by force.[15] There is no textual evidence for this reading, but it helped to maintain Esther's integrity and make her a more acceptable agent of God.

Without question, early modern readers regarded Esther's tale as a demonstration of divine love and justice.[16] And yet, the actual book of Esther contains no mention of either God or prayer. Instead, early modern readers and writers supplied the devotions the Bible fails to provide, assigning to Esther a feminine virtue that is unsupported by her narrative. Aemilia Lanyer's *Salve Deus* poem (1611) demonstrates the heroine's piety:

> . . . vertuous Hester fasted three days space,
> And spent her time in prayers all that while,
> That by Gods powre shee might obtain such grace,
> That shee and hers might not become a spoyle.[17]

Lanyer refers to the period preceding Esther's approach to the king's inner court where she worked to save the Jews from Haman's murderous plot. Esther's uninvited approach is her most prominent episode, and the narrative makes clear her assumed risk: "whosoeever, man or woman, that commeth to the king into the inner court, which is not called, there is a law . . . that he shal dye, except him to whome the king holdeth out the golden rod."[18] Ahasuerus receives his wife warmly, a gesture early modern commentators attribute to "God being hereby inclined to pitty his people."[19] Bentley has Esther recognize a divine hand in her achievement and undermines her agency. He has her acknowledge, "If I perish . . . I perish" (as she says in the Bible), but he also assigns her the lines, "yet will I referre the success to God, seeing it is for the glorye of *his* name, and the deliveraunce of *his* Churche."[20]

There are, however, those early modern readings of Esther's advance that rely less on God's grace and more on Esther's artfulness. In Artemisia Gentilschi's well-known canvas *Esther before Ahasuerus* (1622–23), Esther is fast approaching the king's throne, but there is no extended scepter. Instead, Esther is shown fainting backward into the arms of her waiting women—an action that appears to prompt the king forward. The painting indicates that Ahasuerus will advance toward her. Esther's bold entrance into court is obscured by her display of feminine frailty. This is a clever tactic and arguably a ruse. As the artist Richard McBee observes, "[Esther's] 'artful' collapse is well calculated. . . . She is in fact very much in control of the situation. Her head is tilted back at an angle, her eyes closed and eyebrows arched in theatrical abandon. Until we notice that only one knee has given way. . . . She . . . has turned this into a way of controlling [the king], manipulating him and actually causing him to rise in her presence."[21]

No less artfully, Bentley also attends to Esther's cunning and curiously uses an act of devotion to underscore her deception. His text contains a scripted prayer for the queen: "O Lord, thou knowest that I hate the glorie and worship of the unrighteous and that I abhor the bed of the uncircumcised. . . . Thou knowest my necessitie, that I hate this token of my preeminence, worship and dignitie which I beare upon mine head, what time as I must shew myselfe, and be seene, . . . that I weare it not when I am quiet and alone by my selfe."[22] Modesty might account for Esther's aversion to the crown, but what of her aversion to her husband? *His* is the bed of the uncircumcised; the glory and worship of the unrighteous would include those duties shown *him*. Such a prayer signals Bentley's misgivings about this heroine. Esther's virtue in the story is ostensibly secure because the victory is considered a divine one. Her methods, though, remain suspicious. Bentley's text reveals an uneasiness surrounding feminine power built on artifice. He extends her deceptions in ways the Bible does not, presenting Esther as a woman of secret judgments and desires. Because Esther's victory involves some degree of dishonest behavior, hers becomes a dishonesty without bounds.

The connection Bentley makes between female cunning and holy virtue has a place in biblical women's histories: Judith seduced Holofernes in order to destroy him; Jael offers sanctuary to a fleeing Sisera so that she might drive a tent peg in his head. Esther's cunning is initiated by her disguise and culminates in the disclosure of her identity before her king and her enemy. This disclosure does not occur in the king's court, but at a private party. Esther invites Ahasuerus and Haman to two banquets, and at the second she makes her Jewish self and Haman's evil known. The reason for Esther's private affairs seems clear: she gives Haman a heightened sense of privilege to accentuate his fall.[23] The queen also manages to get Haman into a compromising position. Esther's accusation occurs in her private chamber. The narrative tells us that on hearing of Haman's plot against Esther's people, the king becomes distressed and exits. Haman seizes the moment alone with the queen to beg for his life. The king reenters to see Haman approach Esther on her bed and assumes that the accused intends a sexual impropriety. Haman's execution is swift.[24]

The biblical narrative is silent regarding Esther's motivation for this strategy, but early modern commentary is not. John Trapp writes that the queen "prudently reserveth her selfe till a fitter opportunity" and goes on to describe her choice as good policy given her husband's fondness for banquets. Trapp notes that similarly in the Old Testament, Rebecca provides "such savory meat as [Isaac] loved."[25] Trapp's reference to Rebecca is extremely revealing, for Rebecca's preparation of Isaac's favorite dish marks one of the greatest of biblical deceptions. In Genesis 27 Rebecca orchestrates a plan by which her favorite son Jacob will deceive his father and obtain a stolen blessing.[26] The use of prepared foods in the enterprise is much less significant than the trickery practiced by the entertaining wife. Trapp's comparison acknowledges Esther's blatant manipulation of her husband's authority. Within Trapp's commentary and in others, Esther teeters on the brink between virtue and vice, held in check by a presumed divine endorsement. Esther's reasons for her actions go largely unrevealed. This mystery—so essential to her success in the biblical narrative—defines her character in early modern readings.

Her very name is linked to secrecy. Bentley defines "Esther" as "close, hidden, plucking downe."[27] The first part of this definition is likely based on a Hebrew word that is similar to the root of her name: *seter* means secret. However, the biblical narrative presents the heroine's Hebrew name as *Hadassah*, myrtle; *Esther* is her assumed name and is likened to the Persian *stara*, which referred to "star" or "light."[28] In essence, though, Bentley defines Esther as a dangerous secret.

The achievement that comes as a result of Esther's hidden identity inspired the author of the 1617 text *Ester hath hang'd Haman: or An ansvvere to a lewd pamphlet, entituled, The arraignment of women.* The author uses the pseudonym Ester Sowernam (sour-name) to write in response to Joseph Swetnam's (sweet-name's) *Arraignment of Lewde, idel, froward, and unconstant women* (1615). Ester Sowernam presents herself as one defending a specific people, women, just as it became Esther's task to save her people, the Jews. Though Sowernam refers to the biblical queen only once in her work, her use of the name Ester and the surtitle referencing Haman's defeat invites us to read her engagement with Swetnam through the lens of the biblical story. As Erin Henrikson has observed, Sowernam "identifies herself . . . with a biblical woman who complicated female identity. . . . 'Ester Sowernam' is a strategy as much as it is a name."[29] Critics speculate that Sowernam was male, given the odd description on her title page as "neither Maide, Wife nor Widdow, yet really all, and therefore experienced to defend all."[30] However, this self-portrait is a potential reference to the biblical Esther. Ahasuerus's queen is more concubine than spouse. The Bible tells us that the king placed a crown upon her head, but there is no mention of an actual marriage in the story. The biblical scholar Adele Berlin notes Ahasuerus's confused regard for the women in the tale: he treats his wife as a concubine while his concubine is treated to the crown.[31]

Both Sowernam and the Bible's Esther engage in impressive rhetorical campaigns that would seem to contradict the silence urged on early modern women. Esther's situation requires that she address the king in his inner court. Sowernam must address Swetnam in print. Language is the women's means to stifle opponents. Given that Esther twice addresses Ahasuerus and goes on to dictate Persian law, it is curious that Trapp praises her silence, saying "silence and modesty. . . . are the greatest commendation to a woman that can be."[32] Trapp's consideration of Esther as a silent queen may be prompted by Esther's apology for her speech before the king.[33] Nevertheless, it is clear that the queen's crusade involves a series of discursive achievements that would counter demands for female silence. Bentley's prayer for Esther highlights the importance of her right words: "O Lord. . . . Give me an eloquent and pleasant speech in my mouth before the lion [before King Ahasuerus]."[34]

The necessity of Esther's speech is noted time and again by early modern women. In addition to Lanyer and Sowernam, Bathusa Makin argues for greater care in the education for women and cites Esther as evidence that women possess "understanding of the highest things."[35] Margaret Fell's *Women's Speaking Justified* (1667) also relies on Esther's history: "And see what glorious expressions Queen *Hester* used to comfort the People of God . . . which caused joy and gladness of heart among all the *Jews*, who prayed and worshipped the Lord in all places, who jeoparded her life contrary to the king's command, went and spoke to the king . . . by which means she saved the lives of the People of God; and righteous *Mordecai* did not forbid her speaking."[36] To these writers, Esther authorizes female discourse. Sowernam's, Makin's and Fell's use of Esther as a model demonstrates readings of the character as a rhetorically bold and clever queen. She is not, in these texts, praised for obedience.

Esther's discursive and political authority is most profound in her book's final chapters. Once the queen informs the king of Haman's plot, she begins to direct her husband's actions and discourse. She requests, "let it be written, that the letter of Haman . . . be called again which he wrote to destroy the Jewes."[37] The king rewards Esther with further linguistic freedom: "Write ye also for the Jewes," he says, "as it liketh you *in the kings name*."[38] Esther's words routinely become law. It is she who requests a greater sentence against Haman's household, ordering his ten sons to be hanged on the gallows Haman constructed for Jews; she suggests additional disgraces after their deaths.[39] But Esther's vengeance is not yet exhausted: Esther prompts Ahasuerus to grant the Jews permission to take revenge against their enemies, first for a single day and then for a second. The two-day spree results in the deaths of over 75,000 people at the hands of the Jews. No other biblical heroine is responsible for bloodshed of this magnitude. Early modern readers do not champion the violence at the close of the book, nor can they ignore it. In his poem *The History of Queen Esther*, Francis Quarles brings home images of slaughter:

> And with their fatall hand (their hand disus'd
> To bathe in blood) they made so strong recoyle,
> That with a purple streme, the thirsty soyle
> O'rflowd: and on the pauement (drown'd with blood)
> Where neuer was before, they rais'd a flood:
> There lyes a headlesse body, here a limme
> Newly dis-ioynted from the trunke of him.[40]

It is difficult to reckon the obedient and silent woman applauded as Esther with the woman who enabled this masculine display of force.

The massacre causes Mayer some concern: "[Was] not this a most bloudy minde in *Ester*, to desire that . . . killing and slaying?"[41]

The flip side of Esther's complicated virtue is a vengeance that cannot be contained; it completes her history and confirms her power as queen. To some, the threat she embodied was cause for discomfort; for others, it was a cause for honor. Esther's history was one of the most popular biblical themes among seventeenth-century embroideresses.[42] Such embroidered works, as Roziska Parker has observed, "provided a weapon of resistance to the painful constraints of femininity. . . . women have . . . sewn a subversive stitch."[43] Needlework and other traditionally feminine arts could indoctrinate women to accept a feminine ideal, but they also permitted alternative expression.[44] In embroidered displays, Esther's duty is rendered in small, even stitches, but these contain frightening reminders of her potency. A tablecloth panel from the Burrell collection (1652) depicts Esther's forbidden approach of Ahasuerus.[45] The center shows Esther coming before the throne of male authority, surrounded by flora and fauna, the king's scepter extended toward her. But the upshot of Esther's courage is more than clear: in the upper right corner hangs Haman on the gallows, and below him is a lion with a bloody bone in its mouth; in front of the beast other bones have been gnawed clean. The lion's activity reminds us that Haman's downfall is just the start of the punishment driven by the heroine.

Esther's magnificent force is not always confined to backgrounds. Philips Galle's engraving *Hester with a Scepter* (circa 1600) celebrates Esther as a woman of might.[46] The queen stands in the center of the image. The scepter, so vital a demonstration of male power in the biblical narrative, is held tightly in her right hand; in her left is a large, open volume representing either the book in which she is immortalized or the decrees she and Mordecai direct. Her chest is clad in armor and decorated with horrified, open-mouthed fiends.

In the upper left corner is the hanging body of Haman. The only suggestion of modesty here is Esther's downcast eyes (though it may be that she is engrossed in a text of her own making). Galle presents Esther as a kind of Deborah: her book signifies the wisdom and judgment associated with a prophetess; her breastplate is a sign of strength in battle. Heywood makes a similar connection between the Old Testament heroines, identifying Esther as a "blessed Mother in Israel," the description Deborah uses to celebrate herself in Judges 5:7.[47]

Heywood is not alone in associating Esther with Deborah. "Oh God," wrote Elizabeth I, "persist . . . in giving me strength so that I, like another Deborah, like another Judith, like another Esther may free Thy people . . . from the hands of Thy enemies." Elizabeth penned this prayer in the early part of her reign while assuming the burden of office—a "heavy weight, surely, for a woman's shoulder, but light with [God's] making it light."[48] Unrest in Scotland and France was threatening. It is fitting that each of the heroines named in the queen's prayer preserve their people from bitter enemies—two of these in the midst of war. Elizabeth's heroines challenge boundaries placed on female authority and manipulate others to God's greater glory. Each is defined in feminine terms—a wife, a widow, a virgin—and each goes on to prove herself an emasculating force: Judith beheads a general; Deborah exposes the cowardice of one general and sings the praise of a woman who symbolically rapes (and kills) another; Esther is offered Ahasuerus's phallic scepter and takes hold. The latter's assumption of masculine sovereignty is evident in the close of her narrative as the king seeks to please her. Trapp notes Ahasuerus's repeated attempts to satisfy his queen "rather out of affection . . . then desire of justice."[49] Indeed, Trapp accuses Ahasuerus of being "a sensualist and effeminate," anxiously observing that he was "only [Esther's] clay and wax."[50]

The anonymous 1561 play *The Interlude of the Virtuous and Godly Queen Hester* begins with the injunction:

> *Come near virtuous matrons and womenkind,*
> *Here may you learn of Hester's duty:*
> *In all comeliness of virtue you shall find*
> *How to behave yourselves in humility.*[51]

But to provide the promised example, the playwright engages in a great deal of creative revision: his Hester is ignorant of her Jewish heritage until the day she confronts the king; there appears to be no risk involved in her approach of the inner court (though Assuerus does extend his wand); and no Persian blood is shed in this story with the exception of Aman's off-stage execution. Furthermore, the character Mardocheus instructs his niece,

> Then, if the king choose you to his queen
> It is of his goodness, bounty, and grace;
> And for none your merits. . . .
> Therefore to him repay must you needs obedience,
> True love, and kindness. . . .
> Not forged nor feigned.[52]

Such direction responds all too apparently to the recognition that the biblical heroine's behavior is potentially less than humble, that her devotion to her husband is doubtful, that she is decidedly one who feigns. A similarly fraught attempt to distance Esther from questionable conduct is seen in another comparison made between Esther and England's Elizabeth. During a 1578 progress in Norwich, Elizabeth is addressed by a Hester preoccupied with deception:

> The fretting heads of furious Foes have skill,
> As well by fraude as force to finde their pray:

In smiling lookes doth lurke a lot as ill,

As where both sterne and sturdy streames do sway, . . .

But force nor fraude, nor Tyrant strong can trap,

Those which the Lorde in his defence doth wrap.[53]

Norwich's Hester appears to assign crooked behavior to a sullen enemy and identifies both herself and Elizabeth as victims of such deceit. And yet, the descriptions with which Hester begins her oration are markedly imprecise: in the book of Esther, the greatest forces are the avengers she herself enables: it is she who has great cause for fury; it is she who pointedly identifies her prey. There is much fraud in the biblical narrative, but it is hardly confined to Haman (who is honest concerning his plans for Jewish destruction). If duplicity is characterized by "smiling lookes," there is no question of the heroine's own guilt, twice hostess as she was to her adversary. The attempt at Norwich to distance Esther from fraudulent behavior only accentuates the deception vital to her character. Hester's discourse appears more instructive than cautionary. Even the confident declaration that fraud may not defeat those whom the Lord defends is a reference to Esther's own success: Haman descends from the Amalekite King Agag, a renowned enemy of King Saul's.[54] Saul, a Benjaminite divinely chosen to be Israel's first king, overcomes Agag just as Esther, another Benjaminite, does Haman. The biblical text implies that the cunning used to realize these victories is righteous.

The book of Esther celebrates feminine achievement while showcasing the inadequacy of male rule. The text begins with the challenge of female disobedience, but that challenge is hardly checked by the book's end. It is impossible for readers who endorse Vashti's banishment on the grounds that it is "unfit that the *hen should crow*, that the woman should usurp authority over the man" to be at peace with the conclusion of this story.[55] This is the great irony of the book of Esther: we meet no man in Persia who *is* able to "beare rule in his owne house."[56] The narrative even includes the detail that the king gave Esther Haman's estate after the villain's execution.[57] Ahasuerus is a most ineffectual ruler. His court was "an ill aire for godlinesse to breathe in," and yet, whatever brand of godliness Esther possessed did flourish there.[58] Her good fortune is due in no small part to her resourcefulness: Esther fashions herself as expected so that she might accomplish the unexpected. Early modern men and women recognized the power of this feminine performance, and though obedience is often ascribed to Esther in their readings, it is clear that in the close of the book Esther demands more obedience than she demonstrates. The revenge of the Jews that she enabled resulted in mass conversions of frightened Persians.[59] She accumulates property and political force. Most telling are her final actions within the narrative as she dictates the celebration of the festival of Purim on the fourteenth day of Adar—a celebration of the Jews' ability to overcome their enemies, a celebration of her own part in that triumph.[60] It is an obligation and an honor, note the editors of the 1560 Geneva Bible, "as Jewes do, even to this day."[61]

Notes

1. Thomas Bentley, *The Monument of Matrons* (London: H. Denham, 1582), Lampe 7, 149.

2. Thomas Heywood, *The Exemplary Lives and Memorable Acts of Nine of the Most Worthy Women of the World: Three Jewes, Three Gentiles, Three Christians* (London: Thomas Cotes, 1640), 49.

3. According to rabbinic lore, the king intended for Vashti to dance naked for him and his guests. See A. Berlin, *The JSP Bible Commentary: Esther* (Jewish Publication Society: Philadelphia, 2001), 14.

4. John Trapp, *A Commentary or Exposition Upon the Books of Ezra, Nehemiah, Ester, Job and Psalms* (London: Thomas Newberry, 1657), 111.

5. Book of Esther 1:22. This and all biblical excerpts are quoted from *The Geneva Bible: A Facsimile of the 1560 Edition* (Madison: University of Wisconsin Press, 1969).

6. Esther 2:9, 12.

7. For information on the early modern use of and the controversy surrounding cosmetics, see J. E. Carney, "'God hath given you one face, and you make yourselves another': Face Painting in the Renaissance," *Lamar Journal of the Humanities* 21, no. 2 (Fall 1995): 21–34; and A. Riehl, "Cosmetics and Makeup," in *The Encyclopedia of Women in the Renaissance*, ed. D. Robin, A. Larsen, and C. Levin (Santa Barbara CA: ABC-Clio, 2007), 223–24.

8. Hannah Woolley, *The gentlewomans companion; or, A guide to the female sex containing directions of behaviour, in all places, companies, relations, and conditions, from their childhood down to old age* (London: A. Maxwell, 1673), 242.

9. Esther 2:10, 20. Mordecai's instruction is significant, marked by its repetition in the narrative.

10. Esther 2:5.

11. The association of the left hand with deception is an early modern commonplace: Hugh Blair preaches that left-handed men "for a bribe, or for respect to persons will pervert Justice and Judgement" (*Gods soveraignity, His Sacred Majesties supremacy, the subjects duty asserted in a sermon, preached before His Majesties high commissioner, and the honourable Parliament of the kingdom of Scotland, at Edinburgh, the 31. of March, 1661* [Glasgow: Printed by Robert Sanders, 1661]), 3.

12. Trapp, *A Commentary or Exposition*, 105, 181.

13. Esther 2:14.

14. John Mayer, *Many Commentaries in One: Upon Joshuah, Judges, Ruth, 1 and 2 of Samuel, 1 and 2 of Kings, 1 and 2 of Chronicles, Ezra, Nehemiah, Esther* (London, John Legatt and Richard Cotes, 1647), 57.

15. Trapp, *A Commentary or Exposition*, 116–17.

16. Trapp considers the book of Esther exceptional: "there being no where in Scripture found more remarkable passages and acts of Gods immediate providence for his calamitous people" (*A Commentary or Exposition*, 103).

17. Aemilia Lanyer, *The Poems of Aemilia Lanyer: Salve Deus Rex Judaeorum*, ed. S. Woods (New York: Oxford University Press, 1993), 115.

18. Esther 4:11.

19. Mayer, *Many Commentaries in One*, 64.

20. Bentley, *Monument of Matrons*, Lampe 7, 151.

21. R. McBee, *Review: Artemisia and Esther at Metropolitan Museum of Art*, February 25, 2001, American Guild of Judaic Art online, www.jewishart.org/artemisia/ArtemisiaEsther.html.

22. Bentley, *Monument of Matrons*, Lampe 1, 47.

23. Haman's ego is extreme and sensitive, as is clear in his exchanges with Mordecai. See Esther, chapter 3.

24. Esther 7:8–10.

25. Trapp, *A Commentary or Exposition*, 148.

26. Genesis 27:8–10.

27. Bentley, *Monument of Matrons*, Lampe 7, 146.

28. Berlin writes that Esther could also be a version of the Babylonian name derived from the name of the goddess Ishtar (*JSP Bible Commentary*, 26).

29. E. Henrikson, "Dressed as Esther: The Value of Concealment in Ester Sowernam's Biblical Pseudonym," *Women's Writing* 10, no. 1 (2003): 154–55.

30. Ester Sowernam, *Ester hath hang'd Haman: or An ansvvere to a lewd pamphlet, entituled, The arraignment of women* (London: Nicholas Bourne, 1617), title page.

31. Berlin, *JSP Bible Commentary*, xx.

32. Trapp, *A Commentary or Exposition*, 122.

33. Esther 7:4.

34. Bentley, *Monument of Matrons*, Lampe 1, 47.

35. Bathusa Makin, *An Essay to Revive the Antient Education of Gentlewomen* (London: J.D., 1673), 24.

36. Margaret Fell, *Women's Speaking Justified, Proved and Allowed of the Scriptures* (London: 1667), 15–16.

37. Esther 8:5.

38. Esther 8:8, emphasis mine.

39. Esther 9:25.

40. Francis Quarles, *Hadassa: or The history of Queene Ester with meditations thereupon, diuine and morall* (London: Richard Moore, 1621), sect. 17.

41. Mayer, *Many Commentaries in One*, 71.

42. Lanto Synge, *Art of Embroidery: History of Style and Technique* (Woodbridge: Antique Collector's Club, 2001), 53.

43. R. Parker, foreword to *The Subversive Stitch: Embroidery in Women's Lives, 1300–1900*, selected by P. Barnett (Manchester: Whitworth Art Gallery, Cornerhouse, 1988), 5.

44. Parker, foreword to *The Subversive Stitch*, 5.

45. This image appears in the catalogue *Embroidery 1600–1700 at the Burrell Collection* (Glasgow: Glasgow Museums, 1995), panel 64.

46. This image appears in *The Illustrated Bartsch Vol 56: Netherlandish Artists: Philips Galle* (New York: Abaris Books, 1978), 225.

47. Heywood, *Exemplary Lives and Memorable Acts*, 66.

48. Elizabeth I, *Collected Works*, ed. L. S. Marcus, J. M. Mueller, and M. B. Rose (Chicago: University of Chicago Press, 2000), 157, 158.

49. Trapp, *A Commentary or Exposition*, 185.

50. Trapp, *A Commentary or Exposition*, 114, 185.

51. *The Interlude of the Virtuous and Godly Queen Hester* (1561), in *Six Anonymous Plays*, ed. J. S. Farmer (New York: Barnes and Noble, 1966), 248.

52. *Interlude of the Virtuous and Godly Queen Hester*, 255.

53. John Nichols, ed., *The Progresses and Public Processions of Queen Elizabeth*, vol. 2 (London: Burt Franklin, 1823), 147–48.

54. I Samuel 15.

55. Trapp, *A Commentary or Exposition*, 113.

56. Esther 1:22.

57. Esther 8:7.

58. Trapp, *A Commentary or Exposition*, 119.

59. Esther 8:17.

60. Esther 9:29, 30.

61. *Geneva Bible*, 222.

9

"Shine like an Angel with thy starry crown"

Queen Elizabeth the Angelic

ANNA RIEHL

The inscription under an anonymous seventeenth-century engraving ambitiously entitled *The True Woman* offers to view a "horrible two-headed monster . . . an angel in Church and a devil at home." Françoise Borin comments, "The devil and the woman are perfectly symmetrical, Siamese sisters. The picture suggests no mere change of mood but a simultaneous dual nature: angel and demon."[1] A striking element in this example is that despite its profession of duality, the inscription enforces an identification of the feminine and the angelic: visually, the devilish head is easily recognizable as demonic, whereas the angelic face, without a verbal label, is merely that of a beautiful woman. In the early modern period, angels were habitually evoked as favored descriptors of the appearance and behavior of human, and specifically female, nature. In addition, poetic descriptions often followed Petrarch in praising women's angelic looks, although the serious theological discussions that permeated early modern thinking about angels were less concerned with angelic looks than the nature of angelic intelligence. Evidentially, these two modes of awareness—metaphoric and theological—coexisted and intertwined in various contexts.

My inquiry is concerned with the implications of this conceptual duality in the case of one particular woman, Elizabeth I. With so many time-tested tropes at their disposal, her poets repeatedly favored one particular comparison: Elizabeth as an angel. Scholars point out that Elizabeth's subjects, especially in the last two decades of her reign, frequently exalt her as a goddess, divine, holy, and saintly.[2] It may seem that the angelic trope is but a variant of this type of praise. However, this figure is rich in very specific meanings that, in this queen's peculiar set of circumstances, overarch the political and personal, power and beauty, the supernatural and the natural. Thus, even though the Petrarchan roots of the angelic trope seem to render it fairly conventional in the early modern period, a fresh look at primary documentation indicates that Elizabeth's distinctive position activates the trope's multiple potential associations and hence transforms it from a customary compliment to a praise that is uniquely her own.

The belief in angels in early modern England was sustained both in theological thought and the common consciousness. Although the English queen made occasional references to angels and was apparently pleased to be complimented in the angelic vein, the exact nature of her personal convictions on this matter is unknown; however, to witness what it would mean to believe in angels and to feel the reality of their presence, Elizabeth had to turn no farther than her learned counselor in matters scientific and supernatural, John Dee. Dee spent years in earnest pursuit of knowledge under the mystical tutelage of many angels with whom he conversed regularly through scryers.[3] Elizabeth almost certainly knew about these conversations. Although there is no record that the queen personally participated in the supernatural communications, Dee once treated her, at her request, to a demonstration of his "glass so famous" and showed her "some of the properties of that glass, to her Majesty's great contentment and delight."[4] It is possible, as Deborah Harkness suggests, that this glass was one of Dee's showstones used for communication with the angels.[5] Harkness offers further evidence that Elizabeth was probably informed of Dee's angelic sources when, on another occasion, Dee "delivered in writing the he[a]venly admonition, and Her Majesty to[o]k it thankfully."[6] The likelihood of her positive attitude to his communication with the angels may be inferred from that welcoming reaction. As I will demonstrate shortly, Dee's own enthusiasm to include his queen in the sphere of angelic activity is evident as early as 1577, in the frontispiece to his *General and Rare Memorials pertaining to the Perfect Arte of Navigation*, which I will analyze in detail later on.

A few aspects of the queen's political and personal situation linked Elizabeth to the angelic host in the minds of her contemporaries. The very name of the people she ruled over lent itself to an angelic association: Pope Gregory's famous wordplay, "*Non Angli, sed angeli*" ("Not Angles, but angels"), was well known to the Elizabethans.[7] Because the ruler of England was habitually identified with her country (and this conflation grew more intense as Elizabeth's reign progressed), the queen became the most prominent beneficiary of the angelic flair suggested by this historical pun.

Elizabeth is additionally associated with angels through the conjunction of a specific royal ritual and "angels," coins stamped with angelic imagery. A common currency traditionally used as healing-pieces, given away by the monarch during the touching for scrofula, or King's Evil, angels reinforce the queen's unique ability to heal, a gift that aligns her with supernatural rather than natural beings.[8] The coin itself, whose obverse depicts the Archangel Michael encircled by Elizabeth's name and regalia, subtly draws

Elizabeth into the angelic iconography. These coins were prized because of the consistent purity of the gold used for their production. Their worth (10 shillings) perhaps exceeded the means of some, but no doubt they were mingled in many pouches with the more common coins that bore the image of Elizabeth herself. As Donald Baker explains in his study of the angel coin, it became "almost a national symbol," with "strong religious connotations." The coin originated in the reign of Edward IV and, during the Wars of the Roses, "became a symbol of royal and spiritual authority," and Elizabeth was a subsequent recipient of that English ruler's prerogative.[9] Moreover, the inscription on the reverse of the angel had an additional, personal relation to Elizabeth. The Biblical quotation "*A domino factvm est istvd et est mirabile in ocvlis nostris*" ("It is the doing of the Lord, and that is miraculous in our eyes") was chosen by Mary Tudor as a new inscription for the angel. The saying, however, soon became a part of Elizabeth's own legend. She was reported to have uttered these very words upon receiving the news that Mary was dead and Elizabeth's time to rule had finally come. Whether or not she actually quoted the Psalm as she stood under the oak tree at Hatfield, Elizabeth must have had a fondness for these words: she kept her sister's inscription intact despite the difficulty caused by its Catholic overtones. And because the angel "was recognized abroad as the characteristic coin of England," the angelic aura of the English queen reached, through her currency, beyond the boundaries of her realm.[10]

Even more important, some of Elizabeth's individual attributes ensured a relatively easy fit with the angelic trope. Her personal motto *Semper Eadem* ("Always the Same") evoked one of the prominent angelic properties: the queen's supposed immutability was seen by her contemporaries as reminiscent of the eternal unchangeability of the angels.[11] In addition, such frequently rehearsed virtues as

Elizabeth's chastity, virginity, and Diana-like insusceptibility to sexual desire equipped her with yet another resemblance to an "angel, all pure & clean from the dreggy appetites of this life: that is to say, utterly rid from all passions, the which ever strive against the will of god."[12] In her study of Elizabeth as a woman "who was possessed of both political and spiritual authority," Philippa Berry refers to the "hypothesis that a chaste woman could serve as a bridge between the material world and an invisible spiritual dimension."[13] So described, Elizabeth's virginity and chastity acquire a distinct angelic significance. Once we recognize the latent angelic connotations that surround Elizabeth's persona, overt statements about her angelic properties begin to compose a surprisingly individualized image.

Visual depictions of the queen make a substantial contribution to strengthening her closeness to angels. Even as an iconoclastic wave propelled by the Reformation wreaked havoc on religious imagery across Europe, many angels of the period survived in books and architecture.[14] While Protestants vehemently discouraged angel worship and "minimized angels along with all other intermediaries between God and man," the angelic appeal did not seem to wane.[15] Matters were additionally complicated by a dualistic belief in the existence of both good and evil angels.[16] Whatever the issues of iconoclasm and the early modern theological disputations about the nature of angels, it is evident that visual culture placed these winged creatures quite comfortably in Elizabeth's presence. These images endow the queen with angelic properties in varying degrees, culminating in depictions that show Elizabeth herself as a kind of an angel. Yet even the placement of angels in close proximity to this woman suggests not only the blessing of the queen and her policies from above, but also the affinity of her nature to that of the heavenly messengers and protectors.

Whether as an embodiment of Elizabeth's piety or a reminder of

Fig. 9.1. Portrait of Elizabeth I, title page from *The holie Bible,
conteynyng the olde Testament and the newe*, also called the
Bishops' Bible (London, 1568). Reproduced courtesy of
the Newberry Library, Chicago (Case +C221.568).

oʃ ʒʃe ʃame .&c. Iohn Foxe her humble ʃubiect wiʃheth daily incr
and Grace, with long raigne, perfect health, and ioyfull ʃ
hys flocke committed to her charge, to the example of all ʃ
the comforte of his Churche, and glory of hys
bleʃʃedname.

H R I
Princes ,
throne of N
the Churcʃ
your royall
yeares to ra
felicitie ,to ʃ
laʃting ioy ʃ
When
and MONᵥ
(moʃt dear
ᴮᴱᵀᴴ, *our ʃ*
Maieʃties r
gentle part
trauailes in
well at an eʃ
turned my ʃ
ʃes after my
to write hiʃ

tong. But certaine euill diʃpoʃed perʃons ,of intemperant tongues ,a
would not ʃuffer me ʃo to reʃt, fuming and fretting, and raiʃing ᵥ
at the firʃt appearing of the booke ,as was wonderfull to heare. A n
to haue bene new borne agayne, and that Herode with all the Citʃ
vprore. Such bluʃtring and ʃtirring was then againʃt that poore bʃ
England ,euen to the gates of Louaine : ʃo that no Engliʃh Papiʃt a
himʃelfe a perfect Catholike ,vnleʃʃe he had caʃt out ʃome word or o
Whereupon, conʃidering with my ʃelfe what ʃhould mooue the
with more circumʃpect diligence to ouerlooke agayne that I had dʃ
found the fault both what it was, and where it lay : which was in dʃ

Fig. 9.2. Illumination of Elizabeth I, folio §5r from *Actes and Monuments*
by John Foxe (London, 1583). Reproduced courtesy of the
Newberry Library, Chicago (Case fᴅ78.308).

her divine right, angelic faces inhabit many depictions of the queen. In the frontispiece to *A booke of christian prayers,* two cherubs are hovering atop the prie-dieu as Elizabeth holds her hands folded in prayer,[17] and another pair is holding back the curtain on the title page of the *Bishops' Bible* (fig. 9.1). In the elaborately embellished letter *C* in Foxe's *Actes and Monuments,* the angel is placed directly over and behind Elizabeth's coat of arms: a compositional choice that emphasizes the holy protection of her rulership as well as its derivation from the angelic (fig. 9.2).[18] The countenances of the queen and the angel are placed on the same level, above the faces of the pope and of Elizabeth's counselors. In the depiction of Elizabeth's calling upon her troops at Tilbury, angels appear prominently in the lower panel, as a tribute to the divinely sanctioned victory over the Spanish Armada.[19] The top of the panel hosts a solitary queen praying in her chamber, her crown and wired veil evoking halo and wings, traditional angelic attributes. This angelic portrait completes the metaphoric triangle that connects angels placed at the outmost points of the painting.

The composition of the well-populated title page of John Dee's *General and Rare Memorials* (fig. 9.3) is even more complex than the vision of Elizabeth at Tilbury, with the angel incorporated in a spirited political message to the queen. The title page depicts four principal characters: Elizabeth herself guiding the ship, Britain kneeling on the shore, Occasion standing on the cliff, and a warrior angel hovering above.[20] The accompanying inscription identifies Dee's angel as Michael, a significant choice that is directly related to the iconography of the angel (coin).[21] Dee's selection of this archangel to seal the visual argument for England's imperial expansion clearly corresponds to its use on the coin, which is likewise "allusive to England's position at sea."[22] While the figures of Occasion and Britain are symbolic personifications, the representation of

Fig. 9.3. Engraving on the title page from *General and Rare Memorials pertaining to the Perfect Arte of Navigation* by John Dee (1577). Reproduced by permission of the Huntington Library, San Marino CA (RB 82497).

Elizabeth, enthroned on the ship entitled *Europa*, juxtaposes symbolic and physical reality. The angel, in contrast, belongs neither to the group of symbolic representations nor to that of material bodies. Its position is characteristically liminal, between the concrete human beings riding on the ship or walking on the shore and the abstract figuration of the divine in the solar tetragrammaton. The corresponding passage in Dee's text evokes the "good angel" as an instrument of God, in a plea to "G[u]ard us, with shield and sword, now, and ever."[23] Frances Yates argues that Dee's frontispiece is an expanded version of the embellished letter *C* in Foxe's book (the letter is additionally reproduced in Dee's publication).[24] This intriguing proposition renders insight into Dee's concept of the relation between Elizabeth and the angels: the apparent transformation of the cherubic angel into a fully fledged archangel aptly reflects the gravity of Dee's attitude toward the angelic. If the former is reminiscent of the decorative childish cherubs or putti, the latter encompasses a militant religious conviction. This charismatic angelic presence, in turn, affects Elizabeth's demeanor, converting what may look like a casual sea voyage to a glorious and potentially dangerous imperial venture. The frontispiece conveys purpose and movement and assures Elizabeth of the divine auspices for the expansion of her dominion. Thus, a few years before his conversations with angels, Dee already envisions Elizabeth under the active protection of a winged warrior and, moreover, issues an implicit assertion of the angelic assistance in order to urge his queen to pursue a grand enterprise.[25]

One of the most spectacular angelic images is found on the pages of Anthony Munday's *Zelauto* as well as in William Teshe's manuscript drawing based on that woodcut: a glorious trumpeting angel is perched on the front of Elizabeth's carriage, proclaiming her fame (fig. 9.4).[26] This image supplements Zelauto's impressions of the queen's "heavenly hew, her Princely personage, her rare Sobriety,

Fig. 9.4. "Elizabeth in Procession," by William Teshe (ca. 1580–84).
Copyright © British Library Board. All rights reserved (Sloane.1832 f7v).
Reproduced by permission.

her singular Wisdom"; he even predicts that Mars himself "would
stand aghast at her heavenly behavior."[27] To his interlocutor's skepti-
cal reaction, Zelauto juxtaposes a familiar assertion of Elizabeth's
probable divinity: "Were it possible for a Goddess to remain on
earth at this day: credit me, it were she."[28] As proof, Zelauto goes
on to praise Elizabeth's ability to speak many languages and relates
an episode of her "marvelously mov[ing]" the mind of the "valiant
Marques Vitelli." The touch of holiness is clearly construed here as
manifest in her intellectual abilities. In the accompanying image, the
English queen's divinity is figured forth in the angelic harbinger of
her fame; in conjunction with Zelauto's praise, the angel appears not
only to signify her glory but also to embody a "heavenly" property
specific to Elizabeth.[29]

Such oblique hints and connections may seem subtle. Yet they signal the extent of the contemporary investment in the concept that not only the monarch and her country are protected by the angels but that the queen herself, like an angel, is God-sent. Her supernatural attributes are hailed not only in the visual metaphors like that in the Tilbury commemoration, not only in the flattering poetic encomiums, but also in a serious theological context. As one preacher puts it, "As *queen*, the natural person is a supernatural gift to her people: God sent us his high gift, our most dear Sovereign Lady Queen Elizabeth, with godly, wise, and honourable counsel."[30] Similarly, in 1585, Edmund Bunny records a prayer of gratitude to god "for giving us so gracious a Princess, sent laden unto us with so many and so special gifts and blessings."[31] Articulating the angelic reference even more openly, William Leigh's fiery diatribe against the Jesuits makes a direct identification of sovereigns with angels: "Time was when an Angel durst not reprove a devil, but said, *The Lord rebuke thee.* Now Jesuited devils dare reprove Angels sent from God to be our Sovereigns, and say, *Ravelack* may kill thee."[32] In dramatizing the opposition between Jesuits and Protestants, Leigh reinforces the contrast between devils and angels by rephrasing the Biblical view of kings as gods on earth.[33] The substitution is particularly meaningful because the sovereign at the center of Leigh's sermon is Elizabeth herself.

The specific relation between Elizabeth and angels becomes even tighter in the poetic worship of the queen in which her nearness to the angelic at times leads to explicit identification. When similes give way to metaphors, it still remains clear that Elizabeth's subjects, in calling her an angel, do not invest their words with a full theological belief. Whereas angels were certainly real to the early moderns (after all, their appearance is recorded in the Old and New Testaments[34]) even the proponents of the view that angels possess "subtle bodies" would not go as far as to suggest that an angel would assume a body of the queen and inhabit it throughout the span of her life.[35] In this sense, angel Elizabeth is always a metaphor; however, in some cases, it reaches beyond the figurative and into the realm of exact theological postulations. For instance, during her visit to Harefield in 1602, she is hailed metaphorically as

> Beauty's rose, and Virtue's book,
> Angel's mind, and Angel's look,
> To all Saints and Angels dear,
> Clearest Majesty on earth,
> Heaven did smile at your faire birth,
> And since your days have been most clear.[36]

On her departure, the sadness of the hosts is alleviated by a somber reasoning that, "As it is against the nature of an Angel to be circumscribed in *Place*, so it is against the nature of *Place* to have the motion of an Angel."[37] If the poetic praise of angelic mind and angelic look constitutes a relatively conventional flattery, the parting statement calls on the properties of angels as supernatural beings; the hint of flattery remains insofar as Elizabeth is being discussed as if she fully belongs to the angelic host, but the latter is evoked here in overtly theological terms.

In addition to conceptual angelic properties, Elizabeth's poeticized likeness to an angel is complicated by the semantic range of the term: in the early modern period, the words *angelic* and *angel* were far from being fixed as descriptors of appearance. Recall, for instance, that Hamlet's "What a piece of work is a man!" speech seizes *action*, rather than *form*, as an appropriate point of comparison in its musing about the angelic properties of a human being: "in action how like an angel."[38] The seminal teachings of Marcilio Ficino identify the mind as a nexus where the human meets the angelic; Ficino goes on to outline a neoplatonist path from human rationation to angelic contemplation of the divine mysteries.[39] In early modern England, therefore, not only a comely demeanor but also superior action (behavior) and, most important, exceptional intelligence justify an angelic allusion.

Indeed, for Elizabeth's admirers, as the previous examples suggest, her angelic properties are hardly limited to her looks. This variety is consistent with the range of the auxiliary associations evoked in this queen's specific situation as a virginal ruler of the Angles. The aforementioned implicit similarities are likely to strengthen and, to an extent, justify the repeated recourse to angels in poetry dedicated to this queen. If angels are praised for their supernatural intelligence, Elizabeth is said to have an "angel's mind" and "angel's wit," while her kindly angelic disposition is hinted at in Edmund Spenser's compliment to her "Heavenly haviour."[40]

Admittedly, insofar as sixteenth-century poetry is imbued with a Petrarchan vocabulary of love, the angelic trope continues to be a popular descriptor of Elizabeth's looks. In "Colin Clouts Come Home Again," Spenser comments on his queen's appearance: "Much like an angel in all form and fashion."[41] Focusing more specifically on her attire, Thomas Deloney's ballad fashions the "Queen on prancing steed / attired like an Angel bright."[42] Finally, it is Elizabeth's face that most frequently compels the author to reach for an angelic epithet of praise:

> Tell me, have ye seen her angelic face,
> Like *Phoebe* fair?
> Her Heavenly haviour, her princely grace
> can you well compare?[43]

In this example from Spenser's *Shepheardes Calendar*, and in many others, the primary suggestion is that Elizabeth is "fair." However, even when some verses explicitly validate their angelic similes by

singing praises to the queen's beauty, the comparison immediately
develops into a political commendation, as exemplified in George
Gascoigne's poem:

> My Queen herself comes foremost of them all,
> And best deserves that place in m[u]ch degree,
> Whose presence now must needs thy sprites appall,
> She is so faire, and Angel like to see.
> Behold her well (my Muse!) for this is she
> Whose beauty's beams do spread themselves full wide,
> Both in this Realm, and all the world beside.
>
> This is the Queen whose only look subdued
> Her proudest foes, withouten spear or shield.
> This is the Queen, whom never eye yet viewed,
> But straight the hart was forced thereby to yield.
> This Queen it is, who (had she sat in field,
> When Paris judged that Venus bore the bell,)
> The prize were hers, for she deserves it well.[44]

It would seem that the beams of beauty carry out a tautological
proclamation of Elizabeth's angelic fairness at home and abroad.
However, it is not only her beauty that emanates from the queen's
physical body across the boundaries of her realm; the metaphor
suggests something more than a conquest by means of spectacle.
Fair like an angel, this queen also possesses a supernatural ability to traverse space through a metaphoric extension of her fame
and power beyond her physical presence. Even as her arrival, in
the opening lines, is accompanied with a nod to her worthiness
(she "best deserves that place in much degree"), her beams, her
envoys that move centrifugally from her beautiful face, claim for
her places far beyond her physical reach. The notion of "place"
as a social position is reinforced by "realm" and "world"—the

ever-widening territorial ownership that Elizabeth claims effort-
lessly, simply because the power of her angelic beauty surpasses the
natural law. Moreover, the nature of her power enacted through
her radiating splendor is reminiscent of the messenger function of
angels. If her "only look subdue[s] / Her proudest foes," the rays
of her beauty operate like warrior angels who peacefully conquer
"all the world beside" on her behalf. In this view, Elizabeth herself
comes close to being equated with the divine, whereas the angelic
emanation is conceived of as one of her supernatural assets. The
angelical properties in the poem, therefore, are ultimately put to
use for political purposes.

Similarly to Gascoigne's vision of Elizabeth's conquering beauty,
George Puttenham provocatively extends the use of the angelic
epithet beyond the standard praise of feminine prettiness. Puttenham, however, polishes a different facet of the metaphor and thus
creates a complicated link between the queen's wisdom and her
angelic looks:

> . . . Nature that seldom works amiss;
> In woman's breast by passing art,
> Hath harbored safe the lion's heart;
> And fitly fixed, with all good grace,
> To serpent's head and angel's face.[45]

This "natural" explanation is offered to rationalize why the queen
appears as "no stranger sight for to be seen" that confuses and
destabilizes human visual perception; hence, one "cannot view her
steadfastly." The resulting figure, while it seemingly perpetuates
Elizabeth's own trope of the "heart and stomach of a king" har-
bored in the "body of a weak and feeble woman,"[46] takes the hybrid
imagery even further, crowning the praise with the metaphors that
focus specifically on the queen's head and face, thus localizing the
extraordinary effect of her appearance.

The symbolic significations of the serpent's head and angel's face, respectively, are wisdom and beauty. In the *Arte of English Poesie*, Puttenham explains that he, "commending her Majesty for wisdom, beauty and magnanimity likened her to the Serpent, the Lion and the Angel, because by common usurpation, nothing is wiser then the Serpent, more courageous than the Lion, more beautiful than the Angel."[47] Conjoined, beauty and wisdom seemingly endow Elizabeth with the best of both worlds. However, this overt compliment is fraught with the implied deceit and misleading nature of such conjunction. Even as the unusual juxtaposition is acknowledged, the gendered hierarchy of the body parts is reestablished: the internal organs, lion's heart, and serpent's head (i.e., brain), are aligned on the masculine side, whereas the woman's breast and angel's face, the external embellishments, are unmistakably feminine. As the symbols of courage and wisdom, the masculine elements are extolled; in contrast, the feminine body parts seem to signify only themselves. Furthermore, the juxtaposition of serpent-like wisdom and angel-like beauty borders on supernatural.

As we have seen, the trope of the angel frequently exceeds a merely conventional gesture toward Elizabeth's good looks. In early modern lore, superior intelligence is one of the primary properties of an angel, and the queen's wit is repeatedly praised in the same terms.[48] Elizabeth's beauty, therefore, when evoked in the phrase "angel's face," is, to an extent, already suffused with wisdom: a "serpent's head" thus becomes a fit and graceful completion of the hybrid. In the overt context of this poem, however, the potentially disturbing contrast between Elizabeth's mind and looks is explained away by nature's "passing art" as a phenomenon unmatched by "other women." It is this haste to refer to nature in terms of art that paradoxically renders the link between the queen's beauty and wisdom both unnatural and supernatural.

The visual counterpart of this combination of "brains and beauty"

Fig. 9.5. The Rainbow Portrait of Queen Elizabeth I, ca. 1603. Reproduced by permission of the Marquess of Salisbury, Hatfield House.

is the *Rainbow* portrait (fig. 9.5), whose most prominent elements reinforce Elizabeth's all-knowing divinity imbued with beauty. The symbolic overtones of the rainbow as Elizabeth's fulfillment of the divine promise are reflected in the benevolent glow of her face, while her wisdom is represented by the prominent serpent on her sleeve. The arrangement of the veil above the sitter's shoulders also contributes to the angelic metaphor.[49] The multiplication of eyes and ears on the queen's robe (a testament to her exceeding vigilance and surveillance over both "this Realm, and all the world beside") echoes Gascoigne's vision of Elizabeth's angelic beauty that penetrates the space outside her physical reach. As noted by scholars such as Roy Strong and Louis Montrose, a similar cloak imprinted with eyes and ears appears in the contemporary emblem of Intelligence.[50] Similarly to Puttenham's poem, the portrait constructs the queen's angelic qualities in the complicated combination of her wisdom and beauty, both of which are expressed through facial features: the fairness of her face echoes her angelic intelligence encoded in the eyes and ears scattered over her mantle.[51]

The vision of Elizabeth as an angelic supervisor and protector of England persists after her death, fulfilling the anticipation that, in time, she will "in Heaven a glorious angel stand."[52] Commemorative verses are even more outspoken about the angelic beauty of the late queen: her death transforms the strained assurances of her eternal youthfulness into a nostalgic confidence of posthumous praise. "Thy matchless beauty was Angelical," lament the mourners and thus recall the fiction of the old queen's closing years, endorsing the legend of her nonpareil appearance in no uncertain terms.[53]

> And though for beauty she an Angel was,
> And all our sex did therein far surpass;
> Yet did pure unspotted Chastity
> Her heavenly beauty rarely beautify.[54]

This extraordinary eulogy, penned by Diana Primrose, not only praises the queen's beauty as her credential for being called an angel but goes even further by hinting that Elizabeth's "unspotted chastity" perhaps renders her beauty even more extraordinary than that of an angel. Such qualification suggests that, for this poet, external beauty is an angelic attribute, whereas human chastity endows such beauty with an aura that argues Elizabeth's superiority even to angels. And this preeminence makes her fit to be their queen.

Memorial verses and images, therefore, not only envision the late queen as an angel in heaven but ascribe to her continued political power taken to a higher plane. For instance, Elizabeth's superior position even in heaven is upheld in John Lane's elegy where she is called on to preside among the angels:

> Go blessed soul, and up to heaven climb,
> Among the Angels seat thee there betime,
> Shine like an Angel with thy starry crown,
> And milk-white Robes descending fairly down,
> Washed in the blood of the unspotted Lamb.[55]

In part, the queen's much-discussed appropriation of the cult of the Virgin Mary continues in her afterlife as Elizabeth is awarded Mary's traditional position of the Queen of Heaven. Helen Hackett points out, however, that the "Bible promised all believers the reward of a heavenly crown and throne," and therefore, Lane's imagery is not an exclusive allusion to the Virgin.[56] Moreover, even as Lane calls Elizabeth "most sacred Dame" and "Elysium's Queen," thereby mixing in the vocabulary that constructs Elizabeth as a saint or goddess, his initial, and most articulate, emphasis falls on likening her to an angel. Her imperial crown seems at once to qualify Elizabeth for the angelic status as if it were a type of halo, and also to preserve her monarchical eminence as it remains recognizable as the royal headgear.

Fig. 9.6. Engraving of Elizabeth I, frontispiece from *Annales: The True and Royall History of the Famous Empresse Elizabeth Queene of England France and Ireland* by William Camden (London, 1625). Photo courtesy of the Newberry Library, Chicago (Case F4549.137).

The 1625 frontispiece to William Camden's *Annales* continues the process of "angelicization" of Elizabeth (fig. 9.6). It depicts the late queen in heaven (the verses to the right announce, "Elizabeth that famous Queene lives here"), where she seems to function as a main source of light in the sky while the stars are reduced to form her crown. This heavenly figuration is complete with the aura emanating from Elizabeth's person and pushing back the clouds; the illuminated face; the starry halo; the high wired veil raised over her shoulders, suggestive of angelic wings; and, to seal the argument, a diminutive angel holding up her imperial "starry crown" and compassionately gazing at the queen. Once again, Elizabeth's angelic prerogative is paired with her royal status: the angel holds the scroll listing her queenly accomplishments, and the crown continues to mark her eternal sovereignty. The latter iconography mirrors the imagery of Lane's elegy where it is intensified by Elizabeth's white attire, her flowing "milk-white Robes": an additional link to her queenship since these robes function as Elizabeth's new angelical robes of state, gone from scarlet to white by virtue of Christ's sacrifice.

The peculiar terms of the survival of the angelic trope indicate not only the trope's tenacity but also the new possibilities for praising Elizabeth after her term as the queen of England comes to an end. For instance, despite its initial emphasis on Elizabeth's angelic status, Lane's elegy testifies to a lack of anxiety about conflating various constructions of Elizabeth's holiness and divinity: the Marian echoes in her depictions and references to Elizabeth as angel, saint, goddess, or even Christ figure. Although these symbolic strands often merge in the vocabulary of conventional praise, it is nevertheless useful to draw some basic distinctions among these modes of representation. The most obvious boundary lies between the references to divinity colored by the Christian (or Biblical) overtones and those partaking of the mythological or pagan constructs of

the divine; the latter are exemplified in the numerous inflections of
Elizabeth's image as goddess Diana, Venus, Astraea, Pallas, and so
forth. Angels belong to the former group, whose terms range from
the concept of kings as gods on earth, to the appropriation of the
attributes often typologically associated with the Virgin Mary and
to the metaphoric references to Elizabeth as a saint.[57] As a result, the
angelic trope partakes, to various degrees, from the symbolic palette
of this biblically grounded group. This trope overlaps, for example,
with the Marian frame of reference in such concepts as the queen
being immaculately pure ("withouten blame or blot") and acting
as a mediatrix between God and her subjects.[58] Frequent claims to
her unrepresentability contribute to the view of Elizabeth as holy
and beyond human understanding, while the assertions of her im-
mortality, however complicated and qualified, still usher the queen
toward the realm of the divine.[59] In contrast, clearly gender-specific
elements so evident in the Marian attributes of maternity, fertility,
femininity, and mercifulness, to name just a few, are deactivated
in the comparisons of the queen to an angel: angels were thought
of as asexual spiritual beings. However, insofar as angelic beauty
is perceived as an overwhelmingly feminine value in this period,
some uses of the trope become inevitably gendered. Though beauty
is frequently described as divine, it is not associated with the Virgin
Mary or the saints as consistently as with the angels. Likewise, if
the angelic action falls in a generic category of heavenly, saintly,
or godly behavior, superior intelligence serves as a distinctively
angelic attribute.

Whether as a compliment, good-wishing, or acknowledgement
of Elizabeth's uniqueness, her affinity to the angelic recurs with
increasing frequency toward the end of her reign and beyond. The
implications of the angelic vocabulary in the period, as applied to

this queen, illuminate her personal and political image, helping us understand how her contemporaries imagined this "happy angel to [their] happy Land."

Notes

I would like to thank Carole Levin, Clark Hulse, Thomas Herron, and the wonderful audience at the Queens and Power conference for their valuable input.

1. *The True Woman*, reproduced in Françoise Borin, "Judging by Images," in *A History of Women: Renaissance and Enlightenment Paradoxes*, ed. N. Z. Davis and A. Farge (Cambridge MA: Harvard University Press, Belknap Press, 1993), fig. 21, pp. 215, 216.

2. See, in particular, C. Levin, "Elizabeth as Sacred Monarch," in *"The Heart and Stomach of a King": Elizabeth I and the Politics of Sex and Power* (Philadelphia: University of Pennsylvania Press, 1994); H. Hackett, *Virgin Mother, Maiden Queen: Elizabeth I and the Cult of the Virgin Mary* (New York: St. Martin's Press, 1995).

3. The surviving records of Dee's conversations with the angels indicate that he communicated with them regularly from 1581 to 1586. His last recorded conversation dates from 1607 (D. Harkness, *John Dee's Conversations with Angels: Cabala, Alchemy, and the End of Nature* [Cambridge: Cambridge University Press, 1999], 1).

4. March 16, 1575. Cited in John Dee, *The Private Diary of Dr. John Dee, and the Catalogue of his Library of Manuscripts, from the original manuscripts in the Ashmolean Museum at Oxford, and Trinity College Library, Cambridge*, ed. J. O. Halliwell (London: The Camden Society, 1842; reprint, New York: Johnson Reprint Corporation, 1968), 9n.

5. Harkness, *John Dee's Conversations with Angels*, 54.

6. May 3, 1594, *Private Diary of Dr. John Dee*, 49; Harkness, *John Dee's Conversations with Angels*, 54.

7. Pope Gregory's pun complimented the lovely faces and fair hair of the British slaves. The legend of Pope Gregory playing on England's Latin name, Anglia, was recorded in the Venerable Bede's *Ecclesiastical History*: "'They are called Angles,' he was told. 'That is appropriate,' he said, 'for they have angelic faces, and it is right that they should become joint-heirs with the angels in heaven'" (Bede, *A History of the English Church and People*, trans. L. Sherley-Price [New York: Dorset Press, 1985], 100).

8. C. E. Challis, *The Tudor Coinage* (New York: Manchester University Press, 1978), 167, 212–13; N. Woolf, *The Sovereign Remedy: Touch-Pieces and the King's Evil* (Manchester: British Association of Numismatic Societies, 1990).

ANNA RIEHL

9. D. C. Baker, "The 'Angel' of English Renaissance Literature," *Studies in the Renaissance* 6 (1959): 85–93.

10. Baker, "'Angel' of English Renaissance Literature," 87.

11. "Saint Basil saith, The Angels suffer no mutation or change, for amongst them there is neither Childe, Youth, nor Old man; but in the same state they were created in the beginning, they still persist, and so vnchangeably shall to all eternitie" (Thomas Heywood, *The hierarchie of the blessed angells. Their names, orders and offices the fall of Lucifer with his angels* [London: Adam Islip, 1635], 219 [Folger, STC 13327, copy 1]).

12. Thomas Lupset, *A treatise of charitie* (London: Thomas Berthelet, 1533), 36/E2v (British Library, STC [2nd ed.]/16939). Medieval monastic thought, in particular, binds the virginal state with the angelic: the asexual life of virgins is believed to approximate *vita angelica*. According to Cyprian, for instance, "Virginity makes itself the equal of the angels," and Ambrose teaches, "In holy virgins we see on earth the life of the angels we lost in paradise" (cited in J. Bugge, *Virginitas: An Essay on the History of a Medieval Ideal* [Netherlands: Martinus Nujhoff, 1975], 34, 31).

13. P. Berry, *Of Chastity and Power: Elizabethan Literature and the Unmarried Queen* (London: Routledge, 1989), 1, 2.

14. For a study of visual representations of angels in Protestant England, see A. Walsham, "Angels and Idols in England's Long Reformation," in *Angels in the Early Modern World*, ed. P. Marshall and A. Walsham (Cambridge: Cambridge University Press, 2006), 134–67.

15. R. H. West, *Milton and the Angels* (Athens: University of Georgia Press, 1955), 13. For an array of well-researched studies of the understanding of angels in the period, see P. Marshall and A. Walsham, eds., *Angels in the Early Modern World*.

16. Keith Thomas quotes an apt example of this belief. In his prayer, one Thomas Becon pleads, "An infinite number of wicked angels there are . . . which without ceasing seek my destruction. Against this exceeding great multitude of evil spirits send thou me thy blessed and heavenly angels, which may deliver me from their tyranny" (K. V. Thomas, *Religion and the Decline of Magic* [New York: Charles Scribner's Sons, 1971], 472).

17. "Elizabeth Regina," frontispiece to Richard Day, *A booke of christian prayers* ["The Queen's Prayerbook"] (London, 1581).

18. For the purposes of this study, I do not pose a distinction between Christianized winged figures of antiquity and angels proper. All the visual imagery discussed here represents winged spiritual beings that, as scholars generally agree, were perceived by the early moderns as angelic. For detailed inquiries in the history of the putto and winged Victory, see C. Dempsey, *Inventing the Renaissance Putto* (Chapel Hill: University of North Carolina Press, 2001); and G. Berefelt, *A Study on the Winged Angel: The Origin of a Motif* (Stockholm: Almqvist & Wiksell, 1968).

19. "Elizabeth at Tilbury," St Faith's Church, King's Lynn, Norfolk/Bridgeman Art Library, London. Reproduced in S. Watkins, *The Public and Private Worlds of Elizabeth I* (New York: Thames and Hudson, 1998), 179.

20. For a description of the frontispiece as well as the preliminary drawing attributed to John Dee, see M. Corbett and R. Lightbown, *The Comely Frontispiece: The Emblematic Title-page in England, 1550–1660* (London: Routledge and Kegan Paul, 1979), 49–51. For various analyses of this image, see P. J. French, *John Dee: The World of an Elizabethan Magus* (London: Routledge and Kegan Paul, 1972), 183–85; F. A. Yates, *Astraea: The Imperial Theme in the Sixteenth Century* [1975] (London: ARK, 1985), 48–50; J. N. King, *Tudor Royal Iconography: Literature and Art in an Age of Religious Crisis* (Princeton: Princeton University Press, 1989), 238–41.

21. Baker notes that St. Michael was "second only to St. George in significance to the English" ("'Angel' of English Renaissance Literature," 87).

22. Baker, "'Angel' of English Renaissance Literature," 87. Baker's observation is based on the fact that the obverse of the coin features St. Michael, the "traditional guardian angel of Land's End," while the reverse has an image of a ship.

23. John Dee, *General and Rare Memorials, pertaining to the Perfect Arte of Navigation* (London: John Day, 1577), 53.

24. Dee, *General and Rare Memorials*, 69; Yates, *Astraea*, 49.

25. The first extant entry in Dee's angel diary dates to 1581. Elizabeth remained very well-disposed toward Dee throughout her reign. His private diary records many signs of her benevolence. For instance, he wrote on December 16, 1590: "Mr. Candish receyved from the Quene's Majestie warrant by word of mowth to assure me to do what I wold in philosophie and alchimie, and none shold check, controll, or molest me" (*Private Diary of Dr. John Dee*, 37).

26. Anthony Munday, *Zelauto. The fountaine of fame Erected in an orcharde of amorous aduentures. Containing a delicate disputation, gallantly discoursed betweene to noble gentlemen of Italye. Giuen for a freendly entertainment to Euphues, at his late ariuall into England* (London: Iohn Charlevvood, 1580), 34 (Bodleian Library, STC [2nd ed.]/18283).

27. Munday, *Zelauto*, 32.

28. Munday, *Zelauto*, 33.

29. Stylistically, this angel descends from the pagan figure of Fame. In addition to Munday's running title, "The Fountayne of Fame," Teshe's variant of this image includes the word FAMA issuing from the trumpet.

30. *Sermon of Obedience*, part 1. Quoted in H. Berger, *The Allegorical Temper: Vision and Reality in Book 2 of Spenser's* Faerie Queene (Hamden CT: Archon Books, 1967), 145.

31. Quoted in Hackett, *Virgin Mother, Maiden Queen*, 85, from Edmund Bunny, *Certaine prayers and other godly exercises, for the seuenteenth of Nouember: Wherein we solemnize the blessed reigne of our gracious Soueraigne Lady Elizabeth* . . . (London: Christopher Barker, 1585), E1r.

32. William Leigh, *Queene Elizabeth, Paraleld in her Princely vertues, with Dauid, Iosua, and Hezekia. In Three Sermons, as they were preached three seuerall Queenes dayes* (London: T.C. for Arthur Johnson, 1612), A5r.

33. As Helen Hackett points out, Protestant commentators interpreted the word *Gods* in Psalm 82 as a reference to kings (*Virgin Mother, Maiden Queen*, 21).

34. See, for instance, John Salkeld, who refers to the apparitions of angels in the scriptures as a confirmation of their real visibility to the humans in *A Treatise of Angels: Of the nature, essence, place, power, science, vvill, apparitions, grace, sinne, and all other proprieties of angels. Collected out of the holy Scriptures, ancient fathers, and schoole-diuines* (London: T[homas] S[nodham] with authoritie of superiours, for Nathaniel Butter, 1613), D2/35–36 (Folger, STC 21621).

35. John Salkeld, "Whether Angels be compound of matter and forme, or rather be pure spirits without any matter or body," in *A Treatise of Angels* (1613), 30–34. See also Urbanus Rhegius, *An homely or sermon of good and euill angels*, trans. Richard Robinson (1583; London: Charlwood, 1593).

36. John Nichols, *The Progresses and Public Processions of Queen Elizabeth* (London: Printed by and for J. Nichols, 1823), 3:591–92.

37. Nichols, *Progresses and Public Processions of Queen Elizabeth*, 3:594.

38. William Shakespeare, *Hamlet*, 2.2.293–97, in *The Norton Shakespeare*, ed. Stephen Greenblatt et al. (New York: Norton, 1997), 1697.

39. For Ficino's views about the angelic, see Bruce Gordon, "The Renaissance Angel," in *Angels in the Early Modern World*, ed. Marshall and Walsham, 47–52.

40. For "angel's mind," see Nichols, *Progresses and Public Processions of Queen Elizabeth*, 3:591. John Davies, in *Hymnes to Astraea*, offers several hymns on Elizabeth's angelic mind. See, in particular, Hymne XV, "Of her Wit," and Hymne XIII, "Of her Minde," in *The Complete Poems of Sir John Davies*, ed. A. B. Grosart (London: Chatto and Windus, 1976), 1:143, 141. Spenser's compliment can be found in Edmund Spenser, *The Shepherds Calendar*, in *The Shorter Poems*, ed. R. A. McCabe (Penguin Classics, 1999), 63, line 66.

41. Edmund Spenser, "Colin Clovts Come Home Againe," in *The Shorter Poems*, 362, line 615.

42. Thomas Deloney, *Works*, ed. F. O. Mann (Oxford: Clarendon Press, 1912), 478. Cited in Levin, *Heart and Stomach*, 144.

43. Spenser, *Shepherds Calendar*, 63, lines 64–67.

44. George Gascoigne, "Vanities of Beauty," 2nd song. Cited in Nichols, *Progresses and Public Processions of Queen Elizabeth*, 1:xliv, note 4.

45. George Puttenham, "That her Majestue surmounteth all the Princesses of our tyme in Wisedome, Bewtye, and Magnanimitye: and ys a Thinge verye admirable in nature. Parte IV. Thalia," in *The Principall Addresse, in Nature of a New-year's Gifte*; seeminge therebye the Author intended not to have his Name knowne. Cited in Nichols, *Progresses and Public Processions of Queen Elizabeth*, 3:471.

46. "Queen Elizabeth's Armada Speech to the Troops at Tilbury, August 9, 1588," in *Elizabeth I, Collected Works*, ed. L. S. Marcus, J. M. Mueller, and M. B. Rose (Chicago: University of Chicago Press, 2000), 326.

47. George Puttenham, *Arte of English Poesie Contriued into Three Bookes, the First of Poets and Poesie, the Second of Proportion, the Third of Ornament* (London, 1589), 204/Dd4v.

48. As Deborah Harkness points out, "Dee noted that the angelic intellect was greater and more powerful than the human, and their mental acumen was critical to his rationale for conversing with them" (*John Dee's Conversations with Angels*, 113).

49. The same arrangement is repeated in many visual representations of the queen: for instance, the *Sieve* and *Ditchley* portraits, as well as in the frontispiece to Camden's *Annales* discussed later. The suggestion of wings in this attire was clearly recognized at the time: see, for instance, Inigo Jones's costume design for a "winged masquer" (1605) in S. Orgel and R. Strong, *Inigo Jones: The Theater of the Stuart Court* (Berkeley: University of California Press, 1975), plate 5.

50. R. Strong, *Gloriana: The Portraits of Elizabeth I* (New York: Thames and Hudson, 1987), 159; L. Montrose, "Idols of the Queen: Policy, Gender, and the Picturing of Elizabeth I," *Representations* 68 (Autumn 1999): 108–61, 140–41.

51. The angel representing good fame in the frontispiece of Raleigh's *The History of the World* (1614) bears eyes and ears on its wings (in contrast, the bad fame angel is spotted all over). Not only does this angel recall the mantle of the *Rainbow* portrait, but it is also very similar to the angel of fame in "Elizabeth in Procession," discussed earlier.

52. John Davies, "Royal dedication to *Nosce Teipsum*," in *The Complete Poems of Sir John Davies*, ed. A. B. Grosart (London: Chatto and Windus, 1876), 1:11.

53. T. W., *The Lamentation of Melpomene, for the death of Belphoebe our late Queene* (1603), quoted in E. C. Wilson, *England's Eliza* (New York: Octagon Books, 1966), 385.

54. D. Primrose, "A Chaine of Pearle; or, a Memoriall of the Peerles Graces and heroick vertues of QE of glorious memory," 2nd pearl (Chastity), quoted in Nichols, *Progresses and Public Processions of Queen Elizabeth*, 3:642–50.

55. John Lane, "An Elegie upon the death of the high and renowned Princesse, our late Soueraigne Elizabeth", quoted in Wilson, *England's Eliza*, 377.

56. Hackett, *Virgin Mother, Maiden Queen*, 215.

57. For plentiful examples of these three points of reference, see Hackett, *Virgin Mother, Maiden Queen*.

58. The phrase "withouten blame or blot" is Spenser's (Edmund Spenser, *Faerie Queene*, book 2, canto 3, stanza 22, line 3). On the queen as a mediatrix, see, for instance, Hackett, *Virgin Mother, Maiden Queen*, 109, 129.

59. See Hackett, *Virgin Mother, Maiden Queen*, 121–23, 176–80.

10

Shakespeare's Queen Cleopatra

An Act of Translation

RICHARDINE WOODALL

I n *Antony and Cleopatra*, Cleopatra undergoes a Shakespearean
translation from a contemptible whore at the beginning of the play
to a noble queen at the end. This translation is, arguably, the crux
of Shakespeare's vision of her. The word *translation* connotes the
act of rendering a text from one language to another. In translating
from one language to another, a translation can be faithful to the
original text, or alternatively, a translation can treat the original
text in a loose manner. A translator must first "understand" the
text in the original language; after the translator understands the
text, he or she "interprets" the text; language emerges when the
original text is "translated" into the language of the translator.
Shakespeare is not translating his Greek or Latin sources in the
conventional sense; he is not translating them into English. Yet his
interpretation of Cleopatra is so ambivalent that translation best
conveys the problematic nature of his depiction of her. Shakespeare's
interpretation is such that in the early stages of the play, Cleopatra
is portrayed as a woman of vice, and as her life is drawing to an
end, this shifts completely. Is Shakespeare intimating that even at

her most immodest moments, Cleopatra's nobility was latent, or is he equating vice and virtue? That is, is he suggesting that sexual immorality is noble in the acquisition of power?

In this analysis of *Antony and Cleopatra*, my use of translation is threefold: classical Roman and Greek writers translated Cleopatra; that is, the original or historical Cleopatra was transformed to serve the ideological, political, and imperial desires of the Romans.[1] Second, the play itself manifests from Shakespeare's translation of the conventional representations of Cleopatra found in his sources.[2] And finally, we witness Cleopatra's self-translations. Cleopatra translates herself from a slut into a queen.

Antony and Cleopatra covers the entire spectrum of the lovers' relationship, from their first meeting to their deaths. In particular, Cleopatra is viewed as a fickle, promiscuous whore by a chorus of Roman characters. And when in the closing acts, the text shifts to Alexandria after the military defeat of Antony and Cleopatra, the ground is prepared for the sympathetic representation of her. In acts four and five, Cleopatra translates herself into a faithful and loving wife, and a courageous queen who dies to protect Antony's posthumous reputation. This Shakespearean translation endangers the authority of his text to be a conduit of the "real truth" of Antony and Cleopatra. The play leaves the reader unable to decide on any single truth that would make Cleopatra knowable. Our inability to penetrate fully this translation might well be at the center of Shakespeare's vision of Cleopatra, in that Cleopatra herself is enigmatic and protean, and Shakespeare finds her so such that her mystery is our inheritance.

Earlier commentators often read Shakespeare's play in one of two alternative ways. In one reading, the Roman perspective, which dominates in the first three acts, is offered as the meaning of the play. In the other reading, the meaning of the play is found in the

SHAKESPEARE'S QUEEN CLEOPATRA

final two acts in which Antony and Cleopatra are portrayed as transcendental lovers. Both interpretations advance a "transparent" or unified reading. In the last thirty or so years, however, critics have argued that contradiction and indeterminacy are central to the play's meaning. Contradictions in the play implicitly undermine any fixed or transparent meaning of Cleopatra, because the text ambiguously privileges neither the Roman perspective nor the alternative vision of her redemption and transcendence. Indeed it juxtaposes both perspectives without reducing or minimizing their contrariness. For example, Janet Adelman refuses to ignore the inherent difficulties and paradoxes in the play. She recognizes that the power of the poetry can "dazzle our moral sense and undo the structure of criticism in the play" as well as "transform our sympathies toward the lovers, in spite of the evidence of our reason and our senses."[3] The grandeur of the poetry, she continues, "takes unfair advantage of us by befuddling our clear moral judgment. It is that doubtless delightful but nonetheless dubious means by which the lovers are rescued from our condemnation at the last moment" (58).

Cleopatra seems to elude interpretation. R. H. Case asks, "Did Shakespeare intend to leave her a problem . . . or was he unable to make up his mind about her?"[4] M. R. Ridley's solution to the problem of Cleopatra is to throw up one's hands and give in to the spell of the text: "We may attempt to analyse the play, to apply critical criteria to it, to examine the characters, and so on. . . . But in the end . . . we know in our hearts that what in this play Shakespeare has to offer us is a thrill, a quickening of the pulses, a brief experience in a region where there is an unimagined vividness of life; and we surrender, with Antony."[5] The parallel Ridley draws between Cleopatra and the text is important: as Antony does to Cleopatra, we can surrender to the poetic language. And arguably the most majestic and superb poetry in the play describes or is spoken by

Cleopatra. In Cleopatra, we are offered a glimpse of a woman who offers an inconceivable brilliance and magnificence of life.

As attractive as Ridley's idea is, however, Shakespeare's play demands more of the reader than simple surrender. Shakespeare's play compels us to make choices. We are asked to watch, listen, and be witnesses; we are co-opted into being juries and judges. Do we believe the Roman characters? Can we trust in a transcendental Cleopatra? Is the poetry beguiling our senses? Do we agree with some critics that judgment is impossible? Our judgments are put on trial: are they trustworthy? What the play ushers in is a crisis of meaning. The problem with the surrender to the text Ridley advises is that it also means surrendering ourselves to history, and in particular to the Roman vision of history. The transcendental Cleopatra is not the only representation of her in the play. Harsh and debased judgments of Cleopatra challenge the poetic grandeur of the language. She not only out-pictures Venus, but she is also a "whore," a "strumpet" and "cunning."

Enobarbus is a fascinating character through which to assess Shakespeare's translation of Cleopatra from a whore to a noble queen in the fifth act. Whereas to some of the Roman soldiers Cleopatra is a whore, to Enobarbus she is larger than life and breathtakingly beautiful. In his famous barge speech, Enobarbus seems to surrender himself to Cleopatra's magnificence and grandeur.[6] Indeed, Cleopatra's brilliant style and physical allure on the barge appear to beguile the usually satirical and realistically blunt Roman. His memory of Cleopatra on the barge is especially noteworthy not only because it is the first account of her that is not contemptuous or derogatory, but also because his tribute to her occurs well before the final scene of the play. His glowing idealization of Cleopatra in which she out-pictures Venus would appear to recognize Cleopatra's queenship in that he ennobles her image.

In contrast, however, Enobarbus's famous description of a divinely inspiring Cleopatra is actually very complex and contradictory. His presentation of her on the barge partakes of the tendency in western culture to associate women with the body and sexual desire instead of with the mind and political and moral authority. Over the last two millennia, there has been a noticeable transformation of Cleopatra's image from a figure of moral and political author- ity to a fantastic image of male sexual and imaginative desire. His memory of Cleopatra celebrates her as a sexual body open and available for male conquest and penetration. He famously recol- lects Cleopatra's initial seduction of both Antony and the natural elements. As Mary Hamer has noticed, Enobarbus's speech "verges in fact on the pornographic. The supine Cleopatra is, figuratively speaking at least, flagellated with silver oars . . . and the water itself is imagined as subject to sexual arousal by the action of the oars."[7] Similarly, Dympna Callaghan writes of his barge speech that "the image of female soldiers handling tackles is transmuted into a specifi- cally sexual caress that brings the phallic members to the point of tumescence."[8] Arguably, instead of ennobling Cleopatra, Enobarbus fantasizes her into the erotic or oriental other. Enobarbus sexualizes Cleopatra as a woman of pleasure and luxury. In this he partici- pates in a tradition that can be traced back to the ancient Greeks in which Egypt is represented as an alternative Eastern landscape where rapture and sexual license is possible. The goddess of love is a fit analogue for the eroticism of Cleopatra's image.

Enobarbus's magnificent image of Cleopatra as Venus is double- edged. On the one hand, this perspective of Cleopatra as a quasi- divine figure glows with admiration for her physical beauty and irresistible charisma. On the other hand, Cleopatra's association with Venus as well as Antony's with Mars is a commonplace in the Renaissance that unflatteringly pairs them with the cosmic adulterers.

Renaissance mythographers, as did such classical predecessors as Ovid and Lucretius, interpreted Antony and Cleopatra's classical analogues in competing ways. Her association with Venus has both a moral reading that warns us of the dangers of adultery as well as a reading that celebrates her sexual and cosmic grandeur. Indeed, it is important to realize that Venus is not Cleopatra's only classical analogue in the play; she is also paired with Omphale. Antony's classical relative in the text is Hercules; the association between them is quite explicit in the play. The play alludes to the legend of Omphale and Hercules when Cleopatra gaily remembers wearing Antony's sword (2.5.21–23). In Greek myth Omphale was a Lydian queen for whom for three years Hercules was in service dressed as a woman. According to Janet Adelman, in Renaissance interpretations Hercules was "as gigantic in folly as he was in strength and virtue" (*Common Liar*, 81). The play repeatedly reminds us that this famous meeting with Antony which Enobarbus so magnificently remembers is devastating for Antony; not only does he lose his share of the empire, but also Cleopatra separates the once heroic Antony from his *virtus*.[9]

If our task is to locate her emergence into Queen Cleopatra, then Enobarbus's representation of her on the barge is not it. Although his view of her is full of admiration and praise, it is also very complex and not altogether trustworthy. Indeed the scene does not end with Enobarbus's famous description of her on the barge. He proceeds to describe her to the captivated Romans in less-flattering language. The divine image is tarnished some fifteen lines later when he says that

> vilest things
> Become themselves in her, that the holy priests
> Bless her when she is riggish. (2.2.248–50)

Her earlier image is deflated still further when the vulgar Agrippa comments,

> Royal wench!
> She made great Caesar lay his sword to bed.
> He ploughed her,
> and she cropped. (2.2.236–38)

The oxymoron "Royal wench!" is another contradiction central to the meaning of the play, and it also further illuminates the complexity of Enobarbus's vision of her: she is both queen and quean. Furthermore, after his mythologizing description of her, the next time we see Cleopatra is in scene five in which she physically assaults the messenger and causes the terrified man to flee when she draws a knife on him. Enobarbus's divine and erotic image of Cleopatra does not inspire confidence in her as a queen. Here a queen is understood as more than a hereditary title. A queen is a sovereign capable of demonstrating leadership, displaying intellectual acuity, and providing her people with military, economic, and moral guidance. Early in the play, Cleopatra is none of these things. In the first three acts, Cleopatra's identity as a queen is suppressed or buried beneath her sexual appetites. Neither her strong sexuality nor her disastrous effeminization of Antony displays her queenship in a positive light.

Antony and Cleopatra is a very problematic text. Historically, the play, written around 1607, emerges shortly after the transition from the sixteenth to the seventeenth century and from the reign of Elizabeth I to James I, that is, from feminine to masculine leadership and from domestic to foreign rule. These transitions are no small matter in the seventeenth century. The story of Antony and Cleopatra is deeply political; from classical times, their story has often been used as a cautionary tale about the danger of gynocracy.

In this view, Antony's love for the politically powerful and sexually promiscuous Cleopatra is disastrous; his obsession for her enslaves and effeminizes him, and, more calamitously, it leads to civil war and his loss of empire. Whereas the well-ordered state is ideologically associated with ideal images of women, such as the virgin, figures of transgressive women are indicative of moral and political degeneration. Some writers, such as Fulke Greville in the late sixteenth century, drew comparisons between the governments of Elizabeth I and Cleopatra; indeed, Greville admits that he destroyed his play about the lovers out of fear that it might be "construed, or strained to a personating of vices in the present Governors and government," which might bring him into conflict with the state.[10] Thus, the appearance of Shakespeare's ambivalent portrayal of Cleopatra at this historical juncture can be read as the relegitimization and reconfiguration of political power around a king after decades of female rule, or as a nostalgic yearning for the dead Elizabeth.

A principal feature of Shakespearean criticism is that the reign of Elizabeth I and Renaissance feminist disputations on the legitimacy of female rule contributed to the images of Cleopatra that we find in the drama of the period. There are complex links between the two queens. For instance, through several strategies Elizabeth negotiates and transforms political and gender theories. In one strategy, she figuratively assumes the conventional role of the mother, allaying fears that as an unmarried woman she is a threat to patriarchal power.[11] Here too dramatic representations of Cleopatra as mother intersect with Elizabeth's. The dramatization of Cleopatra in such roles as the mother and wife transforms the meaning of her story from the politics of empire building that it was in the classical period to a narrative about the politics of gender. The anomalous situation of Elizabeth, who unlike her sister Mary ruled without a husband, compelled some sixteenth-century political theorists to change their position on female rule. Whereas John Knox exemplifies patriarchal discomfort with female rule when he argues that female rule is "repugnant to Nature" and is a "subversion of good order," the Protestant polemicist John Foxe, for example, defends Elizabeth as a special case.[12] An ardent defender of Elizabeth's right to rule, Foxe argues that God chose Elizabeth to defend a new faith and safeguard the true Church against the corrupt Roman one.[13] Even Foxe remains, however, ambivalent about female rule.

Despite such strategies to ease her subjects' discomfort and fear of her rule, Elizabeth's sovereignty remained in dispute throughout her reign. Her detractors used her sexuality to malign her. In particular, rumors concerning her sexuality labeled her a whore and the mother of numerous illegitimate children.[14] Her sexual degradation was then interpreted to have contaminated the body politic.[15] Rumors of her illicit sexuality and the threat her female rule posed to the body politic are strong parallels Elizabeth shares with the historical Cleopatra. Cleopatra and Elizabeth's enemies actively produced a defamatory discourse that traduced their sovereignty by viciously attacking their sexuality. Cleopatra's Roman enemies slandered her with rumors that she not only had illicit affairs with countless men, but also was so vile and insatiable that she even copulated with slaves.[16]

Shakespeare's translation of Cleopatra must be understood against the backdrop of this defamatory discourse. His translation of her brings into view a critical contrast between a flesh-and-blood woman and her image. Her sexuality as dramatized in the first three acts of the play is vile and contemptible. Antony's loathing and repulsion cannot be clearer than when he flings at her, "I found you as a morsel, cold upon / Dead Caesar's trencher" (3.13.116–17). Yet this is not her only representation in the first half of the play; she also excites, captivates, and bewitches our senses. She is Antony's

... wrangling queen
Whom everything becomes—to chide, to laugh,
To weep; whose every passion fully strives
To make itself, in thee, fair and admired!" (1.1.49–52)

Cleopatra has a full-bodied subjectivity; every emotion has full range in her being. She plays and teases Antony: "He was disposed to mirth, but on the sudden / A Roman thought struck him" (1.2.87–88). She enrages Antony: "You'll heat my blood. No more" (1.3.81). Like a despondent lover, Cleopatra desires to "sleep out this great gap of time / My Antony is away" (1.5.5–6). She indulges in childish games, as Enobarbus recounts: "I saw her once / Hop forty paces through the public street" (2.2.238–39). And, of course, she is highly sexualized: she evokes the sex act when she commands Antony's messenger "Ram thou thy fruitful tidings in mine ears, / That long time have been barren!" (2.5.24–25).

This perspective of Cleopatra is of a woman with zest and zeal for life. She defies any simple or single definition. Antony desires this passionate, flesh-and-blood woman, not "the holy, / cold and still conversation" of the saintly Octavia (2.6.124–25). Shakespeare conveys Cleopatra's sexual potency and irresistible attraction. The image of Cleopatra in the first three acts of the play is a startling and complex combination of full-bodied femininity and fantasy.

In contrast, the flip side of the image of a full-bodied, sexualized femininity is the vile, contemptible whore. The fantastic vision of Cleopatra that Enobarbus memorializes so magnificently is all too easily tarnished. Shakespeare's Cleopatra is acutely aware that in Rome,

Saucy lictors
Will catch at us like strumpets, and scald
rhymers
Ballad us out o'tune. The quick comedians

Extemporally will stage us and present
Our Alexandrian revels; Antony
Shall be brought drunk forth; and I shall see
Some squeaking Cleopatra boy my greatness
I'th' posture of a whore. (5.2.213–20)

This metatheatrical moment breaks the dramatic illusion of verisimilitude. The illusion of verisimilitude is revealed as just that, an illusion. That is the point. No actress or actor, boy or otherwise, can adequately represent the fantasy that is Cleopatra. The fantastic image of a Cleopatra-as-Venus is as fictitious as Roman depictions of her as a whore. Absent, however, in the first half of the text is a corresponding perspective of Cleopatra as queen.

As was the case with the emergence of a defamatory discourse about Cleopatra and Elizabeth's sexuality, an examination of Elizabeth's queenship helps to focus our analysis of Shakespeare's translation of Cleopatra. The magnificence and spectacle that Queen Elizabeth I conjured up in her coronation procession through the streets of London on January 14, 1559, is a useful point of contrast to their absence in Shakespeare's treatment of Cleopatra early in the play. Unlike the dignity and majesty of Elizabeth's ceremonial procession, which translates her from princess into sovereign, Cleopatra's translation does not have a similar effect. Cleopatra kills herself to avoid being in Caesar's triumphant procession through the streets of Rome. Her transformation into Queen Cleopatra does not legitimize her right to rule; all it prepares her for is the grave.

There is one intriguing image that draws the English queen and Shakespeare's into even greater symmetry. In a famous speech before her first Parliament, Elizabeth declared, "And in the end this shall be for me sufficient, that a *marble* stone shall declare that a queen having reigned such a time, lived and died a virgin."[17] As a point of comparison, Shakespeare's Cleopatra, determined to commit suicide following Antony's death, becomes *"marble-constant"* (5.2.239; emphasis added) and filled with "Immortal longings" (5.2.280). Whether or not Shakespeare was familiar with Elizabeth's speech, he may have had the opportunity to view the two statues, which James I had erected to commemorate the memories of the former queen and his late mother.[18] As Katherine Eggert points out, "James's most public act of homage to his two female progenitors served both to equate and to *marbleize* their memories."[19]

Marble might be a beautiful and costly material, but it is also cold, stony, and dispassionate. A marble statue does not merely memorialize something or someone; it also freezes the subject of the representation into a perpetual state of otherness. As Cleopatra prepares to stage her death, Shakespeare transforms her highly sexualized body into a royal, queenly one. At the completion of her translation, her disobedient, subversive, and dangerous body is fixed, frozen, and stabilized into a beautiful and sublime work of fiction.

It is only after Cleopatra's moment of metatheatrical insight that her self-translation begins. That is, Cleopatra transforms herself from the object of others' speculations into the author of her own representation; in this too she resembles Elizabeth.[20] Cleopatra firmly announces,

> My resolution's plac'd, and I have nothing
> Of woman in me: now from head to foot
> I am marble-constant: now the fleeting moon
> No planet is of mine. (5.2.237–40)

The conditions for her transformation into a sublime work of art are now complete:

Give me my robe, put on my crown, I have
Immortal longings in me
. . . .
methinks I hear
Antony call. I see him rouse himself
To praise my noble act. (5.2.279–80, 282–84)

The audience watches as Cleopatra is attired in clothing befitting a sovereign. Shakespeare is dramatizing the metamorphosis of Cleopatra from her physical body into a royal one. Finally, we witness the emergence of Queen Cleopatra, an identity the text has heretofore denied her. It is only in her final moments that she assumes the role of queen. Cleopatra's queenliness is defined by her absence. That is, her sovereignty is dependent on the literal eradication of a full-bodied, sexualized femininity. The precondition for Cleopatra to embody a noble dignity is her literal death. Over the body of her dead mistress, Charmian defends Cleopatra's decision to commit suicide, as "fitting for a princess / Descended of so many royal kings" (5.2.325–26).

Charmian's participation in the staging of her mistress's suicide is central to the success of Cleopatra's self-translation and to Shakespeare's translation of her into a noble, dignified queen. After all of the imperial business of the preceding acts, Shakespeare confines Cleopatra within the monument. The significance of the monument cannot be stressed enough. A monument is a sacred space; it is a holy place of sanctuary. Cleopatra's seizure in the monument is profane. Cleopatra no longer disarms men of their patriarchal sword; instead, Caesar's soldiers use their swords to penetrate her country and sanctuary. The image of Cleopatra as a seemingly helpless victim has replaced the transgressive Cleopatra of the first half of the play. As a result of her capture, Cleopatra is both figuratively and literally brought down; Caesar's guards force her out of the monument. The staging of this scene has been the focus of much critical debate.[21] The image of Caesar's soldiers forcing Cleopatra down from the top of the monument reinforces the magnitude of her fall. From this bitter low, Shakespeare stages Cleopatra's apotheosis. Out of the ignominy of defeat, Shakespeare dramatizes Cleopatra's courageous and noble rise to claim her queenship, and Charmian ensures that Cleopatra's carefully crafted image will be the final one the audience sees.

Unlike the physical monument that King James erected to Elizabeth, Shakespeare constructs an imaginative one. The monuments of these two queens remain, however, vulnerable. James relocated Elizabeth's body from its original resting place and buried her along with her sister Mary in a joint grave. He erected an enormous monument to his mother, Mary Stuart, and placed her tomb directly opposite Elizabeth's smaller one. James was himself buried in Elizabeth's original burial site.[22] In a similar fashion, Shakespeare's Caesar relocates Cleopatra's body from the monument. He instructs his soldiers, "Take up her bed, / And bear her women from the monument" (5.2.355–56). In both cases, the powerful men who succeed these women revise the carefully crafted images these queens meant to be their final ones.

What motivated Shakespeare to translate his sources must remain a mystery. What is apparent, though, is that his translation of Cleopatra frustrates critics. His translation of her might confuse and irritate us, but it cannot be ignored or dismissed. We must return to his Cleopatra again and again, armed with a barrage of questions that all too often yield no satisfactory answers. One nagging question remains above all: has Shakespeare demonstrated that Cleopatra deserves to be monumentalized? For the majority of the text, there is little holy about Cleopatra. In spite of what her detractors say about her, for instance, Elizabeth showed grandeur; she maintained social order; she defeated the Spanish threat; she deserved the monument because she held Parliament, the nation, and the armed forces together. By these standards, Cleopatra's reign seems to be a failure: her army deserted her; she was defeated; her country was annexed. If we consider Elizabeth's other strength, Cleopatra again falls far short. Elizabeth is known famously as the virgin queen; her reign is founded on a significant measure of virtue. Elizabeth's example of virtue is definitely not Cleopatra's hallmark. Since sexual purity does not hold the key to her mystery, perhaps Shakespeare finds virtue in Cleopatra's suicide. Cleopatra tells her Roman captor,

> Know, sir, that I
> Will not wait pinioned at your master's court,
> Nor once be chastised with the sober eye
> Of dull Octavia. Shall they hoist me up
> And show me to the shouting varletry
> Of censuring Rome? Rather a ditch in Egypt
> Be gentle grave unto me! (5.2.51–57)

The crux of Cleopatra's mystery might well be that she speaks to us about freedom. Cleopatra refuses not only to be Caesar's slave but also Fortune's. Throughout the first half of the play, Cleopatra was a fortunate woman. She was endowed with great beauty, seductiveness, intelligence, healthy children, great wealth, and power as well as Antony's love. As her fortunes change, Cleopatra is deprived of not only these things, but also of her freedom. She is Caesar's slave; her will is not her own. As a slave, her will is buried; she cannot show it. She does not have the right to think, travel, or worship as she chooses. She is stripped of everything, not even recognized as queen any longer. Ultimately, Cleopatra refuses to surrender her will. It is this very act of refusal that, arguably, earns her a monument. It is her indomitable will that also snubbed social conventions, such as sexual virtue. Cleopatra's virtue, her efficacious and beneficial quality, is her relentless struggle for freedom. It is only now as she prepares to end her life that Cleopatra ironically shows genuine leadership. Her faithful waiting women, Charmian and Iras, follow her lead and die courageously alongside their mistress. She shows them that self-representation and courageous action are possible modes of being even for the vanquished and the slave.

Shakespeare's magnificent play has received many accolades; Adelman admits that it dazzles her, and Ridley surrenders to the thrill and unimagined vividness it offers. Shakespeare has erected a glorious monument to Cleopatra. He translates her from a "woman" into a "marble-constant" queen filled with "immortal longings"; and although her lover is dead and her enemy has hunted her down, captured, and imprisoned her, she courageously orchestrates her death-scene (5.2.238–39, 280). Shakespeare's monument to Cleopatra is steeped in sociocultural traditions and rituals.[23] Public monuments convey social value. Societies erect monuments to their heroes and heroines; these distinguished men and women are remembered for their noble achievements and ideals. Monuments address the living; they initiate us into acts of remembering events and lives lived; they are public reminders of our past. Every time Shakespeare's play is staged, Cleopatra is revived and remembered. Like Shakespeare's text, monuments leave a record, a trace. Monuments are erected in the face of our inevitable extinction, a defiance of our ephemerality. Shakespeare asks us to remember her. A monument to Cleopatra says that she is worth remembering; it suggests that her death is worth mourning; it asks us to contemplate her value to us as individuals and as a culture.

Notes

1. For comprehensive studies of the historical Queen Cleopatra VII, see H. Volkmann, *Cleopatra: A Study in Politics and Propaganda*, trans. T. J. Cadoux (London: Elek Books, 1958).

2. See G. Bullough, ed., *Narrative and Dramatic Sources of Shakespeare*, vol. 5 (London: Routledge and Kegan Paul, 1964).

3. J. Adelman, "'Nature's Piece 'gainst Fancy': Poetry and the Structure of Belief in Antony and Cleopatra," in *Antony and Cleopatra: William Shakespeare*, ed. John Drakakis (New York: St. Martin's Press, 1994), 57–58. Further citations to this work are given in the text.

4. R. H. Case is quoted in R. M. Ridley, introduction to *Antony and Cleopatra*, by William Shakespeare (London: Methuen, 1965), xxxii.

5. Ridley, introduction to *Antony and Cleopatra*, xlvi–xlvii.

6. William Shakespeare, *Antony and Cleopatra*, ed. J. Wilders (London: Methuen, 1995), 2.2.237–83. Further citations to this work are given in the text.

7. M. Hamer, "*Antony and Cleopatra* through Irigaray's Speculum," in *Antony and Cleopatra*, ed. Nigel Wood (Buckingham: Open University Press, 1996), 57.

8. D. Callaghan, "Representing Cleopatra in the Post-Colonial Moment," in *Antony and Cleopatra*, ed. Wood, 58.

9. See J. Adelman, *The Common Liar; an Essay on Antony and Cleopatra* (New Haven: Yale University Press, 1973), 79–101.

10. Greville is quoted in Bullough, *Narrative and Dramatic Sources*, 216–17.

11. See L. C. Orlin, "The Fictional Families of Elizabeth I," in *Political Rhetoric, Power, and Renaissance Women*, ed. C. Levin and P. A. Sullivan (Albany: State University of New York Press, 1995), 85–110.

12. John Knox, *The Works of John Knox*, ed. D. Laing, 6 vols. (Edinburgh: James Thin, 1895), 4:369.

13. John Foxe, *Acts and Monuments*, ed. Stephen Reed Cattley, 6 vols. (London: R. B. Seeley and W. Burnside, 1938), 4:45.

14. See C. Levin, "Power, Politics, and Sexuality: Images of Elizabeth I," in *The Politics of Gender in Early Modern Europe*, ed. J. R. Brink, A. P. Coudert, and M. C. Horowitz, (Kirksville: Sixteenth Century Journal Publishers, 1985), 96, 100.

15. See C. Levin, "'We shall never have a merry world while the Queene lyveth': Gender, Monarchy, and the Power of Seditious Words," in *Dissing Elizabeth: Negative Representations of Gloriana*, ed. J. Walker (Durham: Duke University Press, 1998), 77–95.

16. See Propertius, *Propertius*, trans. H. E. Butler (Cambridge MA: Harvard University Press, 1962), Elegy XI.

17. Elizabeth's speech is cited in C. Levin, *"The Heart and Stomach of a King": Elizabeth I and the Politics of Sex and Power* (Philadelphia: University of Pennsylvania Press, 1994), 97, emphasis added.

18. It is likely that Shakespeare did know of these statues. See John Bowers, "'I Am Marble-Constant': Cleopatra's Monumental End," *Huntington Library Quarterly* 46, no. 4 (1983): 290.

19. K. Eggert, *Showing Like a Queen: Female Authority and Literary Experiment in Spenser, Shakespeare, and Milton* (Philadelphia: University of Pennsylvania Press, 2000), 137, emphasis added.

20. Right from the beginning of her reign, Elizabeth sought to control her own representations. See Levin, *Heart and Stomach of a King*, 26–28 and 64–65.

21. For a discussion of the staging of the monument scene, see H. Levin, "Two Monumental Death Scenes: Antony and Cleopatra, 4.15; 5.2," in *Shakespeare Text, Language, Criticism: Essays in Honor of Marvin Spevack*, ed. B. Fabian and K. Tetzeli von Rosador (Hildesheim: Olms, 1987), 147–63; E. L. Rhodes, "Cleopatra's 'Monument' and the Gallery of Fludd's Theatrum Orbi," *Renaissance Papers* (1971): 41–48.

22. J. Walker, "Bones of Contention: Posthumous Images of Elizabeth and Stuart Politics," in *Dissing Elizabeth*, ed. Walker, 252–76.

23. See Bowers, "I Am Marble-Constant"; Levin, "Two Monumental Death-Scenes"; and the valuable collection of essays on the monumental tradition in D. M. Reynolds, ed., *"Remove Not the Ancient Landmark": Public Monuments and Moral Value* (Amsterdam: Gordon and Breach Publishers, 1996).

11

"She is the man, and Raignes"

Popular Representations of Henrietta Maria during the English Civil Wars

MICHELLE A. WHITE

On February 22, 1643, Charles I's French, Catholic queen consort, Henrietta Maria, evaded parliamentary forces and landed successfully at Bridlington, a small fishing port perilously situated midway between the parliamentary strongholds of Hull and Scarborough. For the past year, while civil war raged in England, she had been in Holland cultivating alliances, raising funds, and procuring supplies in support of her husband's cause. Despite facing enormous opposition, the queen managed a considerable measure of success. Upon landing she proudly brought with her an astonishing army of 1,000 men and 300 officers, along with 1,000 saddles, £80,000 in cash and armor for 20,000 men.[1] Five months after arriving in Bridlington, Henrietta reunited with her husband at Oxford and remained there with him for the better part of a year. In April 1644, however, fearing the town would be overtaken by parliamentary forces, the (now pregnant) queen was forced to flee. When Charles and Henrietta departed from one another on April 17, 1644 (as it would turn out), the two would never see one another again.

Throughout this fourteen-month period, the queen garnered much attention in the press. This chapter examines the various and complex ways parliamentary newsbooks and pamphlets wrote about her. Unfortunately, by engaging publicly in the civil wars, Henrietta provided her enemies plentiful ammunition. Her actions, schemes, and interference in state affairs, once publicized and commented on, would have catastrophic repercussions; in the end, interpreted through the prism of contemporary gender roles, they served to lower people's respect for Charles and called into question his ability to govern effectively.

However, before examining exactly how antiroyalist newsbooks discussed Henrietta's actions and intrigues, attention first must be given to the particulars of civil war news culture in general.[2] How were newsbooks produced and circulated? How many were produced? For whom were they written? It is to these issues that we must now turn.

Back on July 11, 1637, the Star Chamber decreed the following regulations with regard to printing: before being published, all new books and pamphlets had to be licensed, authorized, and entered into the Stationers' Company Registers Book; printers were required to put up a good faith bond of £300 to ensure they would only print those books lawfully assigned to them; and, finally, the number of master printers was limited to twenty.[3]

These were the most severe censorship regulations yet established; however, when the Court of Star Chamber was itself abolished on July 5, 1641, they were repealed. The upshot of Charles's consent to this was that now, books no longer required the approval of an official licenser before being printed.[4] As a result of this change, the number of new unlicensed and unauthorized publications soared. According to Christopher Hill, "the number of pamphlets published in England shot up from 22 in 1640 to 1966 in 1642—an increase of nearly 9000 percent."[5] Clearly, eliminating the measures by which censorship and licensing laws had been enforced opened the proverbial floodgates.[6]

Newsbooks in particular can safely be said to have reached virtually every part of England and beyond. From London, parliamentary newsbooks were distributed as far as Scotland, the Isle of Wight, France, and even the Americas.[7] From Oxford, the royalists' newsbook *Mercurius Aulicus* had a substantial print run as well as a wide circulation thanks to the help of a network of carriers and spies.[8]

Without doubt, throughout the 1640s, London was the country's main generator of news. There, people collected and spread news in shops, in streets, in markets, at fairs, in taverns, in restaurants, and at church.[9] From London, news regularly made its way to the countryside. In fact, one civil war newsbook, *The Parliament Scout*, specifically identified provincials as among its target audience. John Dillingham, its editor, wrote that he stood "ingaged to Country friends . . . For their satisfaction."[10] The post (established in 1635) and individual carriers were chiefly responsible for circulating printed works throughout the provinces, but armies also passed on printed news as they moved about the country.[11]

Joad Raymond has identified literate people from all social classes, including members of parliament, academics, merchants, traders, journalists, and poets as among those who read and collected newsbooks.[12] Unfortunately, determining the number of people who were capable of reading at the time is difficult. Literacy scholars and historians estimate that in the 1640s about 30 percent of the national adult male population were literate, but this could be as high as 70 percent in urban areas.[13] For women, the national average was 10 percent but as high as 15 percent in major cities.[14] Nevertheless, these statistics, based almost exclusively on signatures on loyalty oaths, should be used with care. As Margaret Spufford has argued, many of the poorer classes never learned to write, but did learn to read.[15]

Another important point to consider is that many newsbooks were designed to be read aloud.[16] The style of two in particular, *The Welch Mercury* and *Mercurius Britanicus*, gives the impression that they were written with this purpose in mind. The former is significant in the history of journalism because it was the only paper written in the Welsh vernacular.[17] The latter used conversational prose and, in Raymond's words, an "oral-animated style" of writing.[18] Unquestionably, then, members of the literate classes read newsbooks aloud to the illiterate.

News was also spread through ballads, poems, jokes, and rhymes (often with politically and religiously laden messages) which were read, sung, or spoken in alehouses, fairs, markets, and streets.[19] Finally, it cannot be overlooked that some people (perhaps mostly the illiterate) gleaned news from the papers by "reading" their politically and religiously themed woodcuts, engravings, and pictures. In assessing readership, then, it is clear that the printed text reached not only the powerful and educated but those lower down the social scale as well.

We know that civil war newsbooks and pamphlets were effectual because the sheer scale of their production alone indicates that writers and publishers on both sides regarded them as valuable propaganda tools. Most newsbooks in the 1640s probably had an average print run of five hundred copies but could reach as high as 3,000.[20] Clearly, there was a demand for the material; otherwise, production levels would never have reached these heights. However, just because there was a demand for the material, and people purchased newsbooks, read them (alone or aloud to others), discussed them, and passed on the information, does not mean that they always shared the opinions of the authors. Gauging the influence of the press or the "impact of news" is notoriously difficult.[21] In some cases, civil war pamphlets helped mould public opinion; in other cases they helped reflect it (no doubt they expressed the judgments of the authors). There is also the possibility that pamphlets and newsbooks had no effect on a reader's (or listener's) views. Ultimately, people tend to believe whatever they are predisposed to believe. But this we do know of civil war pamphlets and newsbooks: first, a socially heterogeneous group purchased, read, collected, discussed, and circulated them; second, quite often the educated classes referenced them in correspondence; and third, both royalists (including the king himself) and parliamentarians considered them important enough to respond to what was printed in them. So, with all this in mind, let us turn our attention back to Henrietta Maria, with the primary concern of determining how contemporary pamphleteers discussed the queen, her activities, and her relationship with the king.

Antiroyalist pamphlets repeatedly commented on the undue influence Henrietta allegedly held over Charles, a charge levied against the royal couple that predated the outbreak of hostilities.[22] Subsequent to her return to England in 1643, it was often stated that she anticipated a reunion with her husband not because of her love for him, or because she was anxious to see him again after more than a year's absence, but rather to frustrate any progress the king and Parliament were making toward peace.[23] Clearly, for many parliamentarians, the queen's very presence was seen as the greatest obstacle to any settlement with the king. In this vein *The Kingdomes Weekly Intelligencer* remarked that the queen objected to an accommodation of any kind and was dissuading the king from making peace. As such, she was the cause of "all our calamities and miseries."[24] *A Continuation of Certain Speciall and Remarkable Passages* similarly observed "that there can bee no treaty of peace agreed upon at Oxford without the counsell and advice [of the queen and the] Jesuiticall faction about her."[25] An issue of *A Perfect Diurnall* agreed, concluding how virtually nothing was to be done "without her approbation and consent."[26] The same criticism is found in yet another tract entitled, *Accommodation Cordially Desired, and Really Intended*:

> The Queen has now attained to a great height of power as formidable as she is to us, in regard to her sex, in regard to her Nation, in regard of her disposition, in regard of her family, in regard of her Religion, and lastly, in regard of her ingagements in these present troubles; some think shee has an absolute unlimitable power over the Kings sword and Scepter; which if it bee so, no end of our feares and calamities can be, no propositions can profit us, no Accommodation can secure us.[27]

Other pamphlets commented in more general terms on the queen's influence. Published letters between the royal couple left several authors concluding that "great and eminent places of the Kingdom were disposed by her advice and power," and that "the King referreth all affaires to the Queene, and is directed by her Counsel and advice."[28]

But why was such influence seen as so objectionable? An accusation made against Henrietta, and constantly repeated in parliamentary pamphlets, was that as a Catholic, her goal was to return England to Rome.[29] Indeed, this recurring theme that Henrietta was at the centre of a great popish plot to subvert the Protestant faith and the liberties of Englishmen became daily inspiration for dozens of pamphlets and broadsheets during the spring and summer of 1643. "At the entrance of Queene Mary to the Crowne," so one publication read, "great protestations were made to maintaine the Protestant Religion, but we see her actions were destructive to it."[30] The writer enjoined all to "seeke unto God by fasting and praying [to be saved from] the King misled in his Authority by his Queene."[31]

From the outset the queen's army was referred to as that "Popish Army," not only because it comprised papist and recusant soldiers, and had been raised with the help of Catholic contributions, but also because of the cause it was believed to be championing.[32] Evidently, some enlisted men in the Northern Army accepted this view. One report stated that many Protestant soldiers of the East and North Ridings deserted the royalist party "because the Queene would have a new Popish Standard carried in the front of the Army."[33]

Reports of her traveling through England "with an army of outlandish Papists to destroy the religion of the Land, and bring in Popery" continued throughout 1643.[34] In May, *A Continuation of Certain Speciall and Remarkable Passages*, informed readers that the queen "hath brought over forraigne forces, set up her standard in the North, and doth daily raise and maintaine forces of Armed men in this Kingdom against the Parliament, and thereby a great Army of Papists are raised in the North to destroy Parliament and the Protestant Religion."[35]

But accounts not only linked the queen to a sinister Catholic/popish plot, they also drew a tight connection between her and the rebels in Ireland. One long passage from *The Parliament Scout* printed in late June serves to sum up all the charges levied against the king's wife:

That Shee hath countenanced and maintained that horrid . . . Rebellion now on foot in Ireland, whereby many thousand Protestants have been barbarously murdured . . . That Henrietta Maria had traiterously and wickedly conspired with Popish Priests, to subvert the Protestant Religion, and to introduce Popery, and for these ten yeares hath advanced the power and jurisdiction of the Bishop of Rome . . . That she hath by severall wayes and meanes

> traiterously assisted and maintained this unnaturall warre against
> the Parliament and Kingdome of England . . . Hath provided
> monies and armes, pawned and sold the Jewels of the Realm . . .
> Hath brought over with her, not only Armes and Ammunition,
> but strangers and forraigners, and is her selfe at the head of the
> Popish Army.[36]

Clearly, such accounts were used to incite readers against the
queen to the fullest, and to a certain extent, it worked. The Henrietta
Maria presented in parliamentary propaganda was a foreign, bossy,
politically influential Catholic who dominated her husband and in-
terfered in public affairs with the ultimate goal of "re-Catholicizing"
England. But how close was this to reality? Certainly, Henrietta was
foreign and she was a Catholic. She was also a spirited, ambitious,
energetic, and strong-willed woman who made her views on matters
of state known to her husband. As such she presented parliamentary pamphleteers an easy target. But as to the last charge, did she
really hope to use her influence with the king to convert England
back to Catholicism? Curiously, no former historian of Henrietta
has considered this crucial question for the period of the civil wars,
no doubt because it is so difficult to answer. In all probability, the
queen was by this time no longer aiming to sway the king or his
Protestant subjects to Catholicism, and an obscure letter from Hugh
Bourke, the Commissary of the Irish Friars Minors in Germany and
Belgium, to Rome helps illustrate why.

As early as May 1642 Bourke wrote of having met with the queen
on several occasions at The Hague to discuss affairs in England and
Ireland, particularly the plight of Irish Catholics. During the course
of one of their conversations, Henrietta assured the commissary that
"the King has no inclination whatever to the Catholic faith."[37] She
further related that the best course of action for Catholics was for
them to make "moderate demands, not amounting to the entire and

public restoration of the Catholic Religion, or the exclusion of all Protestants."[38] In the end, the queen promised to do all that was in her power with His Majesty, for as Hugh Bourke explained, "she is willing to serve the Catholics, but fears to vex the King."[39]

This incident suggests Henrietta had become a political realist. Whilst back in 1625 she may have been sent to England to, in the words of her godfather, Pope Urban VIII, be the "Esther of her own oppressed people," and whilst during the pre–civil war period, as Caroline Hibbard has effectively argued, she and her "Catholic party" at court genuinely engaged in bona fide "popish plotting,"[40] changing circumstances resulted in the queen's political maturity. Now, evidently, her first duty was to the king, defending him and his prerogatives, and a close second was her desire to achieve a measure of *toleration* of Catholicism in her husband's kingdoms. Contrary to parliamentary pamphleteer accusations, she was not trying to return England to Rome.

During the one-year period when the royal couple were together at Oxford, parliamentary propagandists continued to criticize Henrietta, but on a much more personal level. The subject of the queen's ill health is one such example. Throughout the autumn of 1643, various London pamphleteers reported that the queen was "troubled with a deafnesse."[41] Just how accurate this reporting was is open to question, as no corroborating evidence seems to exist. By April 1644 several antiroyalists were reporting that the queen had died or at least had had a miscarriage, apparently as the result of injuries incurred from a terrible fall.[42] Though these rumors were later discovered to be untrue, her critics did not refrain from passing comment. One pamphlet wrote of how the queen had gone to her chapel to pray for a cavalier victory at Cheriton; the bruises she received as a result of a fall she took upon leaving the chapel were interpreted as God's punishment: "as if God Almightie had told her Majestie how vain such prayers are against his peoples, whose enemies should be thus crushed and bruised."[43] Another, *The Scotish Dove*, speculated that rumors of the queen's death, or her delivery of a stillborn child, might or might not be true but added the snide comment: "she may (if God please) live to be a better woman, and then she will be fitter for death, and heaven."[44] A later edition printed in mid-May tried to settle the matter with a "correct" account, but its writer could not resist the opportunity to denounce the queen: "Many severall reports have formerly beene divulged of the Queenes death, and then of her miscarriage, and of her childs death, all which I never beleeved, nor published any thing of it: onely I had an assured confidence of some miscarriage by her, but it was in the Kindgomes affaires, not of her child."[45] A similar tack was taken the next month in the *Court Mercurie*. Hearing that the queen was "in a deep Consumption," the editor wrote, "she has indeed beene consuming, and has brought the Kingdome into as weake a condition as her selfe."[46] Such reports did not abate after Henrietta had escaped to France. In early September, *Mercurius Britanicus* made the following comment about a ruptured imposthume under the queen's right breast: "I could wish that all her Corruption might be drawne out of her."[47]

Admittedly, these comments were little more than cheap shots. A much more prominent and damaging theme in anti-Henrietta tracts at this time revolves around the issue of gender, specifically the queen's perceived domination over royalist policies. "Never was a whole Junto so infatuated, so led about by the Apron strings," *Mercurius Britanicus* printed in late March: "they dare do nothing, Vote nothing, Act nothing, but first they send out a Privado, and he was to know if it be her Majesties pleasure . . . was there ever such a company of Lords and Gentlemen, that pretend to State affairs, and yet not daring to speake without leave from hoods and petticoats."[48] A later issue reported in a similar vein, telling how people commonly complained, "she is the man, and Raignes."[49]

The queen, for her part, appears not to have taken great offence at such bad press, and it did not deter or intimidate her. Doubtless she was offended that a queen of England could be openly criticized and attacked, but she was not cowed. Furthermore, being unpopular was certainly not new to her, nor was it something that was of particular concern. She had one ultimate goal in mind: to help crush the parliamentarians, and in the process ensure the preservation of her husband's (and her children's) traditional hereditary rights and privileges. She flatly rejected anything that might infringe on monarchical authority and would labor tirelessly to preserve it at all costs. "God forgive them for their Rebellion," she wrote to the Duke of Hamilton in May 1643, "as I assure you I forgive them from my Heart for what they do against Me, and [I] shall ever continue, as I have promised."[50]

The king too made an effort to publicly defend himself and his wife. Galled that his enemies had intercepted, read, and published with scathing commentaries the royal couple's private correspondence, the king lashed out in a formal declaration: "[I] cannot but deplore the Condition of the Kingdome," Charles wrote, "when Letters of all Sorts, of Husbands to Wives, even of His Majesty to His Royall Consort are intercepted, read, brought in Evidence, and publisht to the world."[51] In an attempt to set the record straight (regarding his asking the queen for advice) and to clear himself of any wrongdoing, the king asserted: "That in Places there named in which her Majesties Advice may seeme to be desired, are in not places (as they call it) of the Kingdome, but private meniall Places, a Treasurer of the Household, a Captaine of the Pensioners, and a Gentleman of the Bed-Chamber; That concerning the other more publique Places, His Majesty absolutely declares Himselfe, without leaving Roome for her Advice."[52]

The king's declaration can hardly be considered a resounding defense of the queen; indeed, he downplays her efforts and significance. Charles may have been hoping to shelter his wife from further criticisms, but it also may have been his desire to cover his own tracks. Charles must have realized what was insinuated in parliamentary pamphlets—how could he not? Was it not implied that he was a weak husband and sovereign governed by his wife's counsel?

Be that as it may, Charles's rather dilatory defense of his wife's role at court does raise an important, though vexing, question: What was the accepted role of a queen consort in early modern England? Unquestionably, first in importance was for a queen consort to produce a male heir or, failing a son, a daughter. In this case, Henrietta performed her queenly/wifely duties admirably, for by the time civil war broke out, six heirs were alive: three boys (Charles, James, and Henry) and three girls (Mary, Elisabeth, and Anne). Nevertheless, as Frances Dolan has pointed out, even on this count the queen suffered retribution. She contends that Henrietta's fecundity actually intensified fears about her influence and power. After all, the birth of so many children advertised to the nation the full extent of Charles and Henrietta's intimacy.[53]

Second, a queen consort was expected to conform to certain socially accepted female behavioral standards: (as with any wife) she was supposed to be obedient, passive, submissive, chaste, pious, kind, and deferential. Henrietta's enemies never seriously questioned her chastity, but clearly, they did not regard her as obedient, passive, kind, and deferential. Additionally, they may have considered her pious, but in the wrong religion. Third, the queen was also important for her role as a social leader. Throughout the period of Charles's personal rule, Henrietta exercised a significant influence on moral values, recreations, and tastes in the fine arts.[54]

Finally, a queen consort was supposed to play a formal, symbolic, and ritualistic role, staying completely out of the business of government. The prevailing presumption was that even though a queen consort enjoyed a special legal position, she did not hold sovereign authority. Therefore, she best served the king, and the nation, by disappearing into the background. After all, women in general were regarded as weak by nature and not supposed to interfere in public affairs; to do so would jeopardize the nation and its moral fabric.

One of the underlying assumptions in Charles's explanation to Parliament, however, is the idea that it was perfectly acceptable for his wife to have personal influence (in "private meniall Places," as the king explained) but not for her to have significant political influence ("publique Places," to use the king's phrase).[55] In other words, from Charles's perspective, his wife should be permitted a legitimate "behind-the-scenes" role in helping to staff the court; but this is a terribly thorny issue. During the period of Charles's personal rule Henrietta was an important source of patronage at court, and she used her position as wife of the king to influence appointments. Troubles arose when critics of the king realized that those appointments took on a public, political significance. It must be acknowledged that key members of the queen's inner circles (men like Henry Jermyn, Henry Rich, George Goring, and Henry Percy) were elevated to highly significant government and military posts, often based on her recommendations.[56] The problem, as far as her detractors were concerned, was that the queen had overstepped (or had been permitted to overstep) her proper bounds; her traditionally sanctioned apolitical role had been expanded into a political one—in effect, the personal had been made political, and this was completely out of order.

This examination of the broader culture of politics, as expressed in pamphlets and broadsheets, forces us to acknowledge that for many English men and women, Henrietta's active presence in the war was a crucial factor in fuelling fears of popery and in spreading anxieties about the king's ability to rule effectively. Her ill-starred interference in the political affairs of England was indeed a contributing factor to the rising antimonarchical sentiments that led to Charles's downfall.

Over and over again antiroyalist pamphleteers continued to present the king as a weak, obsequious husband dominated by his foreign-born, Catholic wife. Because of Henrietta Maria, patriarchy, hierarchy, and the established Church of England were threatened. Rather effectively, parliamentarian propagandists drew on common misogynistic opinions of the time, and anxieties about the growth of popery, and pulled them into the debate to communicate to the broader nation the need to rebel against the king. This was a clever strategy, because such fears were not only believable but cut across all class boundaries as well.

Ultimately, then, the queen's interference in affairs of state had a serious impact. Largely because of her, Charles lost the aura of irreproachable legitimacy that normally would have engendered respect for a monarch; instead, he was seen as submissive and weak, and unfit to be a king. Henrietta's political prominence, sexual "power," and religious fervor fused together in propagandists' writings to degrade and diminish the Crown. Unintentionally, Charles's wife inspired a degree of hatred against the royal couple they no doubt could have avoided had Henrietta been a Protestant, as well as a more docile and respected queen consort.

Notes

I am grateful to Ashgate Publications for granting me permission to use portions of my book *Henrietta Maria and the English Civil Wars* (2006) in this volume.

1. *Calendar of State Papers and Manuscripts Relating to English Affairs, Existing in the Archives and Collections of Venice: and in other Libraries of Northern Italy*, ed. H. F. Brown and A. B. Hinds (London: Longman, Green, Longman, Roberts, and Green,

1864–1947), 26:252; P. Newman, "Royalist Armies in Northern England" (PhD thesis, University of York, 1978), 127. An account published in London on December 30, 1642, gives us some idea as to where a portion of this cash came from. *The Queenes Proceedings in Holland. Being the Copie of a Letter sent from the Staple at Middleborough to Mr Vancode a Dutch Marchant in London* (London: Printed by T. F. for I. M., December 30, 1642), Thomason Tracts (hereafter, TT) E 83(33), sig A3r, tallies the following donations Henrietta received from "Priests, Jesuites, Seminaries, Friers, Nuns, and holy sisters": from the Colleges at St. Omers, £3,000, plus £5,000 more "gathered from the Governors of every Towne, Village, or petty Dorpe." Unfortunately, these types of pamphlets were notoriously inaccurate, and I have been unable to independently verify the amounts against other, more reliable, sources.

2. The best accounts on this subject are: J. Raymond, ed., *Making the News: An Anthology of the Newsbooks of Revolutionary England, 1641–1660* (Gloucestershire: Windrush Press, 1993), and his *The Invention of the Newspaper* (Oxford: Clarendon Press, 1996); C. Clair, *A History of Printing in Great Britain* (Oxford: Oxford University Press, 1966); F. S. Siebert, *Freedom of the Press in England, 1476–1776* (Urbana: University of Illinois Press, 1965); J. Frank, *The Beginnings of the English Newspaper* (Cambridge MA: Harvard University Press, 1961).

3. On licensing and entry into the Stationers' Company Registers Book, see T. E. Scrutton, *Laws of Copyright: An Examination of the Principles Which Should Regulate Literary and Artistic Property in England and Other Countries* (London: John Murray, Albemarle Street, 1883), 82–83. On the good-faith bond of £300, see D. Zaret, *Origins of Democratic Culture: Printing, Petitions, and the Public Sphere in Early Modern England* (Princeton: Princeton University Press, 2000), 143. On the number of master printers, see D. F. McKenzie, "Printers of the Mind: Some Notes on Bibliographical Theories and Printing-House Practices," in *Making Meaning: Printers of the Mind and Other Essays*, ed. D. MacDonald and M. F. Suarez (Boston: University of Massachusetts Press, 2002), 59.

4. "The Act for the Abolition of the Court of Star Chamber," printed in S. R. Gardiner, *Constitutional Documents* (Oxford: Oxford University Press, 1899), 170–86.

5. C. Hill, *Some Intellectual Consequences of the English Revolution* (London: Weidenfeld & Nicholson, 1980), 49. The breakdown of censorship and its consequences are also examined in Hill's "Censorship and English Literature," in *Writing and Revolution in Seventeenth-Century England* (Brighton: Harvester Press, 1985), 32–71, and A. Patterson, *Censorship and Interpretation: The Conditions of Writing and Reading in Early Modern England* (Madison: University of Wisconsin Press, 1984).

6. Siebert, *Freedom of the Press*, 203.

7. Raymond, *The Invention of the Newspaper*, 240–41.

8. Raymond, ed., *Making the News*, 333.

9. See Raymond, *Invention of the Newspaper*, 238; R. Cust, "News and Politics in Early Seventeenth-Century England," *Past and Present*, no. 112 (August 1986): 70; T. Cogswell, *The Blessed Revolution: English Politics and the Coming of War, 1621–24* (Cambridge: Cambridge University Press, 1989), 22–24; W. Notestein, "John Chamberlain," in *Four Worthies: John Chamberlain, Anne Clifford, John Taylor, Oliver Heywood* (New Haven: Yale University Press, 1957), 31–32; A. Fox, "Rumour, News and Popular Political Opinion in Elizabethan and Early Stuart England," *Historical Journal* 40, no. 3 (1997): 603–4.

10. *The Parliament Scout*, July 13–20, 1643, TT E 61(13), 25. This newsbook had a print run from June 26, 1643, to January 30, 1645. It was published by George Bishop and Robert White and edited by John Dillingham (Frank, *Beginning of the English Newspaper*, 46).

11. Raymond, *Invention of the Newspaper*, 238; I. Gentles, *The New Model Army in England, Ireland, and Scotland, 1645–1653* (Oxford: Blackwell, 1992), 325.

12. Raymond, *Invention of the Newspaper*, 243–44.

13. D. Cressy, *Literacy and the Social Order: Reading and Writing in Tudor and Stuart England* (Cambridge: Cambridge University Press, 1980), chaps. 4, 6, and 7.

14. Cressy, *Literacy and the Social Order*, chaps. 4, 6, and 7.

15. See M. Spufford, "First Steps in Literacy: The Reading and Writing Experiences of the Humblest Seventeenth-Century Spiritual Autobiographers," *Social History* 4 (1979): 407–35; T. Watt, *Cheap Print and Popular Piety, 1550–1640* (Cambridge: Cambridge University Press, 1991), 7–8; K. V. Thomas, "The Meaning of Literacy in Early Modern England," in *The Written Word: Literacy in Transition*, ed. G. Baubann (Oxford: Clarendon Press, 1986), 102–3; and T. Laqueur, "The Cultural Origins of Popular Literacy in England, 1500–1800," *Oxford Review of Education* 2, no 3 (1976): 255–75.

16. Raymond, *Invention of the Newspaper*, 31–32, 35, 154, 159; Frank, *Beginnings of the English Newspaper*, 48–49; and K. Lindley, "London and Popular Freedom in the 1640s," in *Freedom and the English Revolution: Essays in History and Literature*, ed. R. C. Richardson and G. M. Ridden (Manchester: Manchester University Press, 1986), 115.

17. Frank, *Beginnings of the English Newspaper*, 36.

18. Raymond, *Invention of the Newspaper*, 158.

19. D. Freist, *Governed by Opinion: Politics, Religion and the Dynamics of Communication in Stuart London, 1637–1645* (London: Tauris Academic Studies, 1997), 127, 147.

20. Frank, *Beginnings of the English Newspaper*, 57; Raymond, *Invention of the Newspaper*, 233–38.

21. R. Cust, "News and Politics in Early Seventeenth-Century England," 69.

22. For Henrietta's actual and perceived influence over Charles predating the Civil Wars, see my *Henrietta Maria and the English Civil Wars* (Aldershot: Ashgate, 2006), chaps. 1 and 2.

23. The Treaty of Oxford was the most significant attempt at peace negotiations throughout the winter and early spring of 1643.

24. *The Kingdomes Weekly Intelligencer* (hereafter, *KWI*), July 25–August 1, 1643, p. 86, TT E 63(1).

25. *A Continuation of Certain Speciall and Remarkable Passages*, May 18–25, 1643, p. 4, TT E 104 (6).

26. *A Perfect Diurnall of Passages in Parliament*, May 22–29, 1643, last page, TT E 249 (10). See also, May 15–22, 1643, last page, TT E 249 (8).

27. *Accommodation Cordially Desired, and Really Intended*, London, May 15, 1643, p. 15, TT E 101(23).

28. For "great and eminent places," see *The Proceedings in the Late Treaty of Peace Together with Severall Letters of His Majesty to the Queen* (London: Edward Husbands, May 17, 1643), p. 83, TT E 102(6). For "the King referreth all affaires to the Queene," see *Certaine Informations, From Severall Parts of the Kingdome* (hereafter, *CI*), May 8–15, 1643, p. 132, TT E 101(24).

29. *Accommodation Cordially Desired*, 15.

30. *The Plotts Revealed And The Parliament Vindicated* (London: Printed for F. Coles and F. Leach, August 4, 1643), p. 9, TT E 63(20). Queen Henrietta Maria was known to all her subjects as Queen Marie (pronounced Mary). Initially, Charles had selected Queen Henry for her, but, for reasons not entirely clear, this was later changed to Marie/Mary. Apparently, Charles had hoped, "the land should find a blessing in that name" (Lucy Hutchinson, *Memoirs of the Life of Colonel Hutchinson*, ed. Julius Hutchinson [London: Jurst, Rees, and Orme, 1806], 69).

31. *Plotts Revealed And The Parliament Vindicated*, 20.

32. *A Continuation of Certain Speciall and Remarkable Passages*, March 23–30, 1643, p. 5, TT E 247(12); *Mercurius Aulicus* (hereafter, *MA*), July 16–22, 1643, p. 386, TT E 63(2).

33. *CI*, March 27–April 3, 1643, p. 82, TT E 94(29).

34. *MA*, July 9–15, 1643, p. 369, TT E 62(3). For general mention of the "popish army," see also *KWI*, May 30–June 6, 1643, p. 182, TT E 105(24); *KWI*, March 14–21, 1643, TT E 93 (19); and *KWI*, June 27–July 4, 1643, TT E 59 (11).

35. *A Continuation of Certain Speciall and Remarkable Passages*, May 18–25, 1643, p. 4.

36. *The Parliament Scout*, June 20–27, 1643, TT E 56(7), 4–5.

37. Hugh Bourke to Luke Wadding, O.S.F., Guardian of St. Isidore's Rome, May 10, 1642, Reports of the Royal Commission on Historical Manuscripts: *Report on Franciscan Manuscripts* (Dublin, 1906), 138.

38. Hugh Bourke to Luke Wadding, *Report on Franciscan Manuscripts*, 138.

39. Hugh Bourke to Luke Wadding, *Report on Franciscan Manuscripts*, 139.

40. Mary Anne Evertt Green, ed., *Letters of Henrietta Maria* (London: Richard Bentley, 1857), 7; C. Hibbard, *Charles I and the Popish Plot* (Chapel Hill: University of North Carolina Press, 1983).

41. *The Kingdomes Weekly Post, with his packet of Letters*, November 22, 1643, p. 16, TT E 76(22), and December 28, 1643–January 4, 1644, p. 148, TT E 80(9). This newsbook lasted (on and off) from November 1643 to 1648. See Frank, *Beginnings of the English Newspaper*, 54; *Remarkable Passages, of the Occurrences of Parliament, and the proceedings of the Armie*, December 8–15, 1643, sig. A4r, TT E 78(18).

42. THE WEEKLY ACCOUNT, April 3–10, 1644, sig A5v, TT E 42(3).

43. OCCURENCES of *Certain Speciall and Remarkable Passages in* PARLIAMENT, *and the affaires of the Kingdome* (London: Printed for Andrew Coe, April 5, 1644), p. 5, TT E 40(26). OCCURENCES lasted until October 1649. See Raymond, *Invention of the Newspaper*, 37; Frank, *Beginnings of the English Newspaper*, 57, 69.

44. *The Scotish Dove*, April 5–12, 1644 (London: Printed according to order for L.C.), pp. 207–8, TT E 42(16).

45. *The Scotish Dove*, May 17–24, 1644, pp. 249–50, TT E 49(19).

46. *The Court Mercurie*, July 10–20, 1644, sig. C3r, TT E 2(25).

47. *Mercurius Britanicus* (hereafter MB), September 2–9, 1644, p. 396, TT E 8(21).

48. MB, March 18–25, 1644, p. 219, TT E 39(5).

49. MB, July 15–22, 1644, p. 347, TT E 2(31).

50. Henrietta to the Duke of Hamilton, May 23, 1643, printed in Gilbert Burnet, *The Memoirs of the Lives and Actions of James and William, Dukes of Hamilton and Castleherald* (London, 1677), 229.

51. HIS MAJESTIES DECLARATION *To all His loving Subjects . . . upon the . . . severall Intercepted Letters of His* MAJESTY *to the* QUEENE, *and of* PRINCE RUPERT *to the Earl of North-Hampton* (Oxford: Leonard Lichfield, June 3, 1643), p. 26, TT E 104(31).

52. HIS MAJESTIES DECLARATION, p. 27.

53. F. Dolan, *Whores of Babylon: Catholicism, Gender, and Seventeenth-Century Print Culture* (New York: Cornell University Press, 1999), 130–36.

54. See, for example, E. Veevers, *Images of Love and Religion: Queen Henrietta Maria and Court Entertainments* (Cambridge: Cambridge University Press, 1989); V. Hart, *Art and Magic in the Court of the Stuarts* (London: Routledge, 1994); R. M. Smuts, *Court Culture and the Origins of a Royalist Tradition in Early Stuart England* (Philadelphia:

University of Pennsylvania Press, 1999); K. Britland, *Drama at the Courts of Henrietta Maria* (Cambridge: Cambridge University Press, 2006); and I. Atherton and J. Sanders, eds., *The 1630s: Interdisciplinary Essays on Culture and Politics in the Caroline Era* (Manchester: Manchester University Press, 2006).

55. *HIS MAJESTIES DECLARATION*, p. 27.

56. K. Sharpe, *The Personal Rule of Charles I* (New Haven: Yale University Press, 1992), 168–79.

12

Sex and the Single Queen

*The Erotic Lives of Elizabeth Tudor
in Seventeenth-century England*

MARJORIE SWANN

Although she died in 1603, Elizabeth I was, culturally, very much alive in Stuart England. We can, for example, analyze seventeenth-century English political ideologies by tracing writers' attitudes toward the queen of famous memory. Thus Andrew Marvell, in a republican mood, declared in 1675, "A Tudor a Tudor! wee've had Stuarts enough; / None ever Reign'd like old Besse in the Ruffe."[1] Other seventeenth-century writers, by contrast, assessed the nature of the Tudor queen by contemplating Elizabeth's career below "the Ruffe." John Watkins has recently contextualized Stuart depictions of Elizabeth's sexual status—from the nationalistic, Protestant virgin to the frustrated lover—within "the bourgeois state's emergence from absolutism"; according to Watkins, by the end of the seventeenth century, Elizabeth's love life was reinvented to uphold emerging ideologies of affective marriage and domesticity.[2] As Carole Levin has demonstrated, such creative interest in the queen's sexual history was widespread during Elizabeth's own lifetime, when rumors regularly depicted the queen as producing illegitimate children or, quite to the contrary, suggested she was physically incapable of bearing children at all. Levin sees such rumors as symptomatic of the early modern period's misogynistic construction of gender and believes that they served to relieve cultural anxiety in the face of a powerful woman by either depicting Elizabeth as a whore or suggesting that she was physically flawed.[3]

In this essay, I shall build on these pioneering assessments of the depiction of Elizabeth I by analyzing Stuart representations of the queen's nonreproductive sexuality. Elizabeth reigned during an era in which gender, sexuality, and reproduction were conceptually bound together. It was traditionally understood that God had created the female sex to allow men to reproduce, the purpose of sexual activity was thus procreation, and such activity should take place only within marriage. Because it was believed that women must experience orgasm in order to conceive, female sexual pleasure did have a place in this system of beliefs; however, neither men nor women were supposed to pursue sexual gratification for its own sake. Thus, in the Tudor period, the begetting of legitimate children, not physical pleasure, was, theoretically, the raison d'être of female sexuality.[4] Certainly during her lifetime, attempts to prod Elizabeth to marry were rooted in the related concept of what Valerie Traub terms "reproductive alliance": Elizabeth was to marry and have sex with her husband not for the sake of her sensual fulfillment, but rather so that she would produce a child-successor.[5] Thus, Elizabeth's sexuality was often imagined by her contemporaries in terms of this normative equation of marriage, sex, and reproduction. Many of the attacks on the queen during her lifetime similarly worked within this reproductive paradigm of female sexuality. Elizabeth bore children out of wedlock and was thus a whore; she killed her bastards and was thus a murderess as well as a whore: such slanderous depictions of the queen aligned her sexuality with reproduction and upheld, by counterexample, the social value placed on the chaste wife producing and nurturing children within marriage.

However, not all representations of Elizabeth's love life were so firmly rooted in this normative vision of married, reproductive female sexuality. In analyzing Elizabethan representations of the queen, especially the "Armada" portrait, Valerie Traub argues that Elizabeth's chastity was sometimes depicted as the site of a self-pleasuring female eroticism.[6] Helpfully complicating our understanding of the relationship between chastity and sexuality, Traub suggests that we find in such sixteenth-century portrayals of Elizabeth structures of female eroticism that are *queer*, that is, "eccentric to patriarchal marriage."[7] In this paper, I would like to develop one obvious implication of Traub's groundbreaking work: simply put, in early modern England, Elizabeth's sexuality could be imagined as unrelated to reproduction. The point of this essay is thus not to make a statement about Elizabeth's actual sexuality— the nature of which must remain as much a matter of speculation as it was in her own day—but instead to show the wide possibilities and implications according to which it was constructed during the early modern period. In the seventeenth century, I shall argue, some writers found in Elizabeth's life story narratives that question the traditional alignment of gender, sexuality, and reproduction. To that end, I shall examine several texts that depict, in different ways, a "queer" Elizabeth, a queen whose sexuality exists outside the patriarchal sex/gender system.

Many Stuart tributes to Elizabeth focus on the monarch's standing as "the Virgin Queen." For Elinor James, writing in 1687, the queen's celibacy constituted an admirable form of asceticism, since Elizabeth "denied her Self that blessed happiness of Marriage."[8] Such accounts of Elizabeth's virginal self-renunciation clearly uphold traditional patriarchal norms. At other times, however, Elizabeth is represented as escaping from a reproductive social order altogether—to the greater good of her subjects. In the anti-Stuart pamphlet *The Humble Petition*, the English people call on Elizabeth for relief from the abuses of Stuart rule. Elizabeth, now residing in Heaven, cannot help but savor the irony of the situation, and she reminds the petitioners that during her lifetime, the people "lusted for a King" instead of appreciating their just and competent queen. Turning the tables further on the petitioners, Elizabeth describes the pain the English people now endure in terms of another experience they had yearned for, in vain, during Elizabeth's lifetime: childbirth.

> Your sorrowes yet alas, like womens throwes
> Doe come and goe, but there will follow blowes,
> Ere England will be delivered, it will make
> Your very entralls bleed, your soules to quake,
> The time shall come when bravest mindes shall mourne
> And children wish they never had beene borne.[9]

Neither male monarchs nor fecundity, it turns out, are so desirable after all.

Stuart assessments of the cultural meaning of Elizabeth's virginity could undermine traditional concepts of female sexuality in other ways as well. As a crucial component of the patriarchal sexual economy, early modern virginity was constructed as a temporary state, a premarital way station fleetingly occupied before a woman arrived at her socially approved destination of chaste, legitimate motherhood. From this perspective, a woman who permanently embraced virginity opposed her society's sexual norms. Theodora Jankowski argues that during her lifetime, Elizabeth's own rhetoric of uniqueness, by setting her apart from all other women, prevented her virginity from challenging traditional concepts of reproductive female sexuality, and Kathryn Schwarz concurs that "if the queen is an exception to the general condition of women, and reinforces patriarchy from that position, she embodies a triumph of male-identified power."[10] But what happens if a writer depicts the Virgin Queen not as a patriarchy-enforcing exception but as a new, disruptive sexual norm? In *A Chaine of Pearle. Or, A Memoriall of the Peerles Graces, and Heroick Vertues of Queene* Elizabeth, *of Glorious Memory*, published in 1630, the poem's author, Diana Primrose, praises Elizabeth's "impregnable Virginity" that "Throughout the World Her Fame did dignify." Primrose goes on to extol Elizabeth's virginal chastity as

> a Document to all,
> The Pearle of *Chastity* not to let fall:
> Into the filthy durt of foule Desires,
> Which Satan kindles with his Hell-bred fires.

Primrose concludes,

> For whether it be termed Virginall
> In Virgins, or in Wives stil'd Conjugall,
> Or Viduall [i.e., befitting a widow] in Widdowes, God respects
> All equally, and all alike affects.[11]

Here, of course, Primrose praises the different forms of chastity suitable for the different life stages of a virtuous early modern woman. By depicting Elizabeth as a poster girl of chastity for *all* women, however, Primrose questions both Elizabeth's anomalous status as the Virgin Queen and the supposedly temporary nature of virginity. In portraying Elizabeth's virginity as exemplary rather than exceptional, Primrose offers her readers a model of female chastity that could provide them with an escape from patriarchal norms. As Schwarz argues, in the early modern period "virginity is always at least potentially an alternative and radical mode of sexuality"[12]; should the virginal Elizabeth truly become "a Document to all" women, she could theoretically inspire the entire female sex's renunciation of marriage.

So far, then, I have suggested that some Stuart writers represented the chaste Virgin Queen in ways that threatened to dismantle traditional constructions of virtuous, reproductive female sexuality. Other writers, by contrast, conjured up images of an Elizabeth who was threatening because she was *not* truly chaste. Edmund Bohun opined in 1693 that although Elizabeth had endured "injurious Reports" about her personal life, the queen was, in effect, Teflon-coated and "as easily washed off that slanderous Infamy, which was one of the most raging Crimes of the Age, by the incredible Continence and Chastity of her whole Life."[13] But Bohun's assessment does not do justice to the many salacious narratives about Elizabeth's sexuality that flourished in the seventeenth century. In some of these stories, authors repeat earlier assertions that because of a physical abnormality, Elizabeth was unable to engage in procreative sexual intercourse. Sir John Harington had reported in 1602 that the queen had "in body some indisposition to the act of marriage," and nearly two decades later, Ben Jonson similarly declared that the queen "had a Membrana on her which made her uncapable of man, though for her delight she tryed many."[14] Like Harington, Jonson focuses on the queen's physicality as the key to understanding her sexual behavior. In Jonson's account, however, the queen's prophylactic body becomes the site of an extramarital, nonprocreative female eroticism: Elizabeth took pleasure in sexual activities with men that could not lead to pregnancy. This vision of the queen enjoying nonprocreative erotic practices likewise appears in accounts of the queen's postmenopausal sexuality. Francis Bacon observed in 1608 that the queen "allowed herself to be wooed and courted, and even to have love made to her; and liked it; and continued it beyond the natural age for such vanities."[15] In a similar vein a half-century later, Francis Osborne depicts the queen as striving both to foster and exist in a constant state of arousal, "apter both in her selfe and others to kindle the flames of Love, then quench them." According to Osborne, the queen's zest for such erotic excitement lasted well into old age. Osborne censoriously describes the elderly monarch's "amorous caresses, which age and in a manner an universall distribution of them had by this time rendered tedious if not loathsome," and Osborne darkly hints that even as a senior citizen, Elizabeth, "for her delight," sexually "tryed many" of the younger men at court: *Minions were not so happy as vulgar judgment thought them, being frequently commanded to uncomely and sometimes unnaturall imployments."*[16] Despite the misogynistic and ageist biases of these narratives, I would argue that we find in such comments the basis of a potentially radical separation of female eroticism from normative concepts of gender and sexuality.

It is from this perspective that we should analyze the playwright John Banks's provocative depictions of Elizabeth's love life. We know little about Banks's biography. Born in the early 1650s and trained as a lawyer, Banks "quitted the more profitable Practice of the Law, for some Years, in pursuit of the Bays, till Experience convinc'd him of his Error."[17] Banks apparently began pursuing the bays in the late 1670s by writing conventional dramas about tragic heroes of classical antiquity. When Banks failed to stage his third tragedy (because, it seems, actors refused to appear in it), the writer changed artistic course and in the 1680s began to create what would later be dubbed "she-tragedies."[18] Developing the focus of Restoration tragedy on individuals racked by private suffering, Banks's she-tragedies explore the emotional distress of innocent but doomed female protagonists.[19]

By creatively reinventing the past, Banks found sixteenth-century English history filled with she-tragedy heroines—including Lady Jane Grey, Anne Boleyn, and Mary Stuart—but it was the malleable figure of Elizabeth Tudor who was central to Banks's new tragic vision. In his first she-tragedy, *The Unhappy Favourite*, produced in 1681, Banks depicts Elizabeth as tormented by her hidden love for the Earl of Essex. Manipulated and betrayed by those she trusts, Elizabeth allows Essex to be executed for treason, unaware that he had sought her pardon. When she realizes that she has been duped into executing the man she adores, Elizabeth can only lament that God chooses to "punish" her by giving her "but a Humane Soul" with which to endure "his hardest Task of Rule."[20] In his next play, *Vertue Betray'd* (1682), Banks transforms Elizabeth's mother, Anne Boleyn, into a she-tragedy heroine; but even in this unlikely setting, Elizabeth again appears as a character, assuming the form of a preternaturally loquacious infant who pleads, unsuccessfully, with Henry VIII to spare her mother's life.

It is in Banks's she-tragedy *The Island Queens*, however, that we find the playwright's most innovative portrayal of Elizabeth. In this play, Banks revises Tudor history to fashion both Elizabeth Tudor and Mary Stuart as tragic heroines. *The Island Queens* initially focuses on the doomed Duke of Norfolk's love for Mary, but our attention soon shifts to Elizabeth instead. During the course of the drama, as in *The Unhappy Favourite*, Elizabeth is ill-served by her advisors, this time tricked into signing Mary's death warrant. To create a narrative awash in she-tragedy pathos, Banks must ensure that Elizabeth is emotionally tortured by her action, and he does so by rewriting not only past events but Elizabeth's sexual history as well: in *The Island Queens*, Elizabeth I and Mary, Queen of Scots, fall passionately in love with each other and engage in a torrid but tragically brief love affair. If, as Valerie Traub suggests, scholars need to "take a closer look, not only at the politics and poetics of heterosexual desire enabled by Elizabeth, but the homoerotics as well," we should analyze carefully Banks' depiction of the queen's same-sex eroticism.[21]

It is in Banks's play that Elizabeth Tudor and Mary Stuart meet for the first time.[22] Indeed, Banks is so keen on this aspect of his historical revisionism that he contrives to have the cousins meet not once, but twice. During their initial face-to-face encounter, the women are immediately captivated by each other. As she first embraces Mary, Elizabeth cries,

> Throw thy lov'd Arms as I do mine about thee,
> And never feel less Joy than I do now.
> Oh, 'Tis too great, it is unspeakable!
> Cleave to my Breast, for I want words to tell.[23]

Intriguingly, it is Mary's evocation of the conjugal relationship between her grandparents that elicits Elizabeth's passionate response:

> The beauteous *Margaret*, your Royal Aunt,
> Whose right and lawful Grand-daughter I am,
> Met not my Grand-father, the valiant *James*,
> With such a scornful and revengeful Brow;
> For if she had, I never had been born,
> And you not known the hated Queen of *Scotland*. (37)

Visions of married, procreative sex and the whiff of incest seem to act as an aphrodisiac for Elizabeth. But in *The Island Queens*, marriage is consistently described as inferior to the passionate bond the royal cousins share. Earlier in the play, a character describes marriage as a cynical exercise in financial strategy:

But now Love's bought, and Marriage grown a Trade,
Estate and Dower are in the Ballance weigh'd;
Love still was free till Pride broke in by stealth,
And ne're a Slave till undermin'd with Wealth. (27)

Further denigrating marriage, the Queen of Scots finds her previous experience of married bliss lacking in comparison to her love for Elizabeth:

Pleasures fill my Breast.
Mine were not half so great when I espous'd,
And threw these Arms about young *Francis* Neck,
And laid me down the Queen of half the World. (38)

After spending the night with her cousin, Elizabeth describes her relationship with Mary in highly charged, unmistakably erotic terms:

'Twas but last Night she had another Prison;
When she did throw her Arms about my Neck,
Her cheeks laid close to mine, methought I drew
Such Sweets as *Eden's* Flowers send up to Heav'n,
Whilst from her Lips flew warm *Arabian* Sighs,
And from her Eyes a Shower of Pearls ran down;
Then with a Tone, sweet as an Angels voice,
Now let me dye, she said, 'tis all I wish,
Since I have her within my Arms I love.
And she protests, and says, she loves me too. (47–48)

While marriage becomes in the play a foil for the passion Elizabeth and Mary feel for each other, the women also use a discourse of reproduction and maternity to express the intensity of their emotional bond. Elizabeth portrays her love for Mary in terms of procreation, promising that "Each moment shall beget, each hour bring forth

/ Fresh Pleasures and rich Welcomes to delight her," (39) and as the play reaches its tragic conclusion, both women describe their emotional desolation as a kind of maternal bereavement. Elizabeth compares her response to the loss of Mary with the impassioned sorrow of a mother mourning the horrific death of her child:

> She's gone, dragg'd from me by the cruel Laws,
> Nor can I tear her from these Vultures Claws,
> But oh, like the distracted Mother roar,
> Whose Child a Wolf had from its Cradle bore,
> Hast's to its Aid, and all the way does complain,
> Speaks the Beast kind, till hearing as 'a flies,
> Betwixt his Teeth, her tender Infants Cries;
> Then she adds wings, and in her Flight does rave,
> With eager Hopes its precious Life to save;
> But finds the Monster with her Bowels gor'd,
> And in her sight, its panting Limbs devour'd (53).

Similarly, Mary aligns her downcast state with her grief at losing her son:

> He whom I bore wrack'd from these tender Bowels,
> Scarce blest his joyful Mother for her Labour,
> With his first Infant Beams, but was by Villains,
> Like little *Romulus*, from this Bosome torn,
> And nurst with Wolves. (67)

Their lives no longer grounded in early modern norms of gender and sexuality, Elizabeth and Mary experience a homoerotic love that surpasses the emotional and erotic rewards of marriage, the intensity of their relationship comparable only to a mother's primal love for her child.

In *The Island Queens*, Banks thus revives—and revises—a

sixteenth-century fantasy of Anglo-Scottish alliance. Scotland's queen was, of course, always a source of anxiety in Elizabethan England, and William Cecil daydreamed of the perfect solution that could peacefully unite the two kingdoms: "God could not have blessed these two kingdoms with greater felicity, than, if one of the two queens had been a king."[24] Cecil's sentiment was shared by Nicholas Throckmorton, who yearned in 1559 "that one of these Queens of the Isle of Britain were transformed into the shape of a man, to make so happy a marriage as thereby there might be an unity of the whole isle," and Mary Stuart likewise joked that she and Elizabeth could have married—if one of them had been a man.[25] But it was Elizabeth Tudor who imagined a narrative most like the one invented by John Banks. While conversing with the Spanish ambassador in 1564, Elizabeth inquired about the recently widowed princess Juana of Portugal, "saying how much she should like to see her." Elizabeth then envisioned living happily with Princess Juana as her spouse, with no need for sex-change operations: Elizabeth imagined "how well so young a widow and a maiden would get on together, and what a pleasant life they could lead. She (the Queen) being the elder would be the husband, and her Highness [Princess Juana] the wife. She dwelt upon this for a time."[26] In dramatizing the kind of alternative domestic history fantasized by Elizabeth herself, John Banks thus disassembles the components of the holy trinity of early modern female experience—marriage, procreative sexuality, and motherhood—and rearranges them according to a new, nonreproductive logic of same-sex passion and mutuality.[27]

Although he was able to publish the play in 1684, Banks was forbidden to stage *The Island Queens*. According to Banks's own account, Charles II, after insisting upon a few "judicious Amendments," had initially been disposed to allow the play to be produced, but, under the influence of some "evil Spirits" who "incens'd the

King with a wrong Interpretation of the Scenes, or of the Story," Charles later reversed himself and deemed the play unstageable.[28] Given the anti-Catholic sentiment unleashed by the Exclusion Crisis, it seems likely that the play was banned because of Banks's sympathetic portrayal of Mary, Queen of Scots, and indeed, Banks notes that the king's "Royal Brother"—the Catholic James, Duke of York, whom anti-Catholic factions wished to exclude from the succession—felt that the tragedy should be produced.[29]

In 1704, however, a version of the play apparently revised by Banks himself and now entitled *The Albion Queens* was staged. Reportedly, Banks persuaded a "nobleman" to petition Queen Anne on the play's behalf, and, assured by this "noble person" that *The Albion Queens* was in "every way an innocent piece," the queen allowed it to be produced.[30] The play was subsequently performed more than sixty times by 1779, making it "one of the most popular tragedies of the eighteenth century."[31] Although the advertisement for *The Albion Queens* disavowed the text's earlier incarnation as "wholly incorrect, and imperfect,"[32] the plot remains largely the same as it first appeared in 1684. Throughout *The Albion Queens*, however, Banks's earlier evocations of transgressions against norms of gender and sexuality are toned down or removed: Elizabeth is neither compared to an Amazon (*IQ*, 29) nor termed a "*She-Harry*" (*IQ*, 24), and the deception she experiences at the hands of her advisors is no longer described as the rape of a virgin (*IQ*, 64). By moderating the diction of *The Island Queens*, Banks also recasts the relationship of Elizabeth and Mary in a more muted, ambiguous form. Most strikingly, Banks removes from his text the highly charged, detailed descriptions of physical intimacy between Elizabeth and Mary that we find in *The Island Queens*: in the later play, Elizabeth no longer savors memories of Mary's embraces, the touch of her cheek, and her declarations of love during the night they spent together (*IQ*,

SEX AND THE SINGLE QUEEN

47), while Mary no longer offers to embrace Elizabeth and "sow fresh Kisses where my last are fled" (*IQ*, 49). Although it was the drama's relationship to high politics that led to the censorship of *The Island Queens* in the late seventeenth century, Banks modified his play's sexual politics as he prepared it for the approval of Queen Anne. If, as Jayne Elizabeth Lewis suggests, Banks thus rendered his Albion queens "more delicate and domesticated," he also made their relationship much less overtly erotic.[33] Despite being married and frequently pregnant, Queen Anne identified with Elizabeth, adopting her motto *Semper Eadem* and dressing in imitation of the Virgin Queen's portraits; and later in her reign, Anne's close friendships with female favorites would fuel attacks on the queen's sexual propriety.[34] Perhaps under these circumstances Banks judged it advisable to modify his earlier depiction of a homoerotic Elizabeth I. So much for *Semper Eadem*.

As we have seen, many seventeenth-century depictions of Elizabeth question patriarchal norms of female sexuality. Whether portrayed as beneficently childless, an exemplary virgin, or a passionate yet nonreproductive woman of diverse erotic appetites, Elizabeth Tudor led many "queer" lives in seventeenth-century England. These latter narratives, I would argue, do not function simply as manifestations of misogyny, for writers like Francis Osborne and John Banks also invite us to consider how female sexuality might be ideologically severed from procreation: portrayals of a sexually active, unmarried and child-free Elizabeth thus explore different modes of nonreproductive female sexuality. Appearing as they did during an era in which the emergence of companionate marriage was beginning to drive a conceptual wedge between sexuality and procreation, such accounts of Queen Elizabeth's love life took on new cultural significance in the century after her death. Puritan theorists in the 1620s suggested that sex within marriage could serve purposes other than procreation: William Gouge, for example, advised that husbands should continue to have intercourse with their pregnant wives, since "Conception is not the only end of this duty: for it is to be rendered to such as are barren," while Thomas Gataker remarked that "If Children bee a Blessing, then the root whence they spring ought much more to bee so esteemed."[35] By envisioning Elizabeth as a woman who sought nonprocreative erotic fulfillment outside marriage, Stuart writers further examined how female sexuality might be experienced solely for the sake of pleasure, not reproduction. In their portrayals of an unmarried, childless queen who could occupy multiple structures of eroticism, seventeenth-century authors thus created in Elizabeth I a figure who defied the sexual norms of both an absolutist order predicated on lineage and a domestic sphere of companionate marriage. Yet, as Banks's revision of *The Island Queens* suggests, there were limits to the ways in which the Tudor queen's love life could be portrayed in Stuart England. Thus, by imagining herself leading a "pleasant life" while married to another woman, Elizabeth I entertained a vision that was still dangerously radical generations—and, we might attest, centuries—later.

Notes

1. Andrew Marvell, "A Dialogue between the Two Horses," in *The Poems and Letters of Andrew Marvell*, ed. H. M. Margoliouth et al., 3rd ed., 2 vols. (Oxford: Oxford University Press, 1971), 1:212, lines 149–50. On the dating of the poem, see 415.

2. J. Watkins, *Representing Elizabeth in Stuart England: Literature, History, Sovereignty* (Cambridge: Cambridge University Press, 2002), 174.

3. C. Levin, *"The Heart and Stomach of a King": Elizabeth I and the Politics of Sex and Power* (Philadelphia: University of Pennsylvania Press, 1994), 66–90.

4. On early modern notions of the relationship between sexuality and reproduction, see M. R. Sommerville, *Sex and Subjection: Attitudes to Women in Early-Modern Society* (New York: Arnold, 1995), 114–18. On the biomedical understanding of the role of female orgasm in procreation, see A. McLaren, *Reproductive Rituals: The Perception of Fertility in England from the Sixteenth Century to the Nineteenth Century* (New York: Methuen, 1984), 13–29.

5. V. Traub, *The Renaissance of Lesbianism in Early Modern England* (Cambridge: Cambridge University Press, 2002), 22.

6. Traub, *Renaissance of Lesbianism*, 154.

7. Traub, *Renaissance of Lesbianism*, 153.

8. Elinor James, *Mrs. James's Vindication of the Church of England in an Answer to a Pamphlet Entituled A New Test of the Church of England's Loyalty* (London, 1687), 9.

9. *The Humble Petition of the Wretched, and Most Contemptible, the Poore Commons of England, To the Blessed* ELIZABETH *of Famous Memory* (London, 1642), 12. The anonymously authored pamphlet was written during James's reign (Watkins, *Representing Elizabeth*, 98).

10. T. A. Jankowski, *Pure Resistance: Queer Virginity in Early Modern English Drama* (Philadelphia: University of Pennsylvania Press, 2000), 3–8, 198; K. Schwarz, "The Wrong Question: Thinking through Virginity," *differences: A Journal of Feminist Cultural Studies* 13, no. 2 (2002): 21.

11. Diana Primrose, *A Chaine of Pearle. Or, A Memoriall of the Peerles Graces, and Heroick Vertues of Queene* Elizabeth, *of Glorious Memory* (London, 1630), 4. Lisa Gim observes that throughout her poem, Primrose presents Elizabeth as an "intellectual and ethical model for her sex," and Gim argues that in her account of Elizabeth's chastity, Primrose subverts "traditional representations of chastity as merely virginity preserved for a husband's or father's possession" ("'Faire *Eliza's* Chaine': Two Female Writers' Literary Links to Queen Elizabeth I," in *Maids and Mistresses, Cousins and Queens: Women's Alliances in Early Modern England*, ed. S. Frye and K. Robertson [New York: Oxford University Press, 1999], 188, 192).

12. Schwarz, "Wrong Question," 17.

13. Edmund Bohun, *The Character of Queen Elizabeth* (London, 1693), 72.

14. Sir John Harington, *A Tract on the Succession to the Crown* (New York: Burt Franklin, 1970), 40; Ben Jonson, *Conversations with Drummond*, in *Ben Jonson*, ed. C. H. Herford and P. Simpson, 11 vols. (Oxford: Oxford University Press, 1925), 1:142. Jonson's conversations with Drummond date from 1619.

15. Francis Bacon, *In felicem memoriam Elizabethae*, in *The Works of Francis Bacon*, ed. J. Spedding, R. L. Ellis, and D. D. Heath, 14 vols. (London: Longmans, 1857–74), 6:317.

16. Francis Osborne, *Historical Memoires on the Reigns of Queen Elizabeth and King James* (London, 1658), 32–33.

17. Gerard Langbaine and Charles Gildon, *The Lives and Characters of the English Dramatick Poets* (London, 1699), 6. My account of Banks's life and works also draws on David Wykes, "John Banks," in *Dictionary of Literary Biography, Volume*

80: Restoration and Eighteenth-Century Dramatists, 1st ser., ed. P. R. Backscheider (Detroit: Gale, 1989), 3–13.

18. The term *she-tragedy* was first used by the editor and playwright Nicholas Rowe in 1714 (Wykes, "John Banks," 4).

19. On the subgenre of she-tragedy, see J. I. Marsden, *Fatal Desire: Women, Sexuality, and the English Stage, 1660–1720* (Ithaca NY: Cornell University Press, 2006), 60–99.

20. John Banks, *The Unhappy Favourite, or The Earl of Essex*, ed. T. M. H. Blair (New York: Columbia University Press, 1939), 77. On Banks's adaptation of the contemporary "secret history" narrative of Elizabeth's relationship with Essex, see D. Wykes, "The Barbinade and the She-Tragedy: On John Banks's *The Unhappy Favourite*," in *Augustan Studies*, ed. D. L. Patey and T. Keegan (Newark: University of Delaware Press, 1985), 79–94.

21. Traub, *Renaissance of Lesbianism*, 152.

22. M. Dobson and N. J. Watson, *England's Elizabeth: An Afterlife in Fame and Fantasy* (Oxford: Oxford University Press, 2002), 101.

23. John Banks, *The Island Queens: Or, The Death of Mary, Queen of Scotland. A Tragedy (1684)*, intro. J. E. Lewis. Augustan Reprints, 265–66, William Clark Memorial Library and UCLA Center for Seventeenth- and Eighteenth-Century Studies (New York: AMS, 1995), 37. Future references to *The Island Queens* (*IQ*) are to this edition, and page numbers are included, in parentheses, in the text.

24. Quoted in J. E. Lewis, *Mary Queen of Scots: Romance and Nation* (London: Routledge, 1998), 24.

25. Quoted in L. S. Marcus, *Puzzling Shakespeare: Local Reading and Its Discontents* (Berkeley: University of California Press, 1988), 97.

26. *Calendar of Letters and State Papers Relating to English Affairs, Preserved Principally in the Archives of Simancas*, ed. Martin Hume, 4 vols. (Nendeln, Lichtenstein: Kraus Reprint, 1971), 1:364.

27. By contrast, John Watkins, one of the few scholars to analyze the play's same-sex eroticism, aligns *The Island Queens* with the emerging values of middle-class domesticity, finding in the women's relationship "the bourgeois fantasy of a retreat from the public world first into the household, but ultimately into the self" (*Representing Elizabeth*, 181).

28. Banks, *The Island Queens*, Epistle Dedicatory, n.p.

29. Banks, *The Island Queens*, Epistle Dedicatory, n.p. On the Exclusion Crisis, see R. O. Bucholz and N. E. Key, *Early Modern England, 1485–1714* (Malden MA: Blackwell, 2004), 282–86. Banks's she-tragedy about Lady Jane Grey, *The Innocent Usurper*, was also banned, first in the early 1680s and again in the 1690s; it seems Banks's story of

how religious strife shaped the Tudor succession was as politically unpalatable under William and Mary as it was under Charles II.

30. D. E. Baker, I. Reed, and S. Jones, *Biographia Dramatica; or, a Companion to the Playhouse*, 3 vols. (London, 1812), 2:336.

31. J. E. Lewis, introduction to *The Island Queens*, iv. This was not the first time Banks had tried to elicit Anne's approval for his work, as he had dedicated *The Unhappy Favourite* to her when she was still a princess. The text of *The Albion Queens* was first published in 1714 and frequently reprinted after that date.

32. J. Milhous and R. D. Hume, ed., *A Register of English Theatrical Documents, 1660–1737*, 3 vols. (Carbondale: Southern Illinois University Press, 1991), 1:378.

33. Lewis, *Mary Queen of Scots*, 96.

34. On Anne's self-fashioning as Elizabeth I, see E. Gregg, *Queen Anne* (New Haven: Yale University Press, 2001), 96, 152. Elizabeth Susan Wahl argues that the "insinuations of lesbianism that began to emerge in partisan attacks" on Queen Anne demonstrate how same-sex female relationships were regarded with increasing anxiety after the Restoration (*Invisible Relations: Representations of Female Intimacy in the Age of Enlightenment* [Stanford: Stanford University Press, 1999], 121).

35. Quoted in McLaren, *Reproductive Rituals*, 15–16.

13

The "Stomach of a Queen," or Size Matters

Gender, Body Image, and the Historical
Reputation of Queen Anne

ROBERT BUCHOLZ

The year 2002 marked the 300th anniversary of the accession of Queen Anne. Unlike 2003's extravaganza of Elizabethan necrophilia, which saw three major international exhibits and a host of commemorative publications, the accession anniversary of the first and last Stuart queen of Great Britain passed virtually without notice, even by the academic world.[1] There were but two conferences, one in Florida, the other in Portugal, and seemingly no significant commemorative publications.[2]

Of all the women who ever ruled in Britain, Queen Anne is probably the most obscure. Most educated people know—or think they know—the others: Mary I as a pathetic monster of religious bigotry and cruelty—the "Bloody Mary" of legend; Mary, Queen of Scots, as beautiful but capricious, glamorous but inept; Elizabeth I as an unattainable mistress of Renaissance realpolitik and improbable feminist icon; and Victoria as a sober-sided matron and unthreatening constitutional monarch. In every case, the achievements and failures of the reign in question have been popularly attributed, either directly or indirectly, to the virtues and defects of each ruler's personality. Indeed, the two success stories in the above list—Elizabeth and Victoria—became symbols of the nation while they lived and gave their names to their eras after they died.

In contrast, Queen Anne has made little impact on our collective historical consciousness, whether popular or professional. Most of the styles and objects named after her—lace, bodices, chairs, even houses—have nothing to do with their namesake. Nor did Anne get to lend her name to her period, which is generally called Augustan after some long-dead Roman Emperor. In short, Queen Anne lacks even her own adjective.

And yet it was during Anne's reign that the British state strode onto the European stage to assume a position of leadership that it would retain, for good or ill, for two centuries. When Elizabeth died in 1603, despite the Armada victory, England was at best a second-rate power still under threat from larger neighbors, but when Anne died in 1714, following the victories of Marlborough and the gains of Utrecht, Britain was the arbiter of Europe. Historians and their readers have generally absolved Anne of responsibility for this. The achievements of her reign have been credited to her subjects, accomplished independently of the stolid presence on the throne. In the words of Justin McCarthy, "When we speak of the age of Queen Anne we cannot possibly associate the greatness of the era with any genius of inspiration coming from the woman whose name it bears." Or, as Beatrice Curtis Brown argues in her lugubriously entitled *Alas, Queen Anne*: "Anne as a historical pivot does not exist."[3]

Those who have noticed the last Stuart queen have rarely been complimentary. Fairly typical is the following passage from a current (and, it must be said, generally judicious) survey of English history:

> Princess Anne, daughter of James II, ascended the throne in 1702.
> She was 37 years old, exceedingly fat, red and spotted in complex-
> ion, and wracked by gout. She had to be carried to her coronation.
> She was slow-witted, uninformed, obstinate, and narrow-minded;
> yet also pious, sensible, good-natured, and kind. She bore fifteen
> children and buried them all. She loved the Church and those who
> defended it, but had no interest in art, music, plays, or books. Her
> one hobby was eating; her husband's, drinking.[4]

Despite the rehabilitative efforts of her definitive biographer, Edward Gregg, and other scholars of the caliber of G. S. Holmes and W. A. Speck, this has remained the dominant view of Anne for most of the past 300 years.[5] It has been enshrined in the most learned scholarly treatises and in such popular entertainments as *The First Churchills* and even Monty Python's *Yellowbeard*—in which the last Stuart sovereign of Great Britain suffers the supreme indignity of being played for laughs by a man in drag.

Elizabeth I versus Anne: Setting the Distaff High

Why have historians and their readers discounted Anne? One obvi-ous answer is gender prejudice: as much recent work has reminded us, political power is generally constructed as male.[6] But, then, what are we to make of the continuing popularity of Elizabeth I? The last Tudor is the one female ruler of a British kingdom who has been almost universally praised by professional historians and the general public alike. But this does not necessarily disprove the rule. It might be argued that Elizabeth's qualities of courage, boldness, steadfast-ness, duplicity, and a witty—even sharp—tongue have all appealed to traditional historians and their readers not least because these are virtues traditionally associated with effective male rulers—and, indeed, with "alpha" males generally.[7] The queen's contemporary, William Camden, argued that "by [her] manly cares and counsels, she surpassed her sex," while a more recent biographer asserts that her "assured self-confidence and assertive will were wholly masculine."[8] When Elizabeth has been criticized, it has tended to be for indecisiveness—a traditional attribute of the stereotypical female.[9] She herself portrayed the essential quality of her own gender, in the famous Tilbury speech, as being "weak and feeble."[10] In other words, if Elizabeth *is* the one generally approved female ruler of England, it may be because, having successfully obscured or minimized her gender, she is widely credited with "the heart and stomach of a King," that is, of really being a man inside a woman's body. In short, our love affair with Gloriana may not show us in quite the feminist light that we may think it does.

In contrast, Anne Stuart could never have been mistaken for anything but a woman, and she appears never to have flirted with gender-bending of any kind.[11] Instead, she projected the contemporary ideal of the good housewife: she was well known to be quiet, shy, thrifty, pious, and happy in her marriage to Prince George of Denmark. These qualities have not played well with posterity: in the words of the Earl of Chesterfield, "Queen Anne had always been devout, chaste and formal: in short, a prude."[12] And yet, these attributes, so easily disparaged, rendered her more successful than any other ruler of her line. Reticence saved her from the charges of frivolity that plagued James I and Charles II. Thrift kept her household relatively small and, in contrast to nearly every one of her predecessors, her debts low. Her Anglican piety was popular, viewed by many as a welcome change from Charles II's moral lassitude and James II's and William III's heterodoxy. The happiness of her marriage added to her popularity, and again contrasted with that of both her libertine uncle and her father. And if she was less intelligent than other monarchs who made a mess of the country—Henry VIII comes to mind—she possessed a far larger share of common sense. Perhaps cognizant of her limitations, she delegated her war to the greatest soldier of the age, John, Duke of Marlborough; her treasury to one of its greatest financial minds, Sidney, Earl of Godolphin; and the management of her parliaments to its greatest political operator, Robert Harley, later Earl of Oxford. Politicians found Anne to be anything but a nonentity, but, rather, stubborn and tough. As she wrote to Godolphin during the struggle over the appointment of the Earl of Sunderland as Secretary of State in 1707: "Whoever of the Whigs thinks I am to be hectored or frighted into a compliance, though I am a woman, is mightily mistaken in me. I thank God I have a soul above that, and am too much concerned for my reputation to do anything to forfeit it."[13] If these are not the qualities we look for in our heroes, that may say as much about us as it does about Anne.

Sarah, Duchess of Marlborough, versus Anne: The Limits of Sisterhood

One might expect that a new generation of historians, sensitive to gender and versed in feminist theory, would have engineered a rescue of the last Stuart queen, but a cursory reading of the literature suggests that they do not quite know what to make of Anne. Admittedly, the historiography of women and gender, though relatively recent, is vast in size and various in approach. That for early modern England has, until recently and quite understandably, tended to be drawn to the heroines of protofeminism: women who rejected patriarchal roles and stereotypes, such as the petitioning women just before and during the Civil Wars, or iconoclastic writers like the seventeenth-century playwright Aphra Behn or the eighteenth-century journalist Mary Astell. Consistent with this predilection, historians of women and gender tend to admire Elizabeth but view Anne as a failure. Thus, Rachel Weil: "by the time of her death in 1714, Anne had lost political credibility, and was regarded by whigs and tories alike as weak and pliable, in thrall to favourites and bed-chamber women."[14]

In fact, historians who have examined the women of Anne's court have tended to be far more attracted to the queen's principal favorite and interlocutor, Sarah Churchill, Duchess of Marlborough. Rachel Weil finds the duchess "interesting for the combination of the ideals she embraced, and how she tried to define herself . . . as a virtuous political actor, that is, as a person who put the good of the country ahead of private concerns." While recognizing that Sarah could be unscrupulous and even vicious in her treatment of the queen, her self-definition intrigues Weil because "[m]any feminist historians [have] suggested that political virtue, the capacity to devote oneself to the public good, came to be defined some time in the eighteenth century as a quality available only to men." In other words, however unpleasant and, ultimately, unsuccessful in her political endeavors, Sarah Churchill, like Elizabeth I, merits attention, in part, because she grasped at power and influence in ways that seemed masculine.[15] Indeed, according to Arthur Maynwaring, she was "more capable of business than any man." Sarah herself boasted "I am confydent I should have been the greatest Hero that ever was known in the Parliament House if I had been so happy as to have been a Man."[16]

Unfortunately confined by her gender to court drawing rooms and bedchamber service, the Duchess of Marlborough's only means to exercise her virtue and shape policy was to badger the queen relentlessly in letter and speech.[17] In the end, the immovable object of Anne's stubbornness withstood the irresistible force of Sarah's personality, in part because Anne was so very conventional that she would not listen to another woman in political matters. As the duchess recalled ruefully in later life: "in the late queen's time, tho

I was a favourit, without the help of the Duke of Marlborough and Lord Godolphin I should not have been able to do any thing of any consiquence and the things that are worth naming will ever bee done from the influence of men."[18] Ironically, perhaps, such sentiments render the Duchess of Marlborough a worthy warrior against the patriarchy, an honorable failure: the front flap of her most recent biography states proudly that she was "attacked for traits that might have been applauded in a man."[19]

In contrast, Anne's reliance on the advice of the Duke of Marlborough and his male associates comes across as a disappointing collaboration with patriarchy for those who find so much promise in Elizabeth I and the Duchess of Marlborough. Scholars who take their valuation of Anne from Sarah's memoir, *The Conduct of the Dowager Duchess of Marlborough*, or from partisan political pamphlets with their own axes to grind,[20] rather than from diaries or correspondence, tend to see Anne's reign as a lost opportunity, blaming her failure on her embrace of conventional femininity. For Weil, Anne's compliance and tenderness are too easy to portray as weakness; for Toni Bowers she relies too much on the image of Mother of Her People: "By the end of her reign, the nation's 'Nursing Mother' was little more than a person to be gotten around, a patroness, a metaphor put to use in the interests of others' power. . . . Anne ended her reign in frustration, isolation and loss, a disenfranchised monarch and a bereaved mother."[21] For these scholars, Queen Anne was too much the good girl.

Mary II versus Anne: The Body in Question

For others, Anne Stuart was just too much—in flesh and mass—period. The body is currently a fashionable subject of historical inquiry.[22] Work on royal bodies accounts for no small part of this new historiography. Ernst Kantorowicz long ago delineated the dichotomy between the sovereign's two bodies, one human, physical, and so mortal; the other legal, spiritual, and eternal.[23] Related to this notion is an older idea of the sacrality of the sovereign's physical body and the related convention that the monarch embodied the state (Louis XIV's purported "L'etat c'est moi") and the nation. Hence the elaborate dressing rituals and precise etiquette required at all European courts when in the presence of the royal body. Anne's uncle, Charles II, may have ridiculed the King of Spain because he "will not piss but another must hold the chamber-pot," but even in England the royal body service was extensive.[24]

If royal bodies mattered, female royal bodies were a problem. Contemporary medical opinion was that the female body was more prone to humoral imbalance and passionate drives than its male counterpart.[25] Moreover, pregnancy was a clearer signifier of the flesh—that gross physical reality that medieval theologians had found so troublesome—than male sexuality, which could be concealed or celebrated in the persons of heirs after women had done the messy, corporeal travail of childbirth. Women, queens in particular, were supposed to be fruitful, but the very act of conception was also one of invasion and seeming passivity (compared to male fecundity's phallic aggressiveness).[26] Here Anne was a double failure. She was clearly not impregnable, famously experiencing a total of seventeen health-wrecking pregnancies.[27] Yet none of her children survived to adolescence, so that, in the words of Gilbert Burnet: "though there was a child born every year for many years, yet they have all died: so that the fruitfullest marriage that has been known in our age, has been fatally blasted as to the effect of it."[28]

How did contemporaries construct Anne's body? Though Anne Stuart was, in comparison to her sister Mary, never thought to be "the pretty one," early portrayals of Anne as princess deploy conventional tropes and contain stereotypical references to her virginity and beauty.[29] The first negative portrayals of both sisters appeared in the wake of the Revolution of 1688–89. They mostly focused on their betrayal of their father, James II, but the two women's bodies were also considered fair game.[30] Thus, in "Tarquin and Tullia," Arthur Maynwaring anticipates modern psychosomatic explanations of obesity by suggesting that Mary's appetites and their results were a response to her feelings of guilt:

> She, jolly glutton, grew in bulk and chins
> Feasted on rapine and enjoyed her sin
> With luxury she did weak reason force,
> Debauched good nature, and crammed down remorse.[31]

In fact, though Queen Mary complained occasionally about her weight, most popular criticism centered on her loquacity. As indicated by a popular piece of doggerel, it was Anne who had the famous appetite:

> King William thinks all;
> Queen Mary talks all;
> Prince George drinks all;
> And Princess Anne eats all.[32]

Perhaps because Anne remained relatively slim in the early 1690s (fig. 13.1), perhaps because her subsequently expanding waistline was attributable to her repeated pregnancies, contemporary critics focused on the act of eating rather than its results. The anonymous "Reflection" of 1689 characterizes her as: "Our all-eating Nancy, of more stomach than fancy." Here, Anne's appetite for food indicates not only a lack of self-control but a mind bent on sublunary matters: even before her accession, gluttony is associated with stupidity. The anonymous "Letter to Lady Osborne" of 1688 suggests a usurpation of gender roles by asking: "Prithee what is't to me if

Fig. 13.1. Portrait of Queen Anne [as princess] by Sir Godfrey Kneller, Bt.,
ca. 1690. Copyright © National Portrait Gallery, London (NPG 1616).

Fig. 13.2. Detail of Antonio Verrio's ceiling painting in the Queen's Drawing Room at Hampton Court Palace of Queen Anne holding the Sword of Justice, ca. 1703. Copyright © Historic Royal Palaces, reproduced by permission of Her Majesty the Queen.

Princess Anne / Will eat as much again as any man."[33] The overall implication is that the royal sisters were out of control, greedy, and transgressive, grasping at crowns as they did food.

After her accession, Anne's contemporaries commented frequently on her appearance, but not generally on her avoirdupois. Rather, they were interested in her complexion—which tended to flush—and her lameness. Both were thought to indicate the state of her always precarious health, upon which rested the fates of nations. But the physical characteristic that has animated most of Anne's posthumous critics has been her weight. Queen Anne was fat.[34] There must be no doubt whatsoever about that. It is obvious from her portraits, state and otherwise, though Verrio's "Tory" portrayal on the ceiling at Hampton Court (fig. 13.2) displays a noticeably thinner figure than that offered in her state portrait by her Whig Principal Painter, Sir Godfrey Kneller, source of many derivations (fig. 13.3). There is no evidence in the household accounts to support the Whig accusation that she was buried in a coffin as wide as it was long, but it may be significant that in 1705 reference is made in the Lord Chamberlain's papers to a new, "much larger throne."[35] In September 1712 Lord Berkely complained: "I am sory to see she grows fatter." According to the woman who knew her best, Sarah, Duchess of Marlborough, "Queen Anne had a person and appearance not at all ungraceful, till she grew exceeding gross and corpulent."[36] It is not often recognized that this description of physical change over time is an exact corporeal parallel to the trajectory of their celebrated friendship: people then and now seem to have been unable to separate Anne's body from her character and abilities.

Constructing the Fat Body in Early Modern England

At this point, it would be helpful to place Anne's body and her subjects' reaction to it within the context of contemporary constructions of fatness. Unfortunately, little scholarly work has addressed corpulence in the early modern period. Historians of twentieth-century obesity, art historians, and fat acceptance activists have tended to argue that tastes in physical beauty, standards of body size, and society's acceptance of fatness wax and wane, with the implication that today's widespread distaste for fleshiness is relatively recent and

Fig. 13.3. Engraving of Queen Anne by George Vertue, 1702, after
Sir Godfrey Kneller. Copyright © City of Westminster Archive Centre,
London, reproduced by permission of Bridgeman Art Library (CWA123954).

potentially temporary. Thus, Richard Klein, author of the provocatively entitled *Eat Fat,* refers to "the current fashion for thin." These
scholars assure us, largely on the basis of Rubens's and other artists'
predilection for abundant female bodies, that early modern people
were much more accepting of corpulence than we moderns tend
to be. A few even posit a golden age in which the fleshy body was
positively celebrated in art, literature, and life itself. Borrowing his
typology of painted and sculpted nudes from Kenneth Clark, Klein
asserts that "In the sixteenth and seventeenth centuries, gluttony
was widespread, even at the highest levels of society," while in the
eighteenth century, "even thin was not so skinny."[37] Certainly, the
evidence from the world of Caroline and Restoration portraiture
suggests that a full breast was considered attractive and a bit of em-
bonpoint remained a point of pride for men well into the eighteenth
century. Roy Porter argues that positive constructions of fatness
had deep psychosocial roots: "[I]n traditional national, social and
occupational stereotyping a certain stoutness was a positive property, betokening not just healthiness but the rock-solid strength of
the gentleman, yeoman farmer, magistrate or citizen."[38]

But how, then, do we explain the despairing tone of Lord Berkely's
observation quoted earlier? How do we ignore the sneer in the
Duchess of Marlborough's? Porter qualifies his rosy picture of early
modern plumpness with a distinction that may be significant for
Anne's case: "The truly obese had always been objects of literary and
artistic satire—for grossness bespoke greed, lack of self-control and
the vulgarity of temper associated with low life."[39] In fact, a preliminary survey of contemporary sources suggests plenty of intolerance
for fatness as a sign of excess, a lack of discipline, a stupid wallow-
ing in the physical. Take proverbs. Fat had positive connotations if
referring to land or animals. But people? Early modern Englishmen
and women, like their descendants, compared fat people to hogs

("fat as a hog"), sows, porpoises, and butter. These associations might seem neutral, particularly in an agrarian society. But it was equally a truism that fat people engaged in excess and greed: "A fat housekeeper makes a lean executor."[40] Late medieval and early modern anticlerical polemics are full of references to "fat beneficed priests."[41] But the most common association with fatness seems to have been with ignorance, dullness, or stupidity, as in the phrase "fat as a fool." Similarly, "The fat man knoweth not what the lean thinkith"; "Fat paunches make lean pates"; and, in Shakespeare's variation: "The proverb is as true as common. That a fat belie doth not engender a subtile wit." A century later, Anne's contemporary, John Dryden lamented, "O souls! in whom no heav'nly fire is found, Fat minds, and ever-grov'ling on the ground."[42]

We have seen similar associations in the satires on Mary and Anne following the Glorious Revolution, and indeed, they may have been growing stronger in their time. Roy Porter dates a shift against fatness to around 1750, but the signs appear earlier. While Augustan newspapers are replete with ads for products to restore the stomach and appetite, beginning in January 1710 we also find: "*Pilulae contra Obesitatem*. These Pills have been experienced, and, if taken according to the Directions given with each Box, never fail'd carrying off Fatness, and all gross Humours of the Body to admiration, leaving it perfectly found [*sic*]; and infallibly prevent it in such as are inclinable to be fat."[43] Dr. Thomas Short worried in 1727: "I believe no Age did ever afford more Instances of Corpulency than our own."[44] Porter argues that the decline of humoral medicine elevated the mind over the body and rendered excessive preoccupation with satisfying bodily appetites "low" and shallow.[45] It may be significant that the *zaftig* female courtiers depicted by Sir Peter Lely as the Windsor Beauties in the 1670s seem to have given way to slimmer forms by the time Sir Godfrey Kneller painted their successors, the Hampton Court Beauties, in the 1690s. It was in this decade that Mary II complained of growing stout and patronized a Reformation of Manners to banish vice and excess.[46] Under Anne, cultural critics like Addison and Steele attacked excess and its cousin, luxury. Thus, an Augustan pamphlet decries "the present luxurious and fantastical manner of Eating."[47]

Constructing Anne's Body in Modern Historiography

Perhaps Anne was the victim of a change in body fashions. In any case, what strikes the historian of Anne's body is how, for all periods since her death, there seems to be a direct correlation, in both popular and scholarly accounts, between how an author portrays the queen's physical size and shape—from pleasantly maternal to grossly obese—and his or her estimation of Anne's political abilities and achievements as sovereign. Those who emphasize her unwieldiness also find her weak, dull, and easily led. Thus, according to the nineteenth-century popular author Mrs. Oliphant, the queen was "a fat, placid, middle-aged woman" who was "little more than a puppet in the hands of successive politicians." In the 1960s, David Green described Anne as "huge and unweildy [sic] and prematurely aged" in a popular biography that characterized her as well-meaning but weak and troubled. The Duchess of Marlborough's most recent scholarly biographer, Frances Harris, writing in the early 1990s, contrasts Sarah's brilliance with Anne's dullness while referring to the latter as "grotesquely overweight."[48] Ophelia Field's recent popular biography of the duchess is merciless, beginning with Edith Sitwell's description of a "lymphatic, pasty-faced child-Princess," carrying on with Sarah's "exceedingly gross and corpulent" adult; and finishing Anne off as "riddled with gout, morbidly obese, and strangely resigned to this." Predictably, Field displays a low opinion of the queen's abilities: "Not even twentieth-century efforts to rescue her reputation have managed to deny that she was a bore."[49]

Historians of the arts, used to reading faces for signs of character, have especially tended to draw a connection between the queen's weight and her lack of mental agility. Thus, Nancy Armstrong, writing the history of jewelry, relates girth to lethargy and stupidity: "Anne I [sic] . . . was getting old, overweight, and tired. Her life was one long confusion, never properly resolved. . . . her political views were muddled and easily swayed."[50] But some very distinguished political historians also embrace the mind-body connection: in the 1920s, Sir Keith Feiling presented Anne's intellect as the perfect analogue of her cumbersome body: "The motion of her mind, her affections, and her passion were similarly slow, unwieldy, but determined."[51]

Adherents of the queen tend to be more tactful about her appearance. Writing in the eighteenth century, Tobias Smollett describes her as "of middle size, well proportioned . . . her aspect more comely than majestic." Neville Connell, whose popular biography from the 1930s is, in general, approving, calls her "moderately tall, and well proportioned." More recently, John Cannon and Ralph Griffiths in *The Oxford History of the British Monarchy* describe "a plain, plump woman, somewhat lacking in vivacity, but conscious of her own dignity and with a certain determination."[52] But as words like *plump* and *comely* have ceased to be compliments in our own time, Anne's defenders have been left to dwell sympathetically on her ill health, differing only in tone from her detractors. For example, while noting the queen's "lonely and pain-ridden existence," Sheila Biddle describes her as "[c]autious and deliberate, sensible rather than intelligent, she bore her responsibilities with all the fortitude chronic ill-health allowed."[53] It may be significant that those with the most approving views of Anne—Leopold von Ranke, Geoffrey Holmes, William Speck, and Stewart Ross—do not address her physical state at all.[54]

Then there are the historians who want to have it both ways—or, as Anne might have appreciated, have their cake and eat it too. In the nineteenth century, Agnes and Elizabeth Strickland portray her as "round as a ball" as a child, and "in her youth, as an uneducated and self-indulgent woman." But they chart an "undeniable improvement in her conduct" as queen, during which period she is characterized as being physically "comely."[55] More amusing, seemingly less subtle but actually more so, is Mark Kishlansky. On the surface, his is the conventional Whig portrait. After recounting the tragic story of Anne's seventeen pregnancies, lameness, and general ill-health, he opines: "Anne was dull, taciturn, stubborn and unattractive. Her conversation was mind-numbing, her taste insipid, her pleasures limited to gambling and dining, losing pounds at one set of tables and gaining them at the other." But in his estimation, her physical failings become an asset: "Despite all of her obvious deficiencies—or perhaps because of them—Queen Anne was a monarch beloved. She desired nothing so much as to be a mother, and if she couldn't achieve this with her children then she would with her subjects. Her pitted face and bulging, watery eyes that limited her vision, her ailments and constant pain, all made her seem a monarch of the people."[56] Thus, in Professor Kishlansky's construction, Anne's body becomes a political and propaganda asset, the pathetic frame providing the base of popular support for her royal style.[57] It is a brilliant reversal. While there appears to be no evidence that Anne's people consciously embraced her *because* of her physical frailties, the contrast and connection between the queen's fragile body and her iron determination are appropriately drawn.

Fig. 13.4. Portrait of Queen Anne by Edmund Lilly, 1703.
Blenheim Palace, Oxfordshire, UK, reproduced by permission
of Bridgeman Art Library (BAL72314).

The Fat Lady Sings

But one might go further. Following the Duchess of Marlborough's description of Anne's corpulence, she affirms in the very next sentence that "there was something of majesty in her look."[58] One sees this clearly in the contemporary painting by Charles Lilly that hangs, fittingly, in the entrance foyer of Blenheim Palace (fig. 13.4). Numerous eyewitness accounts confirm the impressive figure the queen made on great state occasions.[59] To judge from the positive crowd reaction Anne always produced, Sarah was not alone in seeing her solid and stolid appearance, her bulk, as a sign of stability and, perhaps, married to her obviously maternal instincts as evidenced by those seventeen pregnancies, motherly care.

Anne consciously portrayed herself as the "mother of her people" in association with, but also in distinction to, the metaphor of Elizabeth as their virgin bride. Her subjects responded with frequent references to her maternal image, in sermons, addresses, and petitions to the throne.[60] In this image was implied many of the queen's most attractive qualities, such as her gracious demeanor and her works of charity. It is not much of a stretch to imagine that Anne's girth, so unfashionable in our own day, may also, along with her tragic obstetrical history, have supported the motherly image to which her people responded with such enthusiasm and, it would seem, affection. Take this anonymous account of the queen's 1706 progress to Newmarket: "Crouds of people from all parts of the Country came to see her Majesty and wish her a long Life and happy Reign; and, indeed, thus it was in whatever part of England she was pleased to appear amongst them . . . they ever looked upon her as their common Parent."[61] The first signifier of parental care was the queen's matronly body: in this alone, that ample frame was not Anne's enemy but an asset.

Toward the end of the textbook portrait quoted earlier, its authors acknowledge that the actions of this fat, dull, "ordinary woman, whom the laws of hereditary monarchy raised to the throne, helped shape events during these years in two ways: first, by naming the Earl of Marlborough in 1702 to command her troops, and second, by dismissing him from that command in 1711. By the first act she brought England unparalleled military victories; by the second she brought peace to her kingdom."[62]

But one could go further still. No previous Stuart was so adept at delegating royal authority to men of ability. Her government sustained the Grand Alliance against Louis XIV, raised great sums of money, fielded vast armies and navies, and won unprecedented victories on the continent against the most powerful state of its time, thwarting the ambitions of the Sun King while leading a political nation wracked by postrevolutionary party strife. This is an achievement that Sir Winston Churchill not only celebrated in his biography of the first Duke of Marlborough but sought to emulate when in power. Anne's regime did all this without the necessity of terror, tyranny, or constitutional chicanery. Indeed, if we date English constitutional monarchy to the Glorious Revolution of 1688–89, then Anne was, arguably, the first fully successful constitutional monarch in British history, maintaining her prerogative in the face of two ambitious and disciplined parties while setting a pattern for delegation and constitutional restraint that did much to render the postrevolutionary regime secure.[63]

If Anne's choice and use of ministers was impeccable, so was her timing. She knew when to fight (1702–10) and when to seek peace (1710–13), often over the inclinations of the majority party in Parliament. The new ministry of 1710, for all of its problems, secured the Treaty of Utrecht. This accord effectively eliminated the French threat to the balance of power, while endowing Britain with Gibraltar (and so control of the Mediterranean); territory in the West Indies (and so control of the sugar trade); and, in a reminder of the barbaric underpinnings of all this prosperity, the *Asiento* slaving contract to the Spanish New World. These ensured that British trade would not only grow but that it would provide the financial underpinning for future victories, culminating on the field of Waterloo in 1815. Britain's triumph in what is sometimes called the Second Hundred Years' War resulted in the military, naval, commercial, and industrial hegemony of the British nineteenth century, for good or ill. Acknowledging all of this makes Queen Anne neither a saint (note the *Asiento*), nor a genius. But it does suggest that she did far more than take up space.

Queen Anne and the Historians

And yet, Anne has been largely stiffed by the scholarly community. Traditional historians have discounted her as a woman: quiet, agreeable, gentle, charitable, and, as we have seen, fat. Historians of gender have seen her as a disappointment, perhaps because she was not, in their view, a pioneer, a resistor, an outlier. Historians of the body ought to find her more interesting because here she *was* an outlier, not so much in her size but in the fact that, unlike her sister Mary II, she never seems to have complained about it. But fat studies is a relatively new endeavor, and it has not, so far, embraced much of a critical historical perspective.[64]

Anne's example calls for a reappraisal, not simply of her role in history, but of the historical representation of women of size. Our tendency toward seeing her size and appearance as indicators of character and ability says a great deal more about us, and our attitudes to leaders, women, and bodies, than it does about this particular woman. Famously moral, a model wife, Anne's one vice was overeating: but could she have picked a worse one from the point of view of prejudices, both longstanding and modern? It has been said that "sizeism" is the last great acceptable prejudice—doubtful, perhaps, given how many remain. Still, no consumer of mass media can fail to note the frequent reportage of academic studies demonstrating that the physically attractive—narrowly defined—get the best jobs, the most dates, even the longer lives. The unruly bodies of the rare public figures who allow themselves to gain weight are splashed across the gutters of tabloid photo spreads and ridiculed by late-night talk-show hosts in a feast of schadenfreude. Apparently, size does matter.

But should it? In particular, how should historians present the significance of physical appearance? The modern historical enterprise is supposed to be rational, and reason tells us that physical appearance has nothing to do with character or ability. But both our subjects and our readers act as if it does. Is the historian's job to give readers what they want—graphic and stereotypically categorized descriptions of bodies à la *People* magazine—or is it to lead them to a promised land of purely rational evaluation in which the bodies of historical actors are portrayed in neutral terms, if at all? Given the fact that size was, in some way, significant to those actors, would that not be a distortion of the past in its own right? Anne's was not a politically correct age, and it clearly did matter that she was fat—though it has perhaps mattered more to posterity. Should it still? If so, how?

Anne's example calls equally for the application to elite women of a wider perspective and a more sophisticated approach to gender and patriarchy—one that has, in fact, been long and successfully applied to ordinary women.[65] Such a perspective problematizes and blurs the old distinctions between oppressors and oppressed. It looks beyond the search for protofeminist heroines to address the experience of *all* women: the brave and the meek, the outspoken and the retiring, the great and the good, the thin and the fat, to get beyond the outlier to the ordinary and the "average." Still, it may be indicative of how far we have to go that a recent search through the online Royal Historical Society Bibliography of British History yields 283 hits for "masculinity," yet only sixty-two for the corresponding feminine ideal, "femininity." We will not fully understand the experience of women in any age until we study the "good girls" too.

Only then will historians, perhaps, be able to contemplate the third project called for in this chapter: a reappraisal of the league table of British rulers. As should have been obvious long ago, Anne's record as sovereign bears comparison with any of her predecessors—even the woman who made female monarchy viable in England and on whom she modeled aspects of her public persona: Queen Elizabeth.[66] Where Elizabeth was conflicted and ambiguous about her gender, often taking the part of a man, Anne was as stereotypical a woman as the times could afford. Where Elizabeth hesitated over and finally rejected the matrimonial state, Anne gloried in her marriage. Where Elizabeth was the Virgin Queen, wedded to her first love, the people of England, with all of the flirtatious play that implies, Anne was their nursing mother, a far less titillating image. Where Elizabeth was quick and profligate with words, Anne was slow and parsimonious with them. Where Elizabeth was ostentatiously courageous, Anne was stubbornly tenacious. And where Elizabeth was glamorously slim, Anne was prosaically (and perhaps morbidly) fat. In the end, both women seem to have been exactly what the nation required at the end of their royal lines, and both achieved success unparalleled in the reigns of their respective ancestors. "Good Queen Bess" has always been so credited. Perhaps, if we can get past our expectations of women's roles and women's bodies, "Good Queen Anne" will similarly receive her due.

Notes

The author wishes to thank his coeditor, the departments of History at Loyola University and Binghamton University, and the participants in the Midwest Conference on British Studies at Notre Dame University in September 2005 and the Conference on Queens and Power at the University of Nebraska–Lincoln in March 2006 for their helpful comments and suggestions on previous versions of this essay.

1. International exhibits on Elizabeth appeared at the National Maritime Museum, Greenwich; the Folger Shakespeare Library, Washington; and the Newberry Library, Chicago. Commemorative publications included C. Levin, *The Reign of Elizabeth I* (New York: Palgrave, 2002); C. Levin, J. E. Carney, D. Barrett-Graves, eds., *Elizabeth I: Always Her Own Free Woman* (Aldershot: Ashgate, 2003); L. Picard, *Elizabeth's London: Everyday Life in Elizabethan London* (London: Weidenfeld and Nicolson, 2003); S. Doran, *Queen Elizabeth I* (London: British Library, 2003); J. M. Mueller and L. S. Marcus, eds., *Elizabeth I: Autograph Compositions and Foreign Language Originals* (Chicago: University of Chicago Press, 2003); J. T. Lynch, *The Age of Elizabeth in the Age of Johnson* (Cambridge: Cambridge University Press, 2003); J. Dunn, *Elizabeth and Mary: Cousins, Rivals, Queens* (London: HarperCollins, 2003); R. Rex, *Elizabeth I, Fortune's Bastard: A Short Account of the Long Life of Elizabeth I* (Stroud: Tempus, 2003); D. M. Loades, *Elizabeth I* (London: Hambledon, 2003); D. M. Loades, *Elizabeth I: The Golden Reign of Gloriana* (Richmond: Public Record Office, 2003); M. Simpson, *Rivals for the Crown* (London: Scholastic, 2003); S. Doran and T. S. Freeman, eds., *The Myth of Elizabeth* (Basingstoke: Palgrave, 2003); F. Pryor, *Elizabeth I: Her Life in Letters* (London: British Library, 2003); S. Adams, *Leicester and the Court: Essays on Elizabethan Politics* (Manchester: Manchester University Press, 2002); J. Watkins, *Representing Elizabeth in Stuart England: Literature, History, Sovereignty* (Cambridge: Cambridge University Press, 2002); L. S. Marcus, J. M. Mueller and M. B. Rose, eds., *Elizabeth I: Collected Works* (Chicago: University of Chicago Press, paperback ed., 2002); M. Dobson and N. J. Watson, *England's Elizabeth: An Afterlife in Fame and Fantasy* (Oxford: Oxford University Press, 2002); F. Edwards, *Plots and Plotters in the Reign of Elizabeth I* (Dublin: Four Courts, 2002); C. Lee, *1603: A Turning Point in British History* (London: Review, 2003).

2. With the possible exception of R. O. Bucholz, "Queen Anne: Victim of her Virtues?" in *Queenship in Britain, 1660–1837: Royal Patronage, Court Culture, and Dynastic Politics*, ed. C. C. Orr (Manchester: Manchester University Press, 2002), 94–129; and the decidedly uncelebratory M. Waller, *Ungrateful Daughters: The Stuart Princesses Who Stole Their Father's Crown* (London: Hodder and Stoughton, 2002); and O. Field, *Sarah Churchill, Duchess of Marlborough: The Queen's Favorite* (New York: St. Martin's, 2003).

3. J. McCarthy, *The Reign of Queen Anne* (London: Chatto & Windus, 1911), 3; B. C. Brown, *Alas, Queen Anne: A Reading of Her Life* (Indianapolis: Bobbs-Merrill, 1929), x.

4. C. Roberts and D. Roberts, *A History of England: Prehistory to 1714*, 2nd ed. (Englewood Cliffs NJ: Prentice Hall, 1985), 1:404.

5. E. Gregg, *Queen Anne* (London: Routledge & Kegan Paul, 1980); G. S. Holmes, *British Politics in the Age of Anne* (London: Macmillan, 1967), 210–16; W. A. Speck, *The Birth of Britain: A New Nation, 1700–1710* (Oxford: Blackwell, 1994), 13–15.

6. See, for example, S. Mendelson and P. Crawford, *Women in Early Modern England, 1550–1720* (Oxford: Oxford University Press, 1998), chap. 7; A. Fletcher, *Gender, Sex, and Subordination in England, 1500–1800* (New Haven: Yale University Press, 1995); M. Suzuki, *Subordinate Subjects: Gender, the Political Nation, and Literary Form in England, 1588–1688* (Burlington VT: Ashgate, 2003); T. Bowers, *The Politics of Motherhood: British Writing and Culture, 1680–1780* (Cambridge: Cambridge University Press, 1996); R. Weil, *Political Passions: Gender, the Family and Political Argument in England, 1680–1714* (Manchester: Manchester University Press, 1999), chap. 1.

7. I except here more recent work informed by feminism, such as that by Carole Levin, Susan Doran, Susan Frye, and Susan Basnett. This work, followed by Mendelson and Crawford in their useful summary (*Women in Early Modern England, 1550–1720*, 353–57), recognizes that Elizabeth picked and chose among male and female characteristics as needed. The point at hand is that the "male" characteristics have most captured the imaginations of historians and the general public.

8. Camden quoted in J. Eales, *Women in Early Modern England, 1500–1700* (London: UCL Press, 1998), 8; W. MacCaffrey, "Politics in an Age of Reformation, 1485–1585," in *The Oxford Illustrated History of Tudor and Stuart Britain*, ed. J. Morrill (Oxford: Oxford University Press, 2000), 322.

9. See, for example, C. Haigh, *Elizabeth I*, 2nd ed.(Harlow, Essex: Longman, 1998), 77–79.

10. See A. Heisch, "Queen Elizabeth and the Persistence of Patriarchy," *Feminist Review* 4 (1980), esp. 53–55.

11. According to Toni Bowers, "Anne . . . was always a *woman* in her subjects' minds" (*Politics of Motherhood*, 68); but cf. Weil, *Political Passions*, 167.

12. Quoted in Philip, Earl Stanhope, *History of England Comprising the Reign of Queen Anne until the Peace of Utrecht, 1701–1713* (London: J. Murray, 1872), 2:310.

13. Anne to Godolphin, September 12, 1707, quoted in *The Letters and Diplomatic Instructions of Queen Anne*, ed. B. C. Brown (New York: Funk & Wagnalls, 1968), 231–32. See also 197, 199–201.

14. Weil, *Political Passions*, 162. Further references to her "failure" may be found on 171 ("loss of her reputation"), and 172 ("Anne's downfall"). For other historians, see later.

15. Weil, *Political Passions*, chap. 8, entitled "Sarah Churchill; or, virtue unrewarded," 188 and *passim*. See also F. Harris, *A Passion for Government: The Life of Sarah, Duchess of Marlborough* (Oxford: Oxford University Press, 1991); Mendelson and Crawford, *Women in Early Modern England*, 377.

16. Quoted in Field, *Duchess of Marlborough*, 198; Mendelson and Crawford, *Women in Early Modern England*, 377.

17. See Gregg, *Queen Anne*, chaps. 6–12; R. O. Bucholz, *The Augustan Court: Queen Anne and the Decline of Court Culture* (Stanford: Stanford University Press, 1993), chaps. 3 and 6, esp. 159–62, both based on the duchess's correspondence with the queen and others in the Blenheim MSS: BL Add. MSS. 61414–61420. The characterization will only seem extreme to those who have not read this correspondence in its entirety.

18. BL Add. MSS. 61444, f. 139v, Sarah, Duchess of Marlborough to Humphrey Fyshe, July 4, 1727, quoted in F. Harris, "Accounts of the Conduct of Sarah, Duchess of Marlborough, 1704–42," *British Library Journal* 8 (1982): 30.

19. Field, *Duchess of Marlborough*, front flap.

20. For the problems with this evidence, see Bucholz, "Queen Anne: Victim of her Virtues?" 113–14; Bucholz, *Augustan Court*, 169–72.

21. Weil, *Political Passions*, 165, 169–74; Bowers, *Politics of Motherhood*, 49–50, and also part 1; C. Barash, *English Women's Poetry, 1649–1714: Politics, Community and Linguistic Authority* (Oxford: Oxford University Press, 1996), 282, 290. For a refutation, see Bucholz, "Queen Anne: Victim of her Virtues?" 103–4.

22. See, for example, M. Foucault, *The History of Sexuality*, trans. A. Sheridan, 3 vols. (New York: Vintage, 1980–85); T. Laqueur, *Making Sex: Body and Gender from the Greeks to Freud* (Cambridge MA: Harvard University Press, 1990); Fletcher, *Gender, Sex, and Subordination*; R. Porter, *Flesh in the Age of Reason: The Modern Foundations of Body and Soul* (New York: Norton, 2003).

23. E. Kantorowicz, *The King's Two Bodies: A Study in Medieval Political Theology* (Princeton: Princeton University Press, 1957). Much of the following discussion has been inspired by P. K. Monod, *The Power of Kings: Monarchy and Religion in Europe, 1589–1715* (New Haven: Yale University Press, 1999), chap. 2; and E. M. McClure, *Sunspots and the Sun King: Sovereignty and Mediation in Seventeenth-Century France* (Urbana: University of Illinois Press, 2006).

24. S. Pepys, *The Diary of Samuel Pepys*, ed. R. Latham and W. Matthews (Berkeley: University of California Press, 1995), 7:201. For the rituals of the English court, see R. O. Bucholz, "Going to Court in 1700: A Visitor's Guide," *Court Historian* 5 (2000):

181–215; A. Keay, "The Ceremonies of Charles II's Court" (PhD thesis, University of London, 2004).

25. See Fletcher, *Gender, Sex, and Subordination*; Eales, *Women in Early Modern England*, chap. 4; Mendelson and Crawford, *Women in Early Modern England*, 18–30.

26. For a different approach to this issue, emphasizing maternal bodies as "political agents," see Bowers, *Politics of Motherhood*, 41.

27. By Edward Gregg's count (*Queen Anne*, 120). For the most complete statement of how Anne's maternal failure implied political failure, see Bowers, *Politics of Motherhood*, part 1.

28. G. Burnet, *A History of His Own Time* (Oxford: Oxford University Press, 1833), 2:391.

29. See *Hymnnaeus Cantabrigiensis* (Cambridge, 1683); *An Heroick Poem on her Highness the Lady Anne's Voyage into Scotland: with a little Digression upon the Time* (London, 1681); *A pastoral Occasion'd by the Arrival of HRH Prince George . . . Design't to marry Her Higness the Lady Ann* (London, 1683). For the political significance of Mary's beauty, see Weil, *Political Passions*, 112–13.

30. See *Poems on Affairs of State: Augustan Satirical Verse, 1660–1714* (hereafter *POAS*), general ed. G. deForest Lord (New Haven: Yale University Press, 1963–75), vol. 4, ed. G. M. Crump, 303; vol. 5, ed. W. J. Cameron, 44–54, 156–57.

31. *POAS*, 5:52, and also 56, 201; H. and B. van der Zee, *William and Mary* (New York: Macmillan, 1973), 381.

32. Quoted in *Encyclopedia Britannica* (Cambridge: Cambridge University Press, 1911), 2:68. For Mary complaining about her weight, see A. Laurence, *Women in England, 1500–1760: A Social History* (London: Weidenfeld and Nicolson, 1994), 100; Waller, *Ungrateful Daughters*, 78, 285.

33. *POAS*, 5:61, 78. For continued fascination with Anne's appetite, see A. Hampson, *The English at Table* (London: Collins, 1944), 33; G. M. Trevelyan, *England under Queen Anne: Blenheim* (London: Longman, 1930), 168–69. For the contemporary association between preoccupation with the belly and vulgarity, see Porter, *Flesh in the Age of Reason*, 60, 62, and later.

34. I here follow the National Association to Advance Fat Acceptance (NAAFA) in using a term that may seem offensive: "'*Fat*' is not a four-letter word. It is an adjective, like short, tall, thin, or blonde. While society has given it a derogatory meaning, we find that identifying ourselves as '*fat*' is an important step in casting off the shame we have been taught to feel about our bodies," http://www.naafa.org/documents/brochures/naafa-info.html#word. It is, in part, precisely to query the automatic use of *fat* as an unambiguously pejorative term that this essay has been written.

35. R. Coke, *Detection of the Court and State of England during the Last Four Reigns* (London, 1719), 3:481–82; PRO LC 5/70, 301–2, 341.

36. *The Wentworth Papers, 1705–1739*, ed. J. J. Cartwright (London: Wyman, 1883), 301; *Memoirs of Sarah, Duchess of Marlborough, Together with Characters of Her Contemporaries*, ed. W. King (London: Routledge, 1930), 229–30.

37. R. Klein, "Fat Beauty," in *Bodies Out of Bounds: Fatness and Transgression*, ed. J. A. Braziel and K. LeBesco (Berkeley: University of California Press, 2001), 20, 28, 33, 35. See also P. Stearns, *Fat History: Bodies and Beauty in the Modern West* (New York: NYU Press, 1997); K. Clark, *The Nude: A Study in Ideal Form* (Princeton: Princeton University Press, 1972); E. St. Paige, *Zaftig: The Case for Curves* (Seattle: Darling, 1999), esp. 40.

38. Porter, *Flesh in the Age of Reason*, 239–40, and also 233–35.

39. Porter, *Flesh in the Age of Reason*, 239.

40. R. Cotgrave, *A French-English Dictionary* (1611), sub. "Testament," repeated right through to B. Franklin, *Way to Wealth* (London, 1736).

41. This reference is from *Mercurius rusticus: the downfall of tythes. The country-man discovering the pride, lewdness, covetousness, and ambition of the fat beneficed priests incroaching tythe-mongers, and oppressing impropriatos, &c.* (London, 1653); see also *Iohn Niccols pilgrimage whrein* [sic] *is displaied the liues of the proude popes, ambitious cardinals, lecherous bishops, fat bellied monkes, and hypocriticall Iesuites* (London: Thomas Butter and Godfrey Isaac, 1581); and Porter, *Flesh in the Age of Reason*, 240.

42. J. Lyly, *Ephues: The Anatomy of wit* (London: Arbor, 1579), 118; G. Herbert, *Jacula Prudentum, or, Outlandish Proverbs, Sentences, &c.* (London, 1640); M. Stephen Guazzo, *The Civile Conversation of M. Steeven Guazzo*, trans. B. Young (London: 1586), 190; W. Shakespeare, *Love's Labour's Lost*, 1.1; J. Dryden, *Second Satire of Persius* (London: Tonson, 1693) lines 110–11.

43. *Daily Courant* no. 2557, January 3, 1710. One wonders if the ad's appearance so soon after the New Year and in two further issues in January and two in February (nos. 2561, 2569, 2587, and 2600) parallels the tendency of modern diet advertisements to appear in magazines just after the Christmas holidays, when people make New Year's resolutions.

44. Quoted in Porter, *Flesh in the Age of Reason*, 233.

45. Porter, *Flesh in the Age of Reason*, 60–61.

46. See Burnet, *History of His Own Time*, 4:181–82. I owe this point to Professor Newton Key.

47. Quoted in Porter, *Flesh in the Age of Reason*, 236, see also 118.

48. M. O. W. Oliphant, *Historical Characters of the Reign of Queen Anne* (New

York: Century, 1894), 2, 77; D. Green, *Queen Anne* (New York: Scribners, 1970), 252; Harris, *Passion for Government*, 77.

49. Field, *Duchess of Marlborough*, 11, 45, 86. See also 319–20.

50. N. Armstrong, *Jewellery: An Historical Survey of British Styles and Jewels* (Guildford: Lutterworth, 1973), 129. See also M. Foss, *The Age of Patronage: The Arts in England, 1660–1750* (Ithaca NY: Cornell University Press, 1976), 111. Toni Bowers, in *Politics of Motherhood*, connects Anne's obesity to her personality: on page 75 she is "the reserved, obese, invalid queen," and on page 79, "the ponderous, impassive queen."

51. K. Feiling, *A History of the Tory Party, 1640–1714* (Oxford: Oxford University Press, 1924), 360. For a modern equivalent, see J. Hoppit, *A Land of Liberty? England, 1689–1727* (Oxford: Oxford University Press, 2000), 281–82. Not all negative portrayals address the queen's appearance: see David Hume and Tobias Smollett, *The History of England: From the Text of Hume and Smollett to the Reign of George III*, ed. T. Gaspey (London: London Printing and Publishing, 1852); T. B. Macaulay, *The History of England from the Accession of James II* (London: Longman, Green and Co., 1895), 2:156–57; Earl Stanhope, *History of England*, 1:42–43; W. H. Lecky, *A History of England in the Eighteenth Century* (London: Longman, 1888), 1:31–32; J. H. Plumb, *The Growth of Political Stability in England, 1675–1725* (London: Macmillan, 1967), 105–6.

52. Hume and Smollett, *History of England*, ed. Gaspey, 3:396; N. Connell, *Anne, The Last Stuart Monarch* (London: Butterworth, 1937), 110–11; J. Cannon and R. Griffiths, *The Oxford Illustrated History of the British Monarchy* (Oxford: Oxford University Press, 1998), 446, and see also their ostensibly sympathetic but ultimately condescending summation on 458–59.

53. S. Biddle, *Bolingbroke and Harley* (London: George Allen & Unwin, 1975), 150–51. See also G. V. Bennett, *The Tory Crisis in Church and State, 1688–1730: The Career of Francis Atterbury, Bishop of Rochester* (Oxford: Clarendon Press, 1975), 63.

54. L. von Ranke, *A History of England Principally in the Seventeenth Century* (New York: AMS Press, 1966), 5:329; Holmes, *British Politics*, 210–15; S. Ross, *The Stewart Dynasty* (Nairn: Thomas and Lochar, 1993), 284–85; Speck, *Birth of Britain*, 13–15, 134–35, 177–78, 195; M. R. Hopkinson, *Anne of England: The Biography of a Great Queen* (New York: Macmillan, 1934), xiii–xv.

55. A. and E. Strickland, *Lives of the Queens of England, from the Norman Conquest* (London: Longman, 1857), 7:5, 8:212, 550–51.

56. M. Kishlansky, *A Monarchy Transformed: Britain, 1603–1714* (New York: Penguin, 1997), 316–17. See also Bowers, *Politics of Motherhood*: "Queen Anne's considerable popularity was largely due to the fact that unlike any monarch before

her, she was defined in terms of what she *shared* with her subjects: she was a model for women insofar as she was ordinary" (44).

57. The Stricklands make a similar point about Anne's appearance when they write that it "bore the national characteristics of the middle classes" (*Lives of the Queens of England*, 8:207, 212–13. See also F. W. Wyon, *The History of Great Britain during the Reign of Queen Anne* (London: Chapman and Hall, 1876), 1:44.

58. *Memoirs of the Duchess of Marlborough*, 229–30.

59. See Bucholz, *Augustan Court*, 205–8, 213, 222, 224; *Flying Post*, no. 1087, April 23–25, 1702.

60. See Bucholz, *Augustan Court*, chap. 7, and 345n43; *Seldom Comes a Better: or, A Tale of a Lady and Her Servants* (London, 1710), 11; J. Bates, *Two (United) are Better than One Alone: a Thanksgiving Sermon Upon the Union* (London, 1707), 27; J. Smith, *The Duty of the Living to the Memory of the Dead. A Sermon Upon the Death of Queen Anne* (London, 1714), 15. For Anne as the Mother of the Church, see *POAS*, 7:147, 460; F. Atterbury, *Sermon Preached Before the Honourable House of Commons . . . March 8 1703/4* (London, 1704), 23.

61. *The Life of her late Majesty Queen Anne As well before her Accession to the Throne as after* (1721), 1:415.

62. Roberts and Roberts, *History of England*, 1:404.

63. See Bucholz, "Queen Anne: Victim of Her Virtues?" 100–101; Gregg, *Queen Anne*, chap. 5.

64. See http://cfp.english.upenn.edu/archive/Cultural-Historical/0362.html for a call for papers for the Popular Culture Association/American Culture Association (PCA/ACA) National Conference in Atlanta, Georgia, April 12–16, 2006, in the area of fat studies. The call for papers defines fat studies as "an interdisciplinary, cross-disciplinary field of study that confronts and critiques cultural constraints against the fat body and creates paradigms for the development of fat acceptance within mass society."

65. A good recent example is A. Froide, *Never Married: Singlewomen in Early Modern England* (Oxford: Oxford University Press, 2006).

66. For Anne borrowing Elizabeth's motto and following her ceremonial and sartorial choices, see Bucholz, *Augustan Court*, 205–7.

14

Two Poems

AMBER HARRIS LEICHNER

Litany for a Princess

After the portrait of Princess Elizabeth by William Scrots, circa 1546

Before the procession followed the velvet-draped horses to Westminster,
Before her throat tightened with ulcers,
Before commissioning *Twelfth Night*,
Before becoming Tilbury's *judge* and *general*,
Before the Armada,
Before the blade at Mary's neck,
Before the plots and traitors, scepter and orb,
Before the skin whitened with lead paste,
Before the poxed taste of death,
Before covered shoulders and ruffs about the neck,
Before the tension: Marry. Do not marry.
Before writing *Much suspected by me, Nothing proved can be*,
Before the Tower,
Before knowing the power of a woman alone,

She is perceptive but serene in crimson folded over gold brocade;
She is the postured awareness of dynasty;
She knows Ascham's humanism, Erasmus and foreign tongues;
She has *a mind she shall never be ashamed to present*;
She has a copy of Cicero in hand, finger marking place;
She has pearls at her collarbones;
>   eyes that know the gaze of tradition;
She stands beside a large leather book,
>   behind her, heavy curtains and darkness;
She owns Diana's mortal strength and the skill,
>   declares it in a crescent at her temples;
She is textured simplicity,
>   favorite sister painted as a brother's gift.

Fifty Sighs at Sunset

> Her heart had been sad and heavy for ten or twelve days; and in
> her discourse she fetched not so few as forty or fifty great sighs.
>
> —ROBERT CAREY, cousin of Queen Elizabeth I of England, 1603

There was frost that February morning at Richmond.
Silver crests coated the windows of the chamber
where they gathered, watching her hold out her hand,
wrist arched like a hundred times before. But this time
instead of the kiss, she waited for the dull grind
of metal teeth meeting the gold band, the slow sawing,
the clink. One half dropped to the floor,
the other still clung to the swollen flesh of her finger.
After that the curtains fell back, and she receded
into the cold privacy of belonging to all but herself.

She insisted on the floor, lingering on embroidered cushions
where her body couldn't rest, couldn't be taken yet.
Her vigil continued through one week, then another.
She never changed from day clothes, preferred the armor
of constant wakefulness, as if she might leave on a whim.
But soon her throat swelled, the words dried up. She took
to her feet. Fifteen hours passed like blood: controlled, slow.

Her councilors convinced her to move to the bed.
She folded into it, accepting this was to be the last place
to lay down for her God, and for her kingdom,
not in the kicked-up dust of armies, hooves
of long processions, but the stale comfort of holland sheets
where finger to cracked lips, prayer to heaven, eyes
following as the Archbishop's mouth curved over
the word *Jesus*, the sound dragging the weight
of too many fears as it moved up beyond the bed.
In the royal chapel courtiers' heads bent
under thoughts of death—not hers, but their own.

The final night the panes were lacquered with spring rain.
And the iron chain loosened while her lids closed, remained
low like her breath, at last lungs empty, no sigh on her lips.
The March night gave over to morning, silence after the rain.

Selected Bibliography

Accommodation Cordially Desired, and Really Intended. London, May 15, 1643, Thomason Tracts, British Library, London (hereafter TT) E 101(23).

Adams, Simon. *Leicester and the Court. Essays on Elizabethan Politics*. Manchester: Manchester University Press, 2002.

Adelman, Janet. *The Common Liar: An Essay on Antony and Cleopatra*. New Haven: Yale University Press, 1973.

Alford, Stephen. *The Early Elizabethan Polity: William Cecil and the British Succession Crisis, 1558–1569*. Cambridge: Cambridge University Press, 1998.

Anderson, James, ed. *Collections Relating to the History of Mary, Queen of Scotland. Containing a Great Number of Original Papers Never Before Printed. Also a Few Scarce Pieces Reprinted, Taken from the Best Copies*. Edinburgh: Printed by J. Mosman and W. Brown, 1727.

Anne. *The Letters and Diplomatic Instructions of Queen Anne*. Edited by Beatrice Curtis Brown. New York: Funk & Wagnalls, 1968.

Armstrong, Nancy J. *Jewellery: An Historical Survey of British Styles and Jewels*. Guildford: Lutterworth Press, 1973.

Ascham, Roger. *The Whole Works of Roger Ascham, Now First Collected and Revised, with a Life of the Author.* Edited by J. A Giles. London: J. R. Smith, 1864.

Aston, Margaret. *The King's Bedpost: Reformation and Iconography in a Tudor Group Portrait.* Cambridge: Cambridge University Press, 1993.

Atherton, Ian, and Julie Sanders, eds. *The 1630s: Interdisciplinary Essays on Culture and Politics in the Caroline Era.* Manchester: Manchester University Press, 2006.

Atterbury, Francis. *Sermon Preached Before the Honourable House of Commons. . . . March 8 1703/4.* London: Printed for Thomas Bennet, 1704.

Augustin, Gonzalex de Amezúa y Mayo. *Isabel de Valois, reina de España.* 3 vols. Madrid: Gráficas Ultra, 1949.

Aylmer, John. *An Harborovve for Faithfvll and Trevve Svbiectes, Agaynst the Late Blowne Blaste, Concerning the Gouerment of VVemen.* Strasbourg, 1559.

Backscheider, Paula R., ed. *Restoration and Eighteenth-century Dramatists: First Series.* Detroit: Gale Research, 1989.

Bacon, Francis. *The Works of Francis Bacon.* Edited by James Spedding, Robert Leslie Ellis, and Douglas Denon Heath. London: Longmans, 1857.

———. *The Works of Francis Bacon, Lord Chancellor of England.* Edited by Basil Montagu. Philadelphia: M. Murphy, 1876.

Baines, Barbara J. *Thomas Heywood.* Boston: Twayne, 1984.

Baker, David Erskine, Isaac Reed, and Stephen Jones. *Biographia Dramatica: or, a Companion to the Playhouse.* London: Longman, Hurst, Rees, Orme, and Brown, 1812.

Baker, Derek, ed. *Medieval Women.* Oxford: B. Blackwell for the Ecclesiastical History Society, 1978.

Baker, Donald C. "The 'Angel' of English Renaissance Literature." *Studies in the Renaissance* 6 (1959).

Bale, John. *A Declaration of Edmonde Bonners Articles Concerning the Cleargye of Lo[n]don Dyocese Whereby That Excerable [sic] Antychriste,*

Is in His Rightecolours Reueled in the Yeare of Our Lord A. 1554. by Iohn Bale. London: By Ihon Tysdall, for Frauncys Coldocke, 1561.

Banks, John. *The Island Queens, Or, the Death of Mary, Queen of Scotland: A Tragedy (1684)*. New York: AMS Press, 1995.

———. *The Unhappy Favourite; Or, the Earl of Essex*. Edited by Thomas Marshall Howe Blair. New York: Columbia University Press, 1939.

Barash, Carol. *English Women's Poetry, 1649–1714: Politics, Community, and Linguistic Authority*. Oxford: Clarendon Press, 1996.

Barbiche, Bernard. *Les institutions de la monarchie française à l'époque moderne: XVIe–XVIIIe siècle*. Paris: Presses universitaires de France, 1999.

Barlow, Frank. *The Feudal Kingdom of England, 1042–1216*. London: Longmans, 1961.

Bartlett, Robert. *England under the Norman and Angevin Kings, 1075–1225*. Oxford: Clarendon Press, 2000.

Bates, J. *Two (United) are Better than One Alone: a Thanksgiving Sermon Upon the Union*. London: Printed by T. Ilve for Jonathan Robinson, 1707.

Baumann, Gerd, ed. *The Written Word: Literacy in Transition*. Oxford: Clarendon Press, 1986.

Baumgartner, Frederic J. *Henry II, King of France, 1547–1559*. Durham NC: Duke University Press, 1988.

Bayer, Mark. "Staging Foxe at the Fortune and the Red Bull." *Renaissance and Reformation* 27 (2003).

Beal, Peter, and Grace Ioppolo, eds. *Elizabeth I and the Culture of Writing*. London: British Library, 2007.

Bede. *A History of the English Church and People*. Translated by Leo Sherley-Price. New York: Dorset Press, 1985.

Beem, Charles, ed. *The Royal Minorities of Medieval and Early Modern England*. New York: Palgrave Macmillan, 2008.

Benkert, Lysbeth. "Translation as Image-Making: Elizabeth I's Translation of Boethius's Consolation of Philosophy." *Early Modern Literary Studies* 6, no. 3 (2001).

Bennett, Gareth Vaughan. *The Tory Crisis in Church and State, 1688–1730: The Career of Francis Atterbury, Bishop of Rochester*. Oxford: Clarendon Press, 1975.

Bennett, Judith. M. "Feminism and History." *Gender and History* 1 (1989).

———. *Medieval Women in Modern Perspective*. Washington DC: American Historical Association, 2000.

Bennett, Judith M., and Amy M. Froide, eds. *Singlewomen in the European Past, 1250–1800*. Philadelphia: University of Pennsylvania Press, 1999.

Bentley, Thomas. *The Monument of Matrons*. London: H. Denham, 1582.

Berefelt, Gunnar. *A Study on the Winged Angel: The Origin of a Motif*. Stockholm: Almqvist & Wiksell, 1968.

Berlin, Adele. *Esther: The Traditional Hebrew Text with the New JSP Translation*. Philadelphia: Jewish Publication Society, 2001.

Berry, Philippa. *Of Chastity and Power: Elizabethan Literature and the Unmarried Queen*. London: Routledge, 1989.

Biddle, Sheila. *Bolingbroke and Harley*. London: George Allen & Unwin, 1975.

Biow, Douglas. *Doctors, Ambassadors, Secretaries: Humanism and Professions in Renaissance Italy*. Chicago: University of Chicago Press, 2002.

Birch, Walter de Gray. *A Fasciculus of the Charters of Mathildis Empress of the Romans and an Account of Her Great Seal*. London, 1875.

Blair, Hugh. *Gods Soveraignty, His Sacred Majesties Supremacy, the Subjects Duty Asserted in a Sermon, Preached Before His Majesties High Commissioner, and the Honourable Parliament of the Kingdom of Scotland, at Edinburgh, the 31. of March, 1661*. Glasgow: Printed by Robert Sanders, 1661.

Bloch, R. Howard. *Medieval Misogyny and the Invention of Western Romantic Love*. Chicago: University of Chicago Press, 1991.

Bohun, Edmund. *The Character of Queen Elizabeth*. London, 1693.

Bowers, John M. "'I Am Marble-Constant': Cleopatra's Monumental End." *Huntington Library Quarterly* 46, no. 4 (1983).

Bowers, Toni. *The Politics of Motherhood: British Writing and Culture, 1680–1760.* Cambridge: Cambridge University Press, 1996.

Bradbury, Jim. *Stephen and Matilda: The Civil War of 1139–53.* Stroud: Alan Sutton, 1996.

Braziel, Jana Evans, and Kathleen LeBesco. *Bodies out of Bounds: Fatness and Transgression.* Berkeley: University of California Press, 2001.

Brink, Jean R., Allison Coudert, and Maryanne Cline Horowitz, eds. *The Politics of Gender in Early Modern Europe.* Kirksville: Sixteenth Century Journal Publishers, 1989.

Britland, Karen. *Drama at the Courts of Henrietta Maria.* Cambridge: Cambridge University Press, 2006.

Brown, Beatrice Curtis. *Alas, Queen Anne: A Reading of Her Life.* Indianapolis: Bobbs-Merrill, 1929.

Brown, Pamela Allen, and Peter Parolin. *Women Players in England, 1500–1660: Beyond the All-male Stage.* Aldershot: Ashgate, 2005.

Bucholz, Robert. "Going to Court in 1700: A Visitor's Guide." *The Court Historian* 5 (2000).

Bucholz, Robert, and Newton Key. *Early Modern England, 1485–1714: A Narrative History.* Malden: Blackwell Publishing, 2004.

Bugge, John. *Virginitas: An Essay in the History of a Medieval Ideal.* The Hague: Martinus Nijhoff, 1975.

Bullough, Geoffrey. *Narrative and Dramatic Sources of Shakespeare.* London: Routledge & Kegan Paul, 1964.

Burnet, Gilbert. *A History of His Own Time.* Oxford: Oxford University Press, 1833.

———. *The Memoirs of the Lives and Actions of James and William, dukes of Hamilton and Castleherald, &c. in Which an Account Is Given of the Rise and Progress of the Civil Wars of Scotland . . . with Many Letters, Instructions, and Other Papers, Written by King Charles the I. Never Before Published. All Drawn Out Of, or Copied from the Originals.* London: Printed by J. Grover, for R. Royston, 1677.

———. *A Sermon Preach'd Before the Queen, and the two Houses of Parliament, at St. Paul's, on the 31st of December, 1706.* London: Printed by W.B. for A. and J. Churchill, 1707.

Burtchaell, George Dames, and J. M Rigg, eds. *Report on Franciscan Manuscripts Preserved at the Convent, Merchants' Quay, Dublin.* Dublin: Printed for H.M. Stationary Office by J. Falconer, 1906.

Calendar of Letters and State Papers Relating to English Affairs, Preserved Principally in the Archives of Simancas [1894]. Vol. 2: *Elizabeth, 1568–1579.* Edited by Martin A. S. Hume. Nendeln, Liechtenstein: Kraus-Thomas Organization, 1971.

Calendar of Letters, Despatches, and State Papers Relating to the Negotiations Between England and Spain Preserved in the Archives at Simancas and Elsewhere. Edited by Royall Tyler. London: Longman, Green, Longman, and Roberts, 1862.

Calendar of State Papers: Domestic Series of the Reign of Mary 1, 1553–58, Preserved in the Public Record Office. Edited by C. S. Knighton. London: Public Record Office, 1998.

Calendar of State Papers and Manuscripts, Relating to English Affairs, Existing in the Archives and Collections of Venice: and in other Libraries of Northern Italy. Edited by R. Brown et al. Vols. 1–38. London: Longman, Green, Longman, Roberts, and Green, 1864–1947.

Calendar of State Papers, Domestic Series, of the Reigns of Edward VI, Mary, Elizabeth, 1547–1580. Edited by Robert Lemon. London: Longmans, 1856.

Calendar of State Papers, Foreign Series, of the Reign of Elizabeth, 1558–1588. Edited by Joseph Stevenson. Nendeln, Liechtenstein: Kraus Reprint, 1966.

Calendar of State Papers, Foreign Series, of the Reign of Mary, 1553–58. Edited by William B. Turnbull. London, 1861.

Camden, William. *Annales: The True and Royall History of the Famous Empresse Elizabeth Queene of England France and Ireland &c.* London, 1625.

———. *The History of the Most Renowned and Victorious Princess*

Elizabeth, Late Queen of England Containing All the Most Important and Remarkable Passages of State, Both at Home and Abroad (so Far As They were Linked with English Affairs) During Her Long and Prosperous Reign. London: Printed by M. Flesher, for R. Bentley, 1688.

Cannon, John Ashton, and Ralph Alan Griffiths. *The Oxford Illustrated History of the British Monarchy.* Oxford: Oxford University Press, 1998.

Carey, John, ed. *English Renaissance Studies Presented to Dame Helen Gardner in Honor of Her Seventieth Birthday.* Oxford: Clarendon Press, 1980.

Carney, Jo. "'God hath given you one face, and you make yourself another': Face Painting in the Renaissance." *Lamar Journal of the Humanities* 21 (Fall 1995).

Carpenter, Jennifer, and Sally-Beth MacLean, *Power of the Weak: Studies on Medieval Women.* Urbana: University of Illinois Press, 1995.

Cartwright, J. J., ed. *The Wentworth Papers, 1705–1739.* London: Wyman, 1883.

Cartwright, Julia Mary. *Christina of Denmark, Duchess of Milan and Lorraine, 1522–1590.* New York: E. P. Dutton, 1913.

Castiglione, Baldassarre. *The Book of the Courtier.* Translated by George Bull. Harmondsworth, England: Penguin Classics, 1976.

Catherine de' Medici. *Lettres de Catherine de Médicis.* Edited by Hector La Ferrière-Percy, Gustave Baguenault de Puchesse et al. 11 vols. Paris: Imprimerie Nationale, 1880.

Cavallo, Sandra, and Lyndan Warner, eds. *Widowhood in Medieval and Early Modern Europe.* Singapore: Longman, 1999.

Certaine Informations, from Severall Parts of the Kingdome. May 8–15, 1643, TT E 101(24); March 27–April 3, 1643, TT E 94(29).

Challis, C. E. *The Tudor Coinage.* Manchester: Manchester University Press, 1978.

Chibnall, Marjorie. *The Empress Matilda: Queen Consort, Queen Mother, and Lady of the English.* Oxford: Blackwell, 1991.

Chibnall, Marjorie, ed. *Anglo-Norman Studies XIII: Proceedings of the Battle Conference, 1990*. Woodbridge, Suffolk: Boydell Press, 1991.

Christopherson, John. *An exhortation to alle menne to take hede and beware of rebellion*. London: John Cawood, 1555.

Clair, Colin. *A History of Printing in Britain*. New York: Oxford University Press, 1966.

Clark, Kenneth. *The Nude: A Study in Ideal Form*. Princeton: Princeton University Press, 1972.

Coch, Christine. "'Mother of my Contreye': Elizabeth I and Tudor Constructions of Motherhood." *English Literary Renaissance* 26 (1996).

Cogswell, Thomas. *The Blessed Revolution: English Politics and the Coming of War, 1621–1624*. Cambridge: Cambridge University Press, 1989.

Coke, R. *Detection of the Court and State of England During the Last Four Reigns*. London: Printed for J. Brotherton and W. Meadows, 1719.

Cole, Mary Hill. *The Portable Queen: Elizabeth I and the Politics of Ceremony*. Amherst: University of Massachusetts Press, 1999.

Coleman, Christopher, and David Starkey, eds. *Revolution Reassessed: Revisions in the History of Tudor Government and Administration*. Oxford: Clarendon Press, 1986.

Collinson, Patrick. "The Elizabethan Exclusion Crisis and the Elizabethan Polity." *Proceedings of the British Academy* 84 (1995).

———. "The Monarchical Republic of Queen Elizabeth I." *Bulletin of the John Rylands University Library of Manchester* 69, no. 2 (July 1986).

Connell, Neville. *Anne, the Last Stuart Monarch*. London: T. Butterworth, 1937.

A Continuation of Certain Speciall and Remarkable Passages. May 18–25, 1643, TT E 104(6); March 23–30, 1643, TT E 247(12).

Coole, Diana H. *Women in Political Theory: From Ancient Misogyny to Contemporary Feminism*. Brighton: Wheatsheaf, 1988.

Corbett, Margery, and R. W. Lightbown. *The Comely Frontispiece: The Emblematic Title-page in England, 1550–1660*. London: Routledge & Kegan Paul, 1979.

Cornette, Joël, ed. *La monarchie entre renaissance et révolution, 1515–1792.* Paris: Seuil, 2000.

Correspondance diplomatique de Bertrand de Salignac de la Mothe-Fénélon. Vol. 2: *Récueil des dépeches, rapports, instructions et mémoires des ambassadeurs de France.* Paris & London, 1840.

Cotgrave, R. *A French-English Dictionary* [1611]. Menston, Yorkshire: Scolar Press, 1968.

The Court Mercurie. July 10–20, 1644, TT E 2(25).

Crawford, Katherine. *Perilous Performances: Gender and Regency in Early Modern France.* Cambridge MA: Harvard University Press, 2004.

Cressy, David. *Literacy and the Social Order: Reading and Writing in Tudor and Stuart England.* Cambridge: Cambridge University Press, 1980.

Cronne, H. A. *The Reign of King Stephen, 1135–1154: Anarchy in England.* London: Weidenfeld & Nicolson, 1970.

Cust, Richard. "News and Politics in Early Seventeenth-Century England." *Past and Present* 112 (1986).

Davies, John. *Hymns to Astroea: The Complete Poems of Sir John Davies.* Edited by Alexander B. Grosart. London: Chatto & Windus, 1976.

Davis, Natalie Zemon, and Arlette Farge, eds. *A History of Women in the West: Renaissance and Enlightenment Paradoxes.* Cambridge MA: Harvard University Press, Belknap Press, 1993.

Davis, R. H. C. *King Stephen, 1135–1154.* London: Longman, 1990.

Dee, John. *The Private Diary of Dr. John Dee: And the Catalogue of His Library of Manuscripts, from the Original Manuscripts in the Ashmolean Museum at Oxford, and Trinity College Library, Cambridge.* Edited by J. O. Halliwell-Phillipps. London: The Camden Society, 1842.

Dempsey, Charles. *Inventing the Renaissance Putto.* Chapel Hill: University of North Carolina Press, 2001.

Digges, Dudley. *The Compleat Ambassador: Or, Two Treaties of the Intended Marriage of Queen Elizabeth of Glorious Memory.* London: Printed by T. Newcomb, for G. Bedell and T. Collins, 1655.

Dobson, Michael, and Nicola J. Watson. *England's Elizabeth: An Afterlife in Fame and Fantasy.* Oxford: Oxford University Press, 2002.

Dolan, Frances E. *Whores of Babylon: Catholicism, Gender, and Seventeenth-century Print Culture.* Ithaca NY: Cornell University Press, 1999.

Doran, Susan. "Elizabeth I and Catherine de Medici." Unpublished manuscript used by permission of the author, n.d.

———. *Elizabeth I and Foreign Policy, 1558–1603.* London: Routledge, 2000.

———. *England and Europe in the Sixteenth Century.* New York: St. Martin's Press, 1999.

———. *Monarchy and Matrimony: The Courtships of Elizabeth I.* London: Routledge, 1996.

———. *Queen Elizabeth I.* London: British Library, 2003.

Doran, Susan, and Thomas S. Freeman, eds. *The Myth of Elizabeth.* Basingstoke: Palgrave Macmillan, 2003.

Drant, Thomas. *Two Sermons preached . . . the other at the Court of Windsor the Sonday after the twelfth day being the viiij of January, before in the yeare 1569.* London, 1570.

Dryden, John. *Second Satire of Persius.* London: Tonson, 1693.

Duffy, Eamon, and D. M. Loades, eds. *The Church of Mary Tudor.* Aldershot: Ashgate, 2006.

Duggan, Anne, ed. *Queens and Queenship in Medieval Europe.* Woodbridge: Boydell Press, 1997.

Dunlop, Ian. *Palaces and Progresses of Elizabeth I.* New York: Taplinger, 1970.

Dunn, Jane. *Elizabeth and Mary: Cousins, Rivals, Queens.* New York: Alfred A. Knopf, 2004.

Eales, Jacqueline. *Women in Early Modern England, 1500–1700.* London: UCL Press, 1998.

Edwards, Francis. *Plots and Plotters in the Reign of Elizabeth I.* Dublin: Four Courts, 2002.

Eggert, Katherine. *Showing Like a Queen: Female Authority and Literary Experiment in Spenser, Shakespeare, and Milton.* Philadelphia: University of Pennsylvania Press, 2000.

Elizabeth I. *Autograph Compositions and Foreign Language Originals*. Edited by Janel M. Mueller and Leah S. Marcus. Chicago: University of Chicago Press, 2003.

———. *Christian Prayers and Meditations in English[,] French, Italian, Spanish, Greeke, and Latine*. London: John Daye, 1569.

———. *Collected Works*. Edited by Leah S. Marcus, Janel M. Mueller, and Mary Beth Rose. Chicago: University of Chicago Press, 2000.

———. *The Letters of Queen Elizabeth I*. Edited by G. B. Harrison. New York: Funk & Wagnalls, 1968.

———. *Precationes Priuat[æ] Regiæ E.R.* London: T. Purfoot, 1563.

Elliott, John Huxtable. *Europe Divided, 1559–1598*. Oxford: Blackwell, 2000.

———. "A Europe of Composite Monarchies." *Past and Present* 137 (1992).

Elton, G. R. *Studies in Tudor and Stuart Politics and Government: Papers and Reviews, 1946–1972*. London: Cambridge University Press, 1974.

Erasmus, Desiderius. *The Education of a Christian Prince*. Translated by Neil M. Cheshire and Michael J. Heath. Edited by Lisa Jardine. New York: Cambridge University Press, 1997.

Fabian, Bernhard, Marvin Spevack, and Kurt Tetzeli von Rosador, eds. *Shakespeare, Text, Language, Criticism: Essays in Honour of Marvin Spevack*. Hildesheim: Olms-Weidmann, 1987.

Farmer, John Stephen, ed. *Six Anonymous Plays (Second Series)*. London: Privately printed for subscribers by the Early English Drama Society, 1906.

Feiling, Keith Grahame. *A History of the Tory Party, 1640–1714*. Oxford: Clarendon Press, 1924.

Fell, Christine E. *Women in Anglo-Saxon England*. London: Colonnade, 1984.

Field, Ophelia. *Sarah Churchill, Duchess of Marlborough: The Queen's Favorite*. New York: St. Martin's Press, 2002.

Fletcher, Anthony. *Gender, Sex, and Subordination in England, 1500–1800.* New Haven: Yale University Press, 1995.

Foliot, Gilbert. *The Letters and Charters of Gilbert Foliot, Abbot of Gloucester (1139–48), Bishop of Hereford (1148–63), and London (1163–87).* Edited by Z. N. Brooke, Adrian Morey, and Christopher Nugent Lawrence Brooke. Cambridge: Cambridge University Press, 1967.

Foss, Michael. *The Age of Patronage: The Arts in England, 1660–1750.* Ithaca NY: Cornell University Press, 1976.

Foucault, Michel. *The History of Sexuality.* Translated by Alan Sheridan. New York: Vintage, 1980.

Fox, Adam. "Rumour, News and Popular Political Opinion in Elizabethan and Early Stuart England." *Huntington Library Quarterly* (1996).

Fox, John. *The Book of Martyrs Containing An Account of the Sufferings & Death of the Protestants in the Reign of Queen Mary the First. Illustrated with Copper-plates. Originally Written by Mr. John Fox. Now Carefully revis'd & Corrected with a Recommendatory Preface by the Revd. Mr. Madan.* London: Published for H. Trapp, 1776.

Fox, Margaret Askew Fell. *Womens Speaking Justified, Proved and Allowed of by the Scriptures All Such As Speak by the Spirit and Power of the Lord Jesus: And How Women Were the First that Preached the Tidings of the Resurrection of Jesus And were Sent by Christ's Own Command Before He Ascended to the Father, John 20:17.* London, 1667.

Foxe, John. *The Acts and Monuments of John Foxe: A New and Complete Edition: With a Preliminary Dissertation, by the Rev. George Townsend.* Edited by Stephen Reed Cattley. London: R. B. Seeley and W. Burnside, 1837.

———. *The First Volume of the Ecclesiasticall History Contaynyng the Actes and Monumentes of Thynges Passed in Euery Kynges Tyme in This Realme, Especially in the Church of England.* London: Printed by John Daye, dwellyng ouer Aldersgate, these bookes are to be sold at hys shop vnder the gate, 1570.

Frank, Joseph. *The Beginnings of the English Newspaper, 1620–1660.* Cambridge MA: Harvard University Press, 1961.

Fraser, Antonia. *The Wives of Henry VIII.* New York: Knopf, 1992.

Freeman, Thomas S. "'As True a Subject being Prysoner': John Foxe's Notes on the Imprisonment of Princess Elizabeth, 1554–5." *English Historical Review* 117, no. 470 (2002).

Freist, Dagmar. *Governed by Opinion: Politics, Religion, and the Dynamics of Communication.* London: I. B. Tauris, 1997.

French, Peter J. *John Dee: The World of an Elizabethan Magus.* London: Routledge & Kegan Paul, 1972.

Frieda, Leonie. *Catherine De Medici: Renaissance Queen of France.* New York: Fourth Estate, 2003.

Frigo, Daniela. *Politics and Diplomacy in Early Modern Italy: The Structure of Diplomatic Practice, 1450–1800.* Translated by Adrian Belton. Cambridge: Cambridge University Press, 2000.

Froide, Amy M. *Never Married: Singlewomen in Early Modern England.* Oxford: Oxford University Press, 2006.

Frye, Susan. *Elizabeth I: The Competition for Representation.* New York: Oxford University Press, 1993.

Frye, Susan, and Karen Robertson, eds. *Maids and Mistresses, Cousins and Queens: Women's Alliances in Early Modern England.* New York: Oxford University Press, 1999.

Gardiner, Samuel Rawson. *The Constitutional Documents of the Puritan Revolution, 1628–1660.* Oxford: Clarendon Press, 1889.

Gaspey, Thomas, ed. *The History of England: From the Text of Hume and Smollett to the Reign of George III.* London: London Print. and Pub., 1852.

The Geneva Bible: A Facsimile of the 1560 Edition. Madison: University of Wisconsin Press, 1969.

Gentles, Ian. *The New Model Army in England, Ireland, and Scotland, 1645–1653.* Oxford: Blackwell, 1992.

Gillingham, John. "Love, Marriage, and Politics in the Twelfth Century." *Forum for Modern Language Studies* 25 (1989).

Goodman, Christopher. *How Superior Powers oght to be obeyd of their subicts.* Geneva: John Crispin, 1558.

A Great Discovery of the Queens Preparation in Holland to Assist the King in England Also How Her Majesty Hath Sent Her Standard, with the Rest of Her Regiments Over to New-castle. London: Printed for J. Wright, December 17, 1642. British Library: Rare Tracts, 1077.f.86.

Green, David Brontë. *Queen Anne.* New York: Scribners, 1970.

Green, Janet M. "Queen Elizabeth's Latin Reply to the Polish Ambassador." *Sixteenth Century Journal* 31 (2000).

Green, Judith A. *The Government of England under Henry I.* Cambridge: Cambridge University Press, 1986.

Gregg, Edward. *Queen Anne.* London: Routledge & Kegan Paul, 1980.

Guazzo, Stefano. *The Civile Conversation of M. Steeven Guazzo.* Translated by Bartholomew Yong. London: By Thomas East, 1586.

Gunn, Steven J. *Charles Brandon, Duke of Suffolk, c. 1484–1545.* Oxford: Blackwell, 1988.

Guy, John. *The Tudor Monarchy.* New York: Arnold, 1997.

Hackett, Helen. *Virgin Mother, Maiden Queen: Elizabeth I and the Cult of the Virgin Mary.* New York: St. Martin's Press, 1995.

Haigh, Christopher. *Elizabeth I.* 2nd ed. Harlow: Longman, 1998.

Hamilton, Adam. *The Angel of Syon: The life and martyrdom of Blessed Richard Reynolds, martyred at Tyburn, May 4, 1535.* Edinburgh: Sands and Co., 1905.

Hampson, A. *The English at Table.* London: Collins, 1944.

Harington, John. *A Tract on the Succession to the Crown (AD 1602).* New York: B. Franklin, 1970.

Harkness, Deborah E. *John Dee's Conversations with Angels: Cabala, Alchemy, and the End of Nature.* Cambridge: Cambridge University Press, 1999.

Harrington, James. *The Art of Law-giving in III Books.* London: Printed for J.C. for Henry Fletcher, 1659.

Harris, Barbara J. *English Aristocratic Women, 1450–1550: Marriage and Family, Property and Careers.* Oxford: Oxford University Press, 2002.

Harris, Frances. "Accounts of the Conduct of Sarah, Duchess of Marlborough, 1704–42." *British Library Journal* 8 (1982).

———. *A Passion for Government: The Life of Sarah, Duchess of Marlborough.* Oxford: Clarendon Press, 1991.

Harrison, Dick. *The Age of Abbesses and Queens: Gender and Political Culture in Early Medieval Europe.* Lund, Sweden: Nordic Academic Press, 1998.

Hart, Vaughan. *Art and Magic in the Court of the Stuarts.* London: Routledge, 1994.

Haynes, Samuel, and William Murdin, eds. *A Collection of State Papers, Relating to Affairs in the Reigns of King Henry VIII. King Edward VI. Queen Mary, And Queen Elizabeth, from the Year 1542 to 1570.* London: Printed by William Bowyer, 1740.

Heisch, Allison. "Queen Elizabeth and the Persistence of Patriarchy." *Feminist Review* 4 (1980).

Henrietta Maria. *Letters of Queen Henrietta Maria, Including Her Private Correspondence with Charles the First.* Edited by Mary Anne Everett Green. London: R. Bentley, 1857.

Henrikson, Erin. "Dressed as Esther: The Value of Concealment in Ester Sowernam's Biblical Pseudonym." *Women's Writing* 10, no. 1 (2003).

Henry of Huntingdon. *The Chronicle of Henry of Huntingdon. Comprising the History of England, from the Invasion of Julius Cæsar to the Accession of Henry II. Also, the Acts of Stephen, King of England and Duke of Normandy.* Edited by Thomas Forester. London: H. G. Bohn, 1853.

Herbert, G. *Jacula Prudentum, or, Outlandish Proverbs, Sentences, &c.* London, 1640.

An Heroick Poem on her Highness the Lady Anne's Voyage into Scotland: with a Little Digression upon the Time. London, 1681.

Heywood, John. *The Spider and the Flie. A Parable of the Spider and the*

Flie, Made by John Heywood [1556]. New York: Spenser Society New Series no. 6, 1967.

Heywood, Thomas. *The Exemplary Lives and Memorable Acts of Nine of the Most Worthy Women in the World. Three Jewes. Three Gentiles. Three Christians. Written by the Author of the History of Women.* Edited by George Glover. London: Printed by Cotes, for Richard Royston, 1640.

———. *The Hierarchie of the Blessed Angells Their Names, Orders and Offices. The Fall of Lucifer with His Angells.* London: Printed by Adam Islip, 1635.

———. *If You Know Not Me, You Know Nobody.* London: Printed for the Malone Society by J. Johnson at the Oxford University Press, 1935.

Hibbard, Caroline M. *Charles I and the Popish Plot.* Chapel Hill: University of North Carolina Press, 1983.

Hill, Christopher. *The Collected Essays of Christopher Hill.* Vol. 1: *Writing and Revolution in 17th Century England.* Boston: University of Massachusetts Press, 1987.

———. *Some Intellectual Consequences of the English Revolution.* Madison: University of Wisconsin Press, 1980.

HIS MAJESTIES DECLARATION *To all His loving Subjects . . . upon the . . . severall Intercepted Letters of His* MAJESTY *to the* QUEENE, *and of* PRINCE RUPERT *to the Earl of North-Hampton.* Oxford: Leonard Lichfield, June 3, 1643, TT E 104(31).

Hollister, C. Warren. "The Anglo-Norman Succession Debate of 1126: Prelude to Stephen's Anarchy." *Journal of Medieval History* 1 (1975).

———. *Henry I.* Edited by Amanda Clark Frost. New Haven: Yale University Press, 2001.

Hollister, C. Warren, ed. *Anglo-Norman Political Culture and the Twelfth-century Renaissance.* Woodbridge, Suffolk: Boydell & Brewer, 1997.

Holmes, Geoffrey S. *British Politics in the Age of Anne.* London: Macmillan, 1967.

Hopkinson, M. R. *Anne of England: The Biography of a Great Queen.* New York: Macmillan, 1967.

Hoppit, Julian. *A Land of Liberty?: England, 1689–1727.* Oxford: Clarendon Press, 2000.

Hudson, John. *Land, Law, and Lordship in Anglo-Norman England.* Oxford: Clarendon Press, 1994.

Huggarde, Miles. *The displaying of the Protestants.* London, 1556.

The Humble Petition of the Wretched and Most Contemptible the Poore Commons of England to the Blessed Elizabeth of Famous Memory: Also a Most Gratious Answer with a Divine Admonition and Propheticall Conclusion. London: Printed for E.P. and E.B., 1642.

Hutchinson, Lucy Apsley. *Memoirs of the Life of Colonel Hutchinson, Governor of Nottingham.* London: G. Routledge, 1906.

Hymnnaeus Cantabrigiensis. Cambridge, 1683.

James, Elinor. *Mrs. James's Vindication of the Church of England in an Answer to a Pamphlet Entituled a New Test of the Church of England's Loyalty.* London, 1687.

Jankowski, Theodora A. *Pure Resistance: Queer Virginity in Early Modern English Drama.* Philadelphia: University of Pennsylvania Press, 2000.

John Niccols pilgrimage whrein [sic] *is displaied the liues of the proude popes, ambitious cardinals, lecherous bishops, fat bellied monks, and hypocriticall Iesuities.* London: Thomas Butter and Godfrey Isaac, 1581.

John of Salisbury. *Memoirs of the Papal Court.* Edited by Marjorie Chibnall. Oxford: Clarendon Press, 1986.

Johns, Susan M. *Noblewomen, Aristocracy and Power in the Twelfth-century Anglo-Norman Realm.* Manchester: Manchester University, 2003.

Johnson, C., and H. A. Cronne, eds. *Regesta Regum Anglo-normannorum, 1066–1154.* Oxford: Clarendon Press, 1968.

Jones, Norman. *The Birth of the Elizabethan Age: England in the 1560s.* Oxford: Blackwell, 1995.

Jonson, Ben. *Ben Jonson*. Edited by C. H. Herford and Percy Simpson. Oxford: Oxford University Press, 1925.

Kantorowicz, Ernst Hartwig. *The King's Two Bodies: A Study in Medieval Political Theology*. Princeton: Princeton University Press, 1957.

Keay, A. "The Ceremonies of Charles II's Court." PhD thesis, University of London, 2004.

Keck, David. *Angels and Angelology in the Middle Ages*. Oxford: Oxford University Press, 1998.

Kelso, Ruth. *Doctrine for the Lady of the Renaissance*. Urbana: University of Illinois Press, 1956.

King, Edmund, ed. *The Anarchy of King Stephen's Reign*. Oxford: Clarendon Press, 1994.

King, John N. "The Godly Woman in Elizabethan Iconography." *Renaissance Quarterly* 38, no. 1 (1985).

———. "Queen Elizabeth I: Representations of the Virgin Queen." *Renaissance Quarterly* 43 (1990).

———. *Tudor Royal Iconography: Literature and Art in an Age of Religious Crisis*. Princeton: Princeton University Press, 1989.

The Kingdomes Weekly Intelligencer. March 7–14, 1643, TT E 93(6); May 30–June 6, 1643, TT E 105(24).

The Kingdomes Weekly Post, with his packet of Letters. November 15–22, 1643, TT E 76(22); December 12–20, 1643, TT E 78(28).

Kingdon, R. *Myths about the St. Bartholomew's Day Massacres, 1572–1576*. Cambridge MA: Harvard University Press, 1988.

Kishlansky, Mark A. *A Monarchy Transformed: Britain, 1603–1714*. London: Penguin, 1996.

Knecht, Robert Jean. *Catherine De' Medici*. London: Longman, 1998.

———. *The Rise and Fall of Renaissance France: 1483–1610*. Oxford: Blackwell, 2001.

Knox, John. *The Works of John Knox*. Edited by David Laing. Edinburgh: James Thin, 1895.

Kyffin, Maurice. *The Blessednes of Brytaine*. London, 1587.

Langbaine, Gerard, and Charles Gildon. *The Lives and Characters of the*

English Dramatick Poets Also an Exact Account of All the Plays That Were Ever yet Printed in the English Tongue, Their Double Titles, the Places Where Acted, the Dates When Printed, and the Persons to Whom Dedicated: With Remarks and Observations on Most of the Said Plays. London: Printed for Thomas Leigh and William Turner, 1699.

Laqueur, Thomas Walter. "The Cultural Origins of Popular Literacy in England 1500–1800." *Oxford Review of Education* 2, no. 3 (1976).

———. *Making Sex: Body and Gender from the Greeks to Freud.* Cambridge MA: Harvard University Press, 1990.

Laurence, Anne. *Women in England, 1500–1760: A Social History.* London: Weidenfeld and Nicolson, 1994.

Layner, Aemilia. *The Poems of Aemilia Lanyer: Salve Deus Rex Judaeorum.* Edited by Susanne Woods. Oxford: Oxford University Press, 1993.

Lecky, William Edward Hartpole. *A History of England in the Eighteenth Century.* New York: Appleton, 1888.

Lee, Christopher. *1603: A Turning Point in British History.* London: Review, 2003.

Leigh, William. *Queene Elizabeth, Paraleld in Her Princely Vertues, with Dauid, Iosua, and Hezekia, Three Sermons, as They Were Preached Three Seuerall Queenes Dayes.* London: Printed by Thomas Creede for Arthur Johnson, 1612.

Lerner, Gerda. *The Creation of Patriarchy.* Oxford: Oxford University Press, 1986.

Letters and Papers, Foreign and Domestic of the Reign of Henry VIII. Edited by J. S. Brewer. London: H.M. Stationery Office, 1862.

A Letter to the Lady Osborne. London, 1688.

Levin, Carole. *"The Heart and Stomach of a King": Elizabeth I and the Politics of Sex and Power.* Philadelphia: University of Pennsylvania Press, 1994.

———. *The Reign of Elizabeth I.* New York: Palgrave Macmillan, 2002.

Levin, Carole, and Patricia Ann Sullivan, eds. *Political Rhetoric, Power, and Renaissance Women.* Albany: State University of New York Press, 1995.

Levin, Carole, Jo Eldridge Carney, and Debra Barrett-Graves, eds. *Elizabeth I: Always Her Own Free Woman.* Aldershot: Ashgate, 2003.

———. *"High and Mighty Queens" of Early Modern England: Realities and Representations.* New York: Palgrave Macmillan, 2003.

Lewis, Andrew W. *Royal Succession in Capetian France: Studies on Familial Order and the State.* Cambridge MA: Harvard University Press, 1981.

Lewis, Jayne Elizabeth. *Mary Queen of Scots: Romance and Nation.* London: Routledge, 1998.

Leyser, Henrietta. *Medieval Women: A Social History of Women in England, 450–1500.* London: Weidenfeld and Nicolson, 1995.

Leyser, Karl. *Medieval Germany and Its Neighbors, 900–1250.* London: Hambledon Press, 1982.

The Life of her late Majesty Queen Anne As Well before her Accession to the Throne as After . . . London: Printed for C. Rivington, 1721.

Llamas, Antonio Martinez. *Isabel de Valois, Reigna de España: una historia de amor y enfermedad.* Madrid: Ediciones Temas de Hoy, 1996.

Loach, Jennifer, and Robert Tittler, eds. *The Mid-Tudor Polity, c. 1540–1560.* London: Macmillan, 1980.

Loades, D. M. *Elizabeth I.* London: Hambledon and London, 2003.

———. *Elizabeth I: The Golden Reign of Gloriana.* Richmond: National Archives, 2003.

———. *Intrigue and Treason: The Tudor Court, 1547–1558.* Harlow: Longman, 2004.

———. *John Foxe and the English Reformation.* Aldershot: Scolar Press, 1997.

———. *Mary Tudor: A Life.* Cambridge MA: Basil Blackwell, 1992.

———. *The Reign of Mary Tudor: Politics, Government, and Religion in England, 1553–1558.* London: Ernest Benn, 1979.

———. *Tudor Government: Structures of Authority in the Sixteenth Century.* Oxford: Blackwell, 1997.

A London Chronicle during the Reigns of Henry VII and Henry VIII. Edited by Clarence Hopper. London: The Camden Society, 1859.

Lyly, John. *Ephues: The Anatomy of Wit.* London: Arbor, 1579.

Lynch, Jack. *The Age of Elizabeth in the Age of Johnson.* Cambridge: Cambridge University Press, 2003.

Macaulay, Thomas Babington. *The History of England: From the Accession of James the Second.* London: Longman, Green, and Co., 1895.

MacCaffrey, Wallace T. *Elizabeth I.* London: E. Arnold, 1993.

———. *The Shaping of the Elizabethan Regime: Elizabethan Politics, 1558–1572.* Princeton: Princeton University Press, 1968.

Machin, Henry. *The Diary of Henry Machyn: Citizen and Merchant-taylor of London, from AD 1550 to AD 1563.* Edited by John Gough Nichols. New York: AMS Press, 1968.

Major, J. Russell. *From Renaissance Monarchy to Absolute Monarchy: French Kings, Nobles, and Estates.* Baltimore: Johns Hopkins University Press, 1994.

Makin, Bathsua. *An Essay to Revive the Antient Education of Gentlewomen In Religion, Manners, Arts & Tongues with an Answer to the Objections Against This Way of Education.* London: Printed by J.D., to be sold by Tho. Parkhurst, 1673.

Marcus, Leah S. *Puzzling Shakespeare: Local Reading and Its Discontents.* Berkeley: University of California Press, 1988.

Marlborough, Sarah Jennings Churchill. *Memoirs of Sarah, Duchess of Marlborough, Together with Her Characters of Her Contemporaries and Her Opinions.* Edited by William King. London: Routledge, 1930.

Marsden, Jean. *Fatal Desire: Women, Sexuality, and the English Stage, 1660–1720.* Ithaca NY: Cornell University Press, 2006.

Marvell, Andrew. *The Poems and Letters of Andrew Marvell.* Edited by Herschel Maurice Margoliouth. Oxford: Oxford University Press, 1971.

May, Steven W., and Anne Lake Prescott. "The French Verses of Elizabeth I." *English Literary Renaissance* 24, no. 1 (1994).

Mayer, John. *Many Commentaries in One Upon Joshua, Judges, Ruth, 1 and*

2 of Samuel, 1 and 2 of Kings, 1 and 2 of Chronicles, Ezra, Nehemiah, Esther. London: Printed by John Legatt and Richard Cotes, 1647.

Maynwaring, Arthur. *The Humble Address of the Clergy of London and Westminister, Paraphras'd*. London, 1710.

McBee, Richard. "Review: Artemisia and Esther at Metropolitan Museum of Art." *American Guild of Judaic Art Online*. February 25, 2001. www.jewishart.org/artemisia/ArtemisiaEsther.html.

McCarthy, Justin. *The Reign of Queen Anne*. London: Chatto & Windus, 1911.

McClure, Ellen M. *Sunspots and the Sun King: Sovereignty and Mediation in Seventeenth-century France*. Urbana: University of Illinois Press, 2006.

McKenzie, Donald Francis. *Making Meaning: "Printers of the Mind" and Other Essays*. Boston: University of Massachusetts Press, 2002.

McLaren, Angus. *Reproductive Rituals: The Perception of Fertility in England from the Sixteenth Century to the Nineteenth Century*. London: Methuen, 1984.

McLaren, Anne N. *Political Culture in the Reign of Elizabeth I: Queen and Commonwealth, 1558–1585*. Cambridge: Cambridge University Press, 1999.

Mendelson, Sara Heller, and Patricia Crawford. *Women in Early Modern England, 1550–1720*. Oxford: Clarendon Press, 1998.

Mercurius Aulicus. July 16–22, 1643, TT E 63(2); July 9–15, 1643, TT E 62(3).

Mercurius Britanicus. September 10–18, 1643, TT E 68(32); September 2–9, 1644, TT E 8(21); March 18–25, 1644, TT E 39(5); July 15–22, 1644, TT E 2(31).

Mercurius rusticus: the downfall of tythes. The country-man discovering the pride, lewdness, covetousness, and ambition of the fat beneficed priests incroaching tythe-mongers, and oppressing impropriatos, &c. London, 1653.

Milbourne, L. *Great Britain's Loss in the death of . . . Queen Anne;*

lamented in a sermon preached at St. Ethelburga's. London: G. Sawbridge, 1714.

Milhous, Judith, and Robert D. Hume, eds. *A Register of English Theatrical Documents, 1660–1737.* Carbondale: Southern Illinois University Press, 1991.

Miller, N. J., and N. Yavneh, eds., *Sibling Relations and Gender in the Early Modern World: Sisters, Brothers, and Others.* London: Ashgate, 2006.

Monod, Paul Kléber. *The Power of Kings: Monarchy and Religion in Europe, 1589–1715.* New Haven: Yale University Press, 1999.

Montrose, Louis Adrian. "Idols of the Queen: Policy, Gender, and the Picturing of Elizabeth I." *Representations* 68 (1999).

———. *The Subject of Elizabeth: Authority, Gender, and Representation.* Chicago: University of Chicago Press, 2006.

Morrill, J. S., ed. *The Oxford Illustrated History of Tudor and Stuart Britain.* Oxford: Oxford University Press, 2000.

Myers, Henry Allen. *Medieval Kingship.* New York: St. Martin's Press, 1982.

Myers, Robin, Michael Harris, and Giles Mandelbrote. *Lives in Print: Biography and the Book Trade from the Middle Ages to the Twenty-first Century.* London: British Library, 2002.

Nadal, Santiago. *Las cuatro mujeres de Felipe II.* Barcelona: Editorial Juventud, 1971.

Naunton, Robert. *The Court of Queen Elizabeth: Originally Written by Sir Robert Naunton, Under the Title of "Fragmenta Regalia." with Considerable Biographical Additions, by James Caulfield.* London: G. Smeeton, 1814.

Newman, Charlotte A. *The Anglo-Norman Nobility in the Reign of Henry I: The Second Generation.* Philadelphia: University of Pennsylvania Press, 1988.

Newman, Peter. "Royalist Armies in Northern England." PhD thesis, University of York, 1978.

Nichols, John. *The Chronicle of Queen Jane: And of Two Years of Queen*

Mary, and Especially of the Rebellion of Sir Thomas Wyat. London: Printed for the Camden Society, 1850.

——. *The Progresses and Public Processions of Queen Elizabeth. Among Which Are Interspersed Other Solemnities, Public Expenditures, and Remarkable Events During the Reign of That Illustrious Princess.* London: J. Nichols, 1823.

Notestein, Wallace. *Four Worthies: John Chamberlain, Anne Clifford, John Taylor, Oliver Heywood.* London: J. Cape, 1956.

Occurences of Certain Speciall and Remarkable Passages in PARLIAMENT, and the affaires of the Kingdome. London: Printed for Andrew Coe, April 5, 1644, TT E 40(26).

Oliphant, Margaret. *Historical Characters of the Reign of Queen Anne.* New York: The Century Co., 1894.

Ordericus Vitalis. *The Ecclesiastical History of Orderic Vitalis.* Edited by Marjorie Chibnall. Oxford: Clarendon, 1998.

"Original Documents Relating to Queen Katharine of Aragon." *The Gentleman's Magazine,* New series, 42 (December 1854).

Orlin, Lena Cowen. *Material London, ca. 1600.* Philadelphia: University of Pennsylvania Press, 2000.

Orr, Clarissa Campbell, ed. *Queenship in Britain, 1660–1837: Royal Patronage, Court, Culture, and Dynastic Politics.* Manchester: Manchester University Press, 2002.

Osborne, Francis. *Historical Memoires on the Reigns of Queen Elizabeth, and King James.* London, 1658.

Osherow, Michelle. "'Give Ear O' Princes': Deborah, Elizabeth and the Right Word." *Explorations in Renaissance Culture* 30, no. 1 (2004).

Palliser, Bury. *History of Lace.* London: Sampson Low, Marston, 1902.

Parker, Geoffrey. *Philip II.* Chicago: Carus, 2002.

Parker, Matthew. *The Holie Bible* [The *Bishops' Bible*]. London: Richard Iugge, 1568.

Parker, Rozsika. *The Subversive Stitch: Embroidery and the Making of the Feminine.* London: Women's Press, 1984.

The Parliament Scout. July 13–20, 1643, TT E 61(13); June 20–27, 1643, TT E 56(7).

Parsons, John Carmi, ed. *Medieval Queenship.* New York: St. Martin's Press, 1993.

A pastoral Occasion'd by the Arrival of HRH *Prince George . . . Design't to marry Her Highness the Lady Ann.* London: N. Thompson, 1683.

Patey, Douglas Lane, and Timothy Keegan, eds. *Augustan Studies: Essays in Honor of Irvin Ehrenpreis.* Newark: University of Delaware Press, 1985.

Patterson, Annabel M. *Censorship and Interpretation: The Conditions of Writing and Reading in Early Modern England.* Madison: University of Wisconsin Press, 1984.

Pepys, Samuel. *The Diary of Samuel Pepys.* Edited by Roger Latham and William Matthews. Berkeley: University of California Press, 1995.

Perez, Joseph. *L'Espagne de Philippe II.* Paris: Librairie Artheme Fayard, 1999.

A Perfect Diurnall of Passages in Parliament. N.p., 1643.

Phillips, James E. "Elizabeth I as a Latin Poet: An Epigram on Paul Melissus." *Renaissance News* 16, no. 4 (1963).

Picard, Liza. *Elizabeth's London: Everyday Life in Elizabethan London.* New York: St. Martin's Press, 2004.

The Plotts Revealed And The Parliament Vindicated. London: Printed for F. Coles and F. Leach, August 4, 1643, TT E 63(20).

Plumb, John Harold. *The Growth of Political Stability in England.* London: Macmillan, 1967.

Poems on Affairs of State: Augustan Satirical Verse, 1660–1714. Edited by G. deForest Lord. 7 vols. New Haven: Yale University Press, 1963–75.

Pollock, Frederick, and Frederic William Maitland. *The History of English Law before the Time of Edward I.* Cambridge: Cambridge University Press, 1968.

Porter, Roy. *Flesh in the Age of Reason.* New York: W. W. Norton, 2004.

Potter, Kenneth Reginald, ed. *Gesta Stephani*. Oxford: Clarendon Press, 1976.

Primrose, Diana. *A Chaine of Pearle. or a Memoriall of the Peerles Graces, and Heroick Vertues of Queene Elizabeth, of Glorious Memory*. London: Printed by John Dawson for Thomas Paine, 1630.

The Proceedings in the Late Treaty of Peace Together with Severall Letters of His Majesty to the Queen. London: Edward Husbands, May 17, 1643, TT E 102(6).

Propertius. *Propertius*. Translated by H. E. Butler. Cambridge MA: Harvard University Press, 1962.

Pryor, Felix. *Elizabeth I: Her Life in Letters*. Berkeley: University of California Press, 2003.

Puttenham, George. *The Arte of English Poesie Contriued into Three Bookes, the First of Poets and Poesie, the Second of Proportion, the Third of Ornament*. London: Printed by Richard Field, 1589.

Quarles, Francis. *Hadassa: Or the History of Queene Ester with Meditations Thereupon, Diuine and Morall*. London: Imprinted by Felix Kingston, 1621.

The Queenes Proceedings in Holland. Being the Copie of a Letter sent from the Staple at Middleborough to Mr Vancode a Dutch Merchant in London. London: Printed by T.F. for I.M., December 30, 1642, TT E 83(33).

Ranke, Leopold von. *A History of England Principally in the Seventeenth Century*. New York: AMS Press, 1966.

Raymond, Joad. *The Invention of the Newspaper: English Newsbooks, 1641–1649*. Oxford: Clarendon Press, 2005.

———. *Making the News: An Anthology of the Newsbooks of Revolutionary England, 1641–1660*. New York: St. Martin's Press, 1993.

Recueil des Depeches, Rapports, Instructions, et Memoires des Ambassadeurs de France. Paris and London, 1838.

The Reflection. London, 1689.

Reilly, Bernard F. *The Kingdom of León-Castilla under Queen Urraca, 1109–1126*. Princeton: Princeton University Press, 1982.

Remarkable Passages, of the Occurrences of Parliament, and Proceedings of the Armie. December 8–15, 1643, TT E 78(18).

Rex, Richard. *Elizabeth I, Fortune's Bastard: A Short Account of the Long Life of Elizabeth I*. Stroud: Tempus, 2003.

Reynolds, Donald M. *"Remove Not the Ancient Landmark": Public Monuments and Moral Values: Discourses and Comments in Tribute to Rudolf Wittkower*. Amsterdam, Netherlands: Gordon and Breach, 1996.

Rhegius, Urbanus. *An Homely or Sermon of Good and Euill Angels*. Translated by Richard Robinson. London: Reprinted by I. Charlwood, 1593.

Rhodes, Ernest L. "Cleopatra's Monument and the Gallery in Fludd's *Theatrum Orbi*." *Renaissance Papers* (1971): 41–48.

Richardson, H. G., and G. O. Sayles. *The Governance of Mediaeval England from the Conquest to Magna Carta*. Edinburgh: Edinburgh University Press, 1963.

Richardson, R. C., and G. M. Ridden, eds. *Freedom and the English Revolution: Essays in History and Literature*. Manchester: Manchester University Press, 1986.

Ridley, Jasper. *Elizabeth I: The Shrewdness of Virtue*. New York: Fromm International, 1989.

Roberts, Clayton, and David Roberts. *A History of England: Prehistory to 1714*. New Jersey: Prentice Hall, 1985.

Robin, Diana, Anne Larsen, and Carole Levin, eds. *Encyclopedia of Women in the Renaissance: Italy, France, and England*. Santa Barbara CA: ABC-Clio, 2007.

Rodríguez-Salgado, M. J. *The Changing Face of Empire: Charles V, Philip II, and Habsburg Authority, 1551–1559*. Cambridge: Cambridge University Press, 1988.

Rodríguez-Salgado, M. J., and Simon Adams, eds. *The Count of Feria's Dispatch to Philip II of 14 November 1558*. London: Offices of the Royal Historical Society, University College London, 1984.

Rosenthal, Joel Thomas. *Patriarchy and Families of Privilege in Fifteenth-*

century England. Philadelphia: University of Pennsylvania Press, 1991.

Ross, Stewart. *The Stewart Dynasty*. Nairn: Thomas & Lochar, 1993.

Salkeld, John. *A Treatise of Angels of the Nature, Essence, Place, Power, Science, Vvill, Apparitions, Grace, Sinne, and All Other Proprieties of Angels. Collected Out of the Holy Scriptures, Ancient Fathers, And schoole-diuines*. London: Printed by Thomas Snodham with authoritie of superiours, for Nathaniel Butter, 1613.

Sarah, Duchess of Marlborough. Correspondence and Papers. British Library Add. MSS, 61414–20.

Scarisbrick, J. J. *Henry VIII*. Berkeley: University of California Press, 1968.

Schramm, Percy Ernst. *A History of the English Coronation*. Translated by Leopold George Wickham Legg. Oxford: Clarendon Press, 1937.

Schwarz, Kathryn. "The Wrong Question: Thinking through Virginity." *differences: A Journal of Feminist Cultural Studies* 13, no. 2 (2002).

The Scotish Dove. April 1–12, 1644, TT E 42(16); May 17–24, 1644, TT E 49(19).

Scott, Walter, and John Somers, eds. *A Collection of Scarce and Valuable Tracts on the Most Interesting and Entertaining Subjects: But Chiefly Such As Relate to the History and Constitution of These Kingdoms*. London: Printed for F. Cogan, 1748.

Scrutton, Thomas Edward. *The Laws of Copyright: An Examination of the Principles which Should Regulate Literary and Artistic Property in England and Other Countries*. London: J. Murray, 1883.

Seldom Comes a Better: or, A Tale of a Lady and Her Servants. London, 1710.

Shakespeare, William. *Antony and Cleopatra*. Edited by John Drakakis. New York: St. Martin's Press, 1994.

———. *Antony and Cleopatra*. Edited by M. R. Ridley. London: Methuen, 1965.

———. *Antony and Cleopatra*. Edited by John Wilders. London: Methuen, 1995.

————. *Antony and Cleopatra*. Edited by Nigel Wood. Buckingham: Open University Press, 1996.

————. *The Norton Shakespeare*. Edited by Stephen Greenblatt. New York: W. W. Norton, 1997.

Sharpe, Kevin. *The Personal Rule of Charles I*. New Haven: Yale University Press, 1992.

————. *Remapping Early Modern England: The Culture of Seventeenth-century Politics*. Cambridge: Cambridge University Press, 2000.

Siebert, Fred S. *Freedom of the Press in England, 1476–1776: The Rise and Decline of Government Controls*. Urbana: University of Illinois Press, 1952.

Simpson, Margaret. *Rivals for the Crown*. London: Scholastic, 2003.

Smith, J. *The Duty of the Living to the Memory of the Dead. A Sermon upon the Death of Queen Anne*. London: Printed for Richard Smith, 1714.

Smuts, R. Malcolm. *Court Culture and the Origins of a Royalist Tradition in Early Stuart England*. Philadelphia: University of Pennsylvania Press, 1987.

Somerset, Anne. *Elizabeth I*. London: Weidenfeld & Nicolson, 1991.

Sommerville, Margaret R. *Sex and Subjection: Attitudes to Women in Early-Modern Society*. New York: Arnold, 1995.

Sowernam, Ester. *Ester Hath Hang'd Haman: Or an Ansvvere to a Lewd Pamphlet, entituled, the Arraignment of Women with the Arraignment of Lewd, Idle, Froward, and Vnconstant Men, and Husbands*. London: Printed by Thomas Snodham, 1617.

Speck, William A. *The Birth of Britain: A New Nation, 1700–1710*. Oxford: Blackwell, 1994.

Spenser, Edmund. *The Shorter Poems*. Edited by Richard A. McCabe. London: Penguin Classics, 1999.

Spufford, Margaret. "First Steps in Literacy: The Reading and Writing Experiences of the Humblest Seventeenth-century Spiritual Autobiographers." *Social History* 4 (1979).

Stafford, Pauline. "The King's Wife in Wessex, 800–1066." *Past and Present* 91 (1981).

———. *Queen Emma and Queen Edith: Queenship and Women's Power in Eleventh-century England*. Oxford: Blackwell, 1997.

Stanhope, Philip Henry. *History of England comprising the Reign of Queen Anne until the Peace of Utrecht*. London: J. Murray, 1872.

Stearns, Peter N. *Fat History: Bodies and Beauty in the Modern West*. New York: New York University Press, 1997.

Stenton, F. M. *The First Century of English Feudalism, 1066–1166*. Oxford: Clarendon Press, 1932.

Storrs, Christopher. *War, Diplomacy and the Rise of Savoy, 1690–1720*. Cambridge: Cambridge University Press, 1999.

Stow, John. *Three fifteenth-century chronicles, with historical memoranda by John Stowe, the antiquary, and contemporary notes of occurrences written by him in the reign of Queen Elizabeth*. Edited by James Gairdner. Westminster: Printed for the Camden Society, 1880.

St. Paige, Edward. *Zaftig: The Case for Curves*. Seattle: Darling, 2003.

Strickland, Agnes. *Lives of the Queens of England, from the Norman Conquest; with Anecdotes of Their Courts, Now First Published From Official Records and Other Authentic Documents, Private As well As Public*. London: H. Colburn, 1840.

Stringer, K. J. *The Reign of King Stephen*. London: Routledge, 1993.

Strohm, Paul. *Hochon's Arrow: The Social Imagination of Fourteenth-century Texts*. Princeton: Princeton University Press, 1992.

Strong, Roy C. *Gloriana: The Portraits of Queen Elizabeth I*. London: Thames and Hudson, 1987.

———. *Portraits of Queen Elizabeth I*. Oxford: Clarendon Press, 1973.

Strype, John. *Ecclesiastical Memorials, relating chiefly to Religion . . . under King Henry VIII, King Edward VI, and Queen Mary I*. Oxford: Clarendon Press, 1822.

Stubbs, John. *John Stubbs's Gaping Gulf with Letters and Other Relevant Documents*. Edited by Lloyd Eason Berry. Charlottesville: University Press of Virginia for the Folger Shakespeare Library, 1968.

Stump, Donald. "Abandoning the Old Testament: Shifting Paradigms for Elizabeth, 1578–82." *Explorations in Renaissance Culture* 30, no. 1 (2004).

Sutherland, N. M. *Catherine de Medici and the Ancien Regime*. London: Historical Association, 1966.

Suzuki, Mihoko. *Subordinate Subjects: Gender, the Political Nation, and Literary Form in England, 1588–1688*. Burlington VT: Ashgate, 2003.

Swanton, Michael, ed. *The Peterborough Chronicle, 1070–1154*. London: J. M. Dent, 1997.

Synge, Lanto. *Art of Embroidery: History of Style and Technique*. Woodbridge: Antique Collectors' Club, 2001.

Taithe, Bertrand, and Tim Thornton. *Prophecy: The Power of Inspired Language in History, 1300–2000*. Stroud: Sutton, 1997.

Talbot Papers. Vol. C. Ms. 3194, n.d. Lambeth Place Library, London.

———. Vol. P. Ms. 3206, n.d. Lambeth Place Library, London.

Tate, William. "Solomon, Gender, and Empire in Marlowe's Doctor Faustus." *SEL: Studies in English Language, 1500–1900* 37, no. 2 (1997).

Taylor, John. *The Needles Excellency a New Booke Wherin Are Diuers Admirable Workes Wrought with the Needle; Newly Inuented and Cut in Copper for the Pleasure and Profit of the Industrious*. London: Printed for Iames Boler and are to be sold at the Signe of the Marigold in Paules Church yard, 1631.

The. Holie. Bible. Conteynyng the Olde Testament and the Newe. London: In povvles Churchyarde by Richarde Iugge, printer to the Queenes Maiestie, 1568.

Thomas, Keith. *Religion and the Decline of Magic: Studies in Popular Beliefs in Sixteenth and Seventeenth Century England*. London: Weidenfeld & Nicolson, 1971.

Trapp, John. *A Commentary or Exposition Upon the Books of Ezra, Nehemiah, Esther, Job and Psalms Wherein the Text Is Explained, Some Controversies Are Discussed . . . : In All Which Divers Other Texts of Scripture, Which Occasionally Occurre, Are Fully Opened.*

London: Printed by T.R. and E.M. for Thomas Newberry . . . and Joseph Barber, 1657.

Traub, Valerie. *The Renaissance of Lesbianism in Early Modern England.* Cambridge: Cambridge University Press, 2002.

Trevelyan, George Macaulay. *England under Queen Anne.* 3 vols. London: Longmans, Green, 1930.

Upon the Vote that Pass'd That the Church was Not in Danger. London, 1705.

Van Houts, Elisabeth M. C., ed. *The Gesta Normannorum Ducum of William of Jumièges, Orderic Vitalis, and Robert of Torigni.* Oxford: Clarendon Press, 1995.

Veevers, Erica. *Images of Love and Religion: Queen Henrietta Maria and Court Entertainments.* Cambridge: Cambridge University Press, 1989.

Vives, Juan Luis. *The Instruction of a Christen Woman.* Edited by Virginia Walcott Beauchamp, Elizabeth Hageman, and Margaret Lael Mikesell. Urbana: University of Illinois Press, 2002.

Volkmann, Hans. *Cleopatra: A Study in Politics and Propaganda.* Translated by T. J. Cadoux. London: Elek Books, 1958.

Wahl, Elizabeth Susan. *Invisible Relations: Representations of Female Intimacy in the Age of Enlightenment.* Stanford: Stanford University Press, 1999.

Walker, Julia. *Dissing Elizabeth: Negative Representations of Gloriana.* Durham NC: Duke University Press, 1998.

Waller, Maureen. *Ungrateful Daughters: The Stuart Princesses Who Stole Their Father's Crown.* London: Hodder and Stoughton, 2002.

Warnicke, Retha M. *Mary Queen of Scots.* New York: Routledge, 2006.

———. *The Rise and Fall of Anne Boleyn: Family Politics at the Court of Henry VIII.* Cambridge: Cambridge University Press, 1989.

Warren, Wilfrid Lewis. *Henry II.* Berkeley: University of California Press, 1973.

Watkins, John. *Representing Elizabeth in Stuart England: Literature, History, Sovereignty.* Cambridge: Cambridge University Press, 2002.

Watkins, John, ed. "Toward a New Diplomatic History of Early Modern Europe." Special issue, *Journal of Medieval and Early Modern Studies* 38 (2008).

Watt, Diane. *Secretaries of God: Women Prophets in Late Medieval and Early Modern England*. Woodbridge, Suffolk: D. S. Brewer, 1997.

Watt, Tessa. *Cheap Print and Popular Piety, 1550–1640*. Cambridge: Cambridge University Press, 1991.

THE WEEKLY ACCOUNT. April 3–10, 1644, TT E 42(3).

Weil, Rachel Judith. *Political Passions: Gender, the Family, and Political Argument in England, 1680–1714*. Manchester: Manchester University Press, 1999.

Wernham, R. B. *After the Armada: Elizabethan England and the Struggle for Western Europe, 1588–1595*. Oxford: Clarendon Press, 1984.

———. *Before the Armada: The Emergence of the English Nation, 1485–1588*. New York: Harcourt, Brace & World, 1966.

———. *The Making of Elizabethan Foreign Policy, 1558–1603*. Berkeley: University of California Press, 1980.

West, Robert Hunter. *Milton and the Angels*. Athens: University of Georgia Press, 1955.

White, Graeme J. "The End of Stephen's Reign." *History* 75 (February 1990).

White, Michelle Anne. *Henrietta Maria and the English Civil Wars*. Aldershot: Ashgate, 2006.

Wiesner, Merry E. *Women and Gender in Early Modern Europe*. Cambridge: Cambridge University Press, 1993.

William of Malmesbury. *Historia Novella: The Contemporary History*. Edited by Edmund King. Translated by K. R. Potter. Oxford: Clarendon Press, 1998.

———. *William of Malmesbury's Chronicle of the Kings of England: From the Earliest Period to the Reign of King Stephen; with Notes and Illustrations*. Edited by J. A. Giles. London: Henry Bohn, 1897.

Wilson, Derek A. *A Tudor Tapestry: Men, Women, and Society in Reformation England*. Pittsburgh: University of Pittsburgh Press, 1972.

Wilson, Elkin Calhoun. *England's Eliza*. New York: Octagon Books, 1966.

Wood, Mary Anne Everett, ed. *Letters of Royal and Illustrious Ladies of Great Britain*. London, 1846.

Woolf, Noel. *The Sovereign Remedy: Touch-pieces and the King's Evil*. Manchester: British Association of Numismatic Societies, 1990.

Woolley, Hannah. *The Gentlewomans Companion; Or, a Guide to the Female Sex Containing Directions of Behaviour, in All Places, Companies, Relations, and Conditions, from Their Childhood down to Old Age*. London: Printed by A. Maxwell for Dorman Newman at the Kings-Arms in the Poultry, 1673.

Wright, Thomas. *The Romance of the Lace Pillow: Being the History of Lace-making in Bucks*. Olney, Buckinghamshire: Thomas Wright, 1919.

Wriothesley, Charles. *A Chronicle of England during the Reigns of the Tudors, from AD 1485–1559*. New York: Johnson Reprint, 1965.

Wyon, Frederick William. *The History of Great Britain during the Reign of Queen Anne*. London: Chapman and Hall, 1876.

Yates, Frances Amelia. *Astraea: The Imperial Theme in the Sixteenth Century*. London: Routledge & Kegan Paul, 1975.

Zanger, Abby E. *Scenes from the Marriage of Louis XIV: Nuptial Fictions and the Making of Absolutist Power*. Stanford: Stanford University Press, 1997.

Zaret, David. *The Heavenly Contract: Ideology and Organization in Pre-revolutionary Puritanism*. Chicago: University of Chicago Press, 1985.

———. *Origins of Democratic Culture: Printing, Petitions, and the Public Sphere in Early Modern England*. Princeton: Princeton University Press, 2000.

Zee, Henri A. van der, and Barbara van der Zee. *William and Mary*. New York: Knopf, 1973.

Contributors

CHARLES BEEM is an Assistant Professor of History at the University of North Carolina, Pembroke, the author of *The Lioness Roared: The Problems of Female Rule in English History* (2006), and the editor of the *Royal Minorities of Medieval and Early Modern England* (2008). He is currently at work on a study of the colorful but obscure Tudor Renaissance figure George Ferrers.

ROBERT BUCHOLZ is a Professor of History at Loyola University, Chicago. He is the author of *The Augustan Court: Queen Anne and the Decline of Court Culture* (1993) and, with Newton Key, *Early Modern England, 1485–1714: A Narrative History* and *Sources and Debates in English History, 1485–1714* (2004). He is also the Director of the online Database of Court Officers, 1660–1837: http://www.luc.edu/history/fac_resources/bucholz/DCO/DCO.html.

SARAH DUNCAN is a PhD candidate at Yale University. She is currently teaching at Spring Hill College in Mobile, Alabama, and is completing her dissertation, "'A queen and by the same title a king also': Gender, Power, and Ceremony in the Reign of Mary I." Her work appears in *Explorations in Renaissance Culture* and in the forthcoming *Elizabeth*

I and the "Sovereign Arts": Essays in History, Literature, and Culture. Her research interests include gender politics and Anglo-Spanish cultural relations at the court of Mary I of England.

TIMOTHY G. ELSTON is the Chair of the Department of History and Social Sciences at Newberry College. Dr. Elston earned his PhD from the University of Nebraska–Lincoln where he focused his academic interests in late medieval and early modern England, emphasizing women's history. Among Dr. Elston's previous publications is an essay on Catherine of Aragon and Juan Luis Vives in the edited collection *"High and Mighty Queens" of Early Modern England.*

AMY GANT recently completed her MA in history at the University of Nebraska–Lincoln. She is interested in the history of religion and religious publications in seventeenth-century England. Her essays have appeared in *The Encyclopedia of Women in the Renaissance.*

ELAINE KRUSE is the Huge-Kinne Professor of History at Nebraska Wesleyan University. She is the author of a number of articles, including "Passion, Property, or Politics? The Implications of the Kornmann Affair," "The Blood-stained Hands of Catherine de Médicis," and "The Woman in Black: The Image of Catherine de Medici from Marlowe to Queen Margot." She is currently at work on a book on divorce during the French Revolution.

AMBER HARRIS LEICHNER is pursuing her PhD in American literature at the University of Nebraska–Lincoln with a focus on the recovery of early twentieth-century women writers. Her poems have appeared in *The Dos Passos Review*, *Relief*, and elsewhere. Her chapbook *Just This Proof* is available from FootHills Press.

CAROLE LEVIN is the Willa Cather Professor of History at the University of Nebraska–Lincoln. She has coedited a number of collections, including *"High and Mighty Queens" of Early Modern England: Realities and Representations* and *Elizabeth I: Always Her Own Free Woman*, both published in 2003. She is the author of *"The Heart and Stomach of a*

King": Elizabeth I and the Politics of Sex and Power (1994), The Reign of Elizabeth I (2002), and Dreaming the English Renaissance: Politics and Desire in Court and Culture (2008). With John Watkins, she is the coauthor of Shakespeare's Foreign Worlds: National and Transnational Identities in the Elizabethan Age (2009).

SHANNON MEYER is a PhD candidate in history at the University of Nebraska–Lincoln, where she specializes in early modern English women's history. Her essays have appeared in The Encyclopedia of Women in the Renaissance.

MICHELE OSHEROW is a Clinical Assistant Professor of English and Associate Director of the Dresher Center for the Humanities at the University of Maryland, Baltimore County. She also serves as dramaturge for the Folger Theatre in Washington DC and for other professional theaters. She is the author of Biblical Women's Voices in Early Modern England (2009).

ANNA RIEHL, Assistant Professor of English at Auburn University, received her PhD from the University of Illinois at Chicago. She is currently working on a book manuscript titled "The Face of Power: Early Modern Representations of Queen Elizabeth I." Her research and teaching interests lie at the intersection of early modern literature, visual culture, history, and cultural studies, with a special focus on the body, visual rhetoric, Elizabeth I, court culture, and gender issues. Her essay "Eying the Thought Awry: The Anamorphosis of John Donne's Poetry" is forthcoming in the journal English Literary Renaissance. Another essay, "Persuading the Prince: Raleigh, Keymis, Chapman, and The Second Voyage to Guiana" is forthcoming in the collection Tudor Court Culture. Dr. Riehl's research has been sponsored by an American Association of University Women's Educational Foundation Dissertation Fellowship, English-Speaking Union Scholarship, and a University Fellowship at the University of Illinois at Chicago.

LISA SCHUELKE is a PhD candidate in history at the University of Nebraska–Lincoln, where she specializes in women's history and has published articles in this field, including "Overcoming Obstacles: Marguerite

CONTRIBUTORS

Higgins Reports from Korea," in the 2005 *Proceedings* for the Center for the Study of the Korean War.

LINDA S. SHENK is an Assistant Professor at Iowa State University, where she teaches Elizabethan court poetry and drama. She has published on Elizabeth I as a learned queen; Robert Devereux, Earl of Essex; Shakespeare; and the seventeenth-century mnemonician John Willis. She is currently working on a book manuscript titled "Learned Queen: The Imperial Image of Elizabeth I," a project that investigates the political ramifications of Elizabeth's learned persona both as a strategy of her own image-making as well as a persona useful to her internationally ambitious court figures as they pursued their own expansionist agenda.

MARJORIE SWANN, Associate Professor of English at the University of Kansas, specializes in Renaissance literature, feminist criticism, and material culture studies. She is the author of *Curiosities and Texts: The Culture of Collecting in Early Modern England* (2001). She is currently working on a book about the frustration of reproductive sexuality in Renaissance culture and literature, as well as a study of Izaak Walton's *The Compleat Angler*.

JOHN WATKINS is a Professor of English, Italian Studies, and Medieval Studies at the University of Minnesota. Associate editor of *The Journal of British Studies*, he is the author of *The Specter of Dido: Spenser and Virgilian Epic* (1995), *Representing Elizabeth in Stuart England: Literature, History, and Sovereignty* (2002), and numerous articles on premodern literature and culture. With Carole Levin, he is the coauthor of *Shakespeare's Foreign Worlds: National and Transnational Identities in the Elizabethan Age* (2009). He is currently finishing a book on marriage diplomacy in medieval and early modern Europe.

MICHELLE A. WHITE is the UC Foundation Associate Professor of History at the University of Tennessee, Chattanooga. She is the author of *Henrietta Maria and the English Civil Wars* (2006) and presently is at work examining English cases of sedition for the period 1646–48.

314

RICHARDINE WOODALL received her PhD from York University, where she teaches English literature. Her area of specialization is the literatures of the English Renaissance, in particular Shakespearean drama. Her research focuses on the ways in which Western fictions have superimposed such categorizers as the "female" and the "east" onto the historical Cleopatra such that she has become a cultural icon in Western culture. She has published articles on representations of Cleopatra and on blacks in British literature and history.

Index

Guildhall speech of, xix; marriage
of, 32, 38, 59, 67, 76, 79, 194;
passivity and submissiveness of, xvi;
queen's mercy during reign of, xxiii–
xxiv, xxx, 31–46, 49n51
Mary II, Queen of England, xix, xxi,
241n29, 249–50, 256, 257, 263
Mary Beatrice of Modena, xv,
xxxiiin14
Mary of Guise, 29n13, 126
Matilda, Empress, xvi, xvii, xx–xxii,
xxvii, xxix–xxx, 1–14, 15n16
Matzger, Marcia Lee, 45
May, Steven W., 120n2
Mayer, John, 143, 150
Maynwaring, Arthur, 247, 250
McBee, Richard, 144–45
McCarthy, Justin, 243
McLaren, A. N., 100, 118
Medici family, 81
Melinsende, Queen of Jerusalem, 2
Mendelson, Sara, xxiv, 18, 267n7
Mendicant orders, 21–22
Mercurius Aulicus (newsbook), 207
Mercurius Britanicus (newsbook), 208,
214
Michieli, Giovanni, 39
Miles of Gloucester, 9
Montmorency, Diane de France, Duch-
ess of, 94
Montmorency, François, Duke of, 81,
94
Montrose, Louis, 176
Monty Python, *Yellowbeard*, 244
Moray, James Stuart, Earl of, 115
Mordecai (biblical figure), 142, 148,
150
More, Thomas, 20
Mueller, Janel, 99
Munday, Anthony, 193n29; *Zelauto*,
167–68

National Association to Advance Fat
Acceptance (NAAFA), 269n34

Noailles, Antoine de, 68
Norfolk, Thomas Howard, Duke of,
xxiv, 121n7, 130, 131, 231
Northern Rebellion, 44
Northumberland, John Dudley, Duke
of, xxiv, 40, 55, 56

Oliphant, Margaret, 257
Omphale (mythological figure), 192
Orlin, Lena, 128
Osborne, Francis, 230, 237
Osherow, Michele, xx, xxiii, xxv,
xxviii–xxx, 100, 141–57
Ovid, 192
Owen, George, 60
Oxford, Robert Harley, Earl of, 246

Page (printer), 135
Paget, Lord, 41, 49n37, 56
Palliser, Fanny Bury, *History of English
Lace*, 25
Parker, Archbishop Matthew, 117
Parker, Toziska, 150
Parliament, English, 78, 81–82, 86, 93,
101, 201, 247, 262; during Civil
Wars, 209, 211, 212, 217; Eliza-
beth's accession announced to, 78;
and royal marriages, 92
The Parliament Scout (newsbook), 207,
211, 220n10
Parr, Katherine, 51
Parsons, John Carmi, 32
Pembroke, William Herbert, Earl of, 41
Penny, Paul, 66
Percy, Henry, 217
A Perfect Diurnall (pamphlet), 210
Petrarch, 158, 159, 171
Philip II, King of Spain, xxiii, xxiv,
xxvii, 38–41, 48n34, 66, 68, 78–80,
97n18, 109, 114; courtship of
Elizabeth by, 80, 82, 85–93; mar-
riages of, xvi, 32, 38, 59, 67, 76,
79, 82–87, 94, 129
Pilgrimage of Grace, 36